Writing History in the Digital Age

DIGITAL HUMANITIES

The Digital Humanities series provides a forum for ground-breaking and benchmark work in digital humanities, lying at the intersections of computers and the disciplines of arts and humanities, library and information science, media and communications studies, and cultural studies.

Series Editors:
Julie Thompson Klein, Wayne State University
Tara McPherson, University of Southern California
Paul Conway, University of Michigan

Teaching History in the Digital Age
T. Mills Kelly

Hacking the Academy: New Approaches to Scholarship and Teaching from Digital Humanities
Daniel J. Cohen and Tom Scheinfeldt, Editors

Writing History in the Digital Age
Jack Dougherty and Kristen Nawrotzki, Editors

DIGITALCULTUREBOOKS, an imprint of the University of Michigan Press, is dedicated to publishing work in new media studies and the emerging field of digital humanities.

Writing History in the Digital Age

Jack Dougherty and Kristen Nawrotzki, editors

The University of Michigan Press
Ann Arbor

Published in the United States of America by
The University of Michigan Press
Manufactured in the United States of America
⊗ Printed on acid-free paper

2016   2015   2014   2013   4   3   2   1

A CIP catalog record for this book is available from the British Library.

DOI: http://dx.doi.org/10.3998/dh.12230987.0001.001

Library of Congress Cataloging-in-Publication Data

Writing history in the digital age / Jack Dougherty, Kristen Nawrotzki,
editors.
        pages   cm. — (Digital humanities)
     ISBN 978-0-472-07206-4 (hardback) — ISBN 978-0-472-05206-6 (paper) — ISBN
   978-0-472-02991-4 (e-book)
        1. History—Methodology.   2. Academic writing—Data processing.   3. History—
   Research—Data processing.   4. Historiography.   5. Electronic data processing.
   I. Dougherty, Jack.   II. Nawrotzki, Kristen.
   D16.12.W75   2013
   902'.85—dc23
                                                        2013025449

About the Web Version

A freely accessible version of this book, including the original essay ideas, preliminary drafts, and comments by readers during the open-review period, is available on the web at http://WritingHistory.trincoll.edu.

All web links in this book were functional as of April 2012. Due to the changing nature of the Internet, all external links have been cited in the notes to assist future researchers.

Acknowledgments

This volume of essays would not have been possible without the numerous contributors and commenters who participated in the process and helped shape our vision of what it means to be writing history in the digital age. We thank those who played a part in our pilot project for the fall 2010 conference of the History of Education Society, as well as those who submitted an essay or posted a comment on the web-book between its launch in May 2011 and the conclusion of the open-review period in November 2012: Trudi Abel, Dan Allosso, Zayde Antrim, Davarian Baldwin, Jean Bauer, Chad Black, Daniela Blei, Lauren Braun-Strumfels, Kevin J. Brehony, Sheila Brennan, Anne-Elizabeth Brodsky, Timothy Burke, William Caraher, Alex Sayf Cummings, Jed Dobson, Sherman Dorn, Thomas Dublin, David Elder, Ansley Erickson, Daniel Faltesek, Nadine Feuerherm, Nancy Friedland, Courtney Fullilove, Sandra Gabriele, Alex Galarza, Susan Garfinkel, Fred Gibbs, Shawn Graham, Cheryl Greenberg, Trevor Griffey, Robbie Gross, Peter Haber, Christopher Hager, Eric Hansen, Tom Harbison, Katherine Hart, Jason Heppler, Michael Hevel, Jonathan Jarrett, Jason Jones, Julie Judkins, Judith Kafka, Hillary Kativa, Mills Kelly, Charles Klinetobe, Shane Landrum, Adrea Lawrence, Cindy Loch-Drake, Brandon Locke, Abbey Lowe, Leslie Madsen-Brooks, Sarah Manekin, Katya Maslakowski, Austin Mason, Guy Massie, Jeff McClurken, John McClymer, Jeremy McGinniss, James B. McSwain, Natalia Mehlman Petrzela, Corey Meyer, Sylvia K. Miller, Sara Morris, Hilary Moss, Kaci Nash, Rob Nelson, Scott Nesbit, Andrea Nichols, Ellen Noonan, Bethany Nowviskie, Mike O'Malley, Y. P. Ong, Trevor Owens, Marshall Poe, Miriam Posner, Heather Munro Prescott, Jenny Presnell, Michelle Purdy, Svetlana Rasmussen, Penny Richards, Stephen Robertson, Charlotte D. Rochez, Barbara Rockenbach, Oscar Rosales Castañeda, Lisa Rosner, Katherine Rowe, Paul Rowland, Allison Ruda, Brian Sarnacki, Martha

Saxton, Frank Schloeffel, Julia Schreiner, Steven Schwinghamer, Amanda Seligman, Jen Seltz, Ryan Shackleton, Ryan Shaw, Tim Sherratt, Amanda Sikarskie, Kathryn Kish Sklar, Margery Sly, Anna Smith, Lisa Spiro, Stefan Tanaka, Mark Tebeau, John Theibault, William G. Thomas, Dee Thompson, Michelle Tiedje, Kathryn Tomasek, Andrew J. Torget, Hannah Ueno, Ted Underwood, Jason Verber, Luke Waltzer, Ethan Watrall, Marcin Wilkowski, Jacqueline Wilson, Rebecca S. Wingo, Mark Winokur, Gail Wolfe, Robert Wolff, and Laura Zucconi.

We also appreciate the timely WordPress support provided by Carlos Espinosa and David Tatem at Trinity College in Hartford, Connecticut; the creation of CommentPress by Eddie Tejeda and the Institute for the Future of the Book, with subsequent revisions by Christian Wach; our Trinity College research assistant, Katie Campbell; a manuscript fellowship from the Trinity Institute for Interdisciplinary Scholarship; Tom Scheinfeldt at the Roy Rosenzweig Center for History and New Media at George Mason University, for early words of encouragement on creating this volume; and our publishing partners at the University of Michigan: Tom Dwyer, Shana Kimball, Korey Jackson, Christopher Dreyer, Alexa Ducsay, Andrea Olson, Jill Butler Wilson, and their colleagues.

Contents

Part 7. Collaborative Writing: Yours, Mine, and Ours

Illustrations

Introduction

Kristen Nawrotzki and Jack Dougherty

Has the digital revolution transformed how we write about the past? Have new technologies changed our essential work-craft as scholars and the way in which we think, teach, author, and publish? Does the digital age have broader implications for individual writing processes or for the historical profession at large? These are the questions addressed in this collection of essays. Here, historians discuss how our means of creating interpretations about the past are challenged and reshaped by a range of electronic tools and techniques, including crowdsourcing, blogging, databases, spatial analysis, visual media, gaming simulations, and online collaborations. Bound together as a book in paper and electronic forms, our essays seek to explicate and embody the promise that the digital age holds for writers of history, while at the same time upending conventional beliefs about and practices of publishing scholarship.

Embedded within this book are arguments for rethinking how we academics create and share knowledge, particularly in history and other humanities fields that have been relatively slow to embrace change in this new era of digital tools and publishing. We historians tend to research and write in isolation. Hiding behind our respective curtains, we typically author long monographs that may take several years to reach any sort of audience at all. Then, after such a long period of investment, the stakes are often especially high for the newly revealed work to be well received within its field. Even when we do share shorter works, such as a chapter in a collection of essays, the results can be disappointing. Reviewers politely refer to poorly implemented volumes as having "uneven quality" or, less politely, as "staple jobs." Although individual essays in conventional edited volumes may represent good scholarship, the lack of intellectual relationship or at least of recognition between them often results in volume-level flaws ranging from sheer repetitiveness to perplexing contradiction, with many steps in between.

Part of the problem traces back to conventional practices of creating this knowledge. Traditionally, a "call for papers" announcement is circulated, individual contributors submit completed chapters, and volume editors make cuts, suggest revisions, and strive to package the compilation as a whole. Under this model, authors typically have little access to each other's ideas or drafts during the generative or revision periods and therefore lack the capacity to share comments and build connections across the volume. A common result is a whole that is not greater than the sum of its parts. To challenge convention, we asked ourselves: Could technology help us to create a more intellectually collaborative volume, with a more transparent process, in a relatively shorter period of time? And if so, would it produce a better book?

This volume represents the results of our experiment and, in three ways, exemplifies for historians a radically different approach to publishing. First, the book is born digital, meaning that we published it on the web in stages, as it developed, and relied on collaborative web tools for contributors to share ideas, drafts, and comments. Some even coauthored their essays on the web. What better way for historians to reflect on digital tools than to use them to write a book? In the spirit of the open web, we made the normally behind-the-scenes development of the book more transparent. In the section "How this book evolved" on our project website, we trace the development of the volume, beginning with our fall 2010 pilot project and continuing through our subsequent correspondence and contract with the University of Michigan Press and early exchanges between authors during the essay idea phase in the spring of 2011. Similarly, the "How it works" section of our website shares details on the open-source WordPress platform that hosts our essays and commentary.

Second, instead of being subjected to anonymous private review, this book benefited from open peer review on the web. During an eight-week period in the fall of 2011, four experts appointed by the press, along with general readers and many of our authors, posted over 940 online comments on our essays. As our "How to comment" tutorial on the website explained, we invited public responses on three levels: general comments on the book as a whole, an individual essay page, or a specific paragraph. All commenters had to identify themselves, using a full name; no anonymous feedback was permitted. The objective was to encourage all readers—

invited experts and general audiences, senior scholars and students alike, regardless of professional status or institutional affiliation —to openly participate in the process of peer review and to engage in dialogues about what "good writing" means in history. Our approach draws from open peer review innovations in other humanities fields, such as Kathleen Fitzpatrick and Katherine Rowe's reflections on their experience with *Shakespeare Quarterly*.[1] Furthermore, to publicly recognize the work of the open peer reviewers, we invited two of the most thoughtfully engaged commentators to collaborate with us in writing this volume's concluding reflections about the process.

Finally, the digital version of this volume is open-access, shared freely with readers on the public web. Unlike proprietary models, no subscription fee or password is required to view or comment on our scholarship. Based on open-source software, the web-book version of this volume can be read on current versions of all major browsers for desktop or laptop computers (and on most tablet and phone devices, though with limited ability to post comments). We embrace the arguments, advanced by historian Roy Rosenzweig and others, that open-access scholarship is more widely discoverable, useful, and consistent with the principles of our scholarly societies.[2] As described in our "Editorial and intellectual property policy" on the website, all contributors agreed to distribute the content of their essays under the Creative Commons Attribution-Noncommercial (BY-NC) license for the site, whereby authors retain the copyright to their work while making a nonexclusive agreement to freely share it with others, as long as the original source is cited.[3] Furthermore, as outlined in our book contract, upon approval of the final manuscript, the University of Michigan Press also agreed to publish it under a Creative Commons license in at least two formats: a print edition (for sale) and an online version (for free).

Wrapping all three qualities—born digital, open peer review, and open access—into one volume makes a unique contribution to our field and illustrates our rethinking of the meaning of "publishing," how we do it, and why. In *Writing History in the Digital Age*, our proposition is simply that wisely implemented web technology can help us to collaboratively create, constructively criticize, and widely circulate our writing in ways more consistent with our scholarly values. Our challenge was to openly test and demonstrate a different way of working together as writers to build a better-quality edited volume. Our call for essay ideas, conducted in the spring of 2011, required prospective contributors to express their initial ideas on the public web, where others could respond and cross-fertilization could take place before essays were fully drafted. Welcoming invited experts and general readers to participate in our open peer review in the fall of 2011 allowed the "wisdom of the crowd" to shape our developmental editing and our final decisions on which essays should advance to the final round. Finally, partnering with an innovative academic press to publish the volume in dual formats (paper for sale and online for free) vastly increases its audience beyond the typical high-priced hardbound-only edition. In all of this, we have seen technology not as the goal but, rather, as a tool that enables us to rethink scholarship-as-usual.

Changing the Culture of History Writing

Historians value good writing. All scholars construct new forms of knowledge, but we historians tend to hold our profession to a particularly high standard when it comes to writing about our discoveries. As readers, we prefer clear and persuasive prose over data tables or abstract jargon. As a discipline, we favor book-length monographs over the article-based publishing traditions of the social sciences. As writers, we aspire to wrap meaningful insights about the past into a good story.

Despite the central role that writing plays within our profession, its practice remains mostly hidden from public view. By and large, we historians do our work—the acts of researching, writing, and publishing—alone, rather than in collaboration with others. While we prize the influential books that hold a special place on our bookshelves and in our minds, historians rarely reveal the underlying processes that led to these finished products. Writing is our shared craft, the glue that unites our profession, but we tend to be private about it. "Do not circulate or cite without permission of the author" is an all-too-familiar warning label appearing on drafts of papers delivered at our conferences. Given this state of secrecy, how do we expect historians-in-training to learn our craft? How do we expect them to develop their skills as writers, particularly of dissertations and books, without openly sharing and comparing our writing processes? How can we advance the overall quality of writing in the profession without asking each of us to reinvent the wheel for ourselves? Collectively, the ideas presented here seek to interrupt this norm of silence within our profession, pull back the curtain, and make our individual work processes more public.

The fact that this volume about writing has been digitally conceived, developed, and published is anything but coincidental. We see this volume and the essays in it as an intervention into a complex and changing landscape of digital scholarship and scholarly publishing. On the one hand, in the last decade, self-described digital humanists have delineated and demonstrated the numerous and wide-ranging ways in which technology might speed up and improve the quality of research and writing in the humanities.[4] Discipline-specific efforts in the field of digital history have been led by such institutions as the Roy Rosenzweig Center for History and New Media (CHNM) at George Mason University,[5] encouraged by the American Historical Association, and undertaken by individuals and groups of scholars both in and outside the academy.[6] As CHNM's Dan Cohen and Roy Rosenzweig explained in their seminal 2005 how-to guide, digital technology allows historians to "do more, reach more people, store more data, [and] give readers more varied sources; [with it] we can get more historical materials into classrooms, give students more access to formerly cloistered documents, hear from more perspectives."[7] In addition, digital media both extend and fundamentally change the way we read and understand information, by rendering it manipulable and interactive and allowing us to access it in nonlinear form.

Despite these potential benefits, however, scholars in humanities disciplines—and historians in particular—have been especially slow to embrace digital technology for the research, writing, and dissemination of their scholarship. The findings of recent surveys indicate that the vast majority of history faculty are neither engaging with digital tools for analysis nor digitally disseminating their in-progress or completed work.[8] These same scholars use e-mail, word processing software, online search engines, and digital archives in the course of producing scholarship, but they do not avail themselves of the many technologies designed to assist in data analysis, text composition, and public dissemination.[9] Approximately 20 percent of historians claim to have published scholarship online, but more than half of those publications may have been digitized versions of articles published in print journals.[10] That leaves only about 10 percent of historians who have shared their scholarship in digital form on the open web, whether on personal blogs or institutional or project-specific websites, as digital documentaries, through games or apps, or as essays in web-born journals or in *Wikipedia*. Why have so few shared their scholarship in this way? Clues to understanding this phenomenon lie both in the circumstances that shape the process and products of historians' writing and in the reasons why historians publish in the first place.

For historians—as for all authors—writing is an individual and highly personal process, as well as one that is materially and culturally situated.[11] There is something understandable and even commendable about scholars wanting to stay with what they know, appreciate, and do well. Until very recently, people who wanted to publish short pieces to be read by a broad readership on a regular basis became journalists, not historians. So although we might all benefit from having more historians blogging their scholarship, for example, it hardly comes as a surprise that most do not. Moreover, as applied linguist Ken Hyland emphasizes, "Academic writing is not just about conveying an ideational 'content,' it is also about the representation of self."[12] In other words, we are what we write—and what we read—and historians on the whole appear disinclined to alter themselves, however compelling the arguments for doing so may be.[13] Yet, as the essays in this volume attest, the arguments are indeed compelling, as is our responsibility as intellectuals, in Donald Hall's words, "to question, reinterrogate, unsettle, and dissipate familiarities," since "we—*our selves*—should hold no privileged position vis-à-vis that critical engagement."[14]

Beyond the personal, historians' willingness to engage in digital history hinges, too, on perceived and real material, technological, and temporal constraints. By definition, digital history utilizes different tools, differently, than most historians are used to. It has its own vocabulary and requires different skills sets (emphasizing, for example, curation as opposed to detective work).[15] Would-be digital historians who are accustomed to working alone, with only a word processor, may be daunted or dismayed by the prospect of managing a multisoftware or multicontributor project. Many of us lack the basic literacy in digital genres, technologies, and information architecture to be able to articulate our ideas, and some are hesitant to immerse themselves in the new technologies, lest these technologies become obsolete before the historian's work is even finished.[16] Historians may not have access to the time, money, or technical support necessary to realize some forms of digital scholarship.[17] Or we may be unaware that we do in fact have access to these resources or that we can do some forms of digital history—including joining extant projects—without them.

The third major influence on historians' engagement with digital history has been the culture of scholarship within the discipline itself.[18] To date, historians' culture and modus operandi have typically been the opposite of the speed and openness, the collaborative spirit and do-it-yourself mentality, that characterize the Internet at its best. In their work, historians largely seek to be comprehensive rather than (necessarily) innovative—and comprehensiveness takes time.[19] "On the 'slow side of sharing,'" we hoard and hone our ideas prior to publication rather than widely circulate working papers or preprints like those in other disciplines. Once submitted for peer review, our articles and monographs may take up to three years to appear in print.[20] In the interim, we fear that the exposure of our messy path to supposed perfection will lead others either to scoop our ideas or else to discover that we are not as clever as our peer-reviewed published works would have them believe.[21] Ultimately, secrecy about our work may indeed support the harsh competitiveness that some feel has come to define the academy more broadly.[22] To the contrary, in accordance with the do-it-yourself culture of the Internet, the sharing of thinking-in-progress seems to encourage more collaboration than competition among scholars (and others), while at the same time modeling the "historical habits of mind" we seek to teach our students.[23]

Why Do We Publish?

Pose that question to any humanities scholar, particularly a historian in today's uncertain publishing and academic job markets, and you're likely to hear a confusing mix of answers that reveal the competing interests we face. Historians are an anxious breed. As we write our conference papers, journal articles, and book manuscripts, we worry about money, ownership, status, and tenure. While obsessing over these individualistic factors, we often lose track of the broader scholarly values that fundamentally motivate us to share our knowledge and engage with the ideas of others. The current disruption caused by digital publishing leads us to pause and sort through the different arguments for why scholars do what we do.

Publishing for Financial Gain

For most historians, we can quickly dispense with the money argument. If your primary goal is to get rich quickly, then publishing scholarly monographs in the humanities is not your best route. Based on our general knowledge of the field, today's typical academic press considers a book to be successful if it sells at least 1,000 print copies. Assuming a royalty of 5 percent based on books retailed at $30 each, this arrangement yields the author a modest sum of $1,500. But most historians probably have spent an equal or greater sum on out-of-pocket expenses in researching and producing a book such as this. In addition to time that is uncompensated for many of us, many historians commonly pay their own costs for research travel, photocopying, copyright permissions, and indexing. Indeed, the financial payoff for a best-selling trade book or popular textbook published by a trade press is far greater. But those experiences are not the norm, and the primary motivator for most historians is something other than money.

In fact, our current models of scholarly publishing place a growing financial burden on university and college libraries. In practice, faculty members effectively give away journal and book manuscripts to publishers for the privilege of seeing them in print. In turn, publishers sell faculty scholarship back to our academic libraries and charge them a price for the right to lend out print copies or disseminate digital copies on proprietary databases. As a result, higher education pays twice for scholarship produced by its own faculty: first, in the form of salary or sabbatical support for individual professors, and second, in fees for the right to distribute the work. (The financial burden is more extreme in the grant-funded sciences, where commercial publishers charge substantially higher journal subscription fees to libraries and publication fees to contributing authors.) The current business model benefits neither the average historian nor the institutions of higher education that employ many of us.

Publishing for Professional Status

Another argument is that academics publish to avoid perishing. Writing an important book matters greatly to the gatekeepers of academic success—the committees and deans that hire faculty and evaluate them for tenure. While an individual history book may yield only modest author's royalties, it may indirectly determine whether a candidate receives a job offer with a stable long-term salary or is promoted to a higher-paying rank. But for most historians, what matters most is our reputation within the profession, and this tends to be based largely on our publications, which are more widely visible to our peers than is, for example, our teaching. The problem arises when scholars insert their perception of a publisher's status as a proxy for the quality of a particular book, without evaluating the latter directly. Many historians carry with us a vague pecking order of scholarly publishers, assuming that those near the top exercise more selective editorial filtering than those below. With so many books produced and so little time to read, we tend to substitute our vague notions of the publisher's prestige in place of informed judgment about the quality of the text. Moreover, publishers have warned universities against basing faculty tenure decisions solely on their decision to accept or reject a manuscript. When academic publishers rely on revenue from book sales to pay their editorial and production costs, their definition of a "good" book is inevitably tied up with a "marketable" one. Of course, quality, status, and marketability are neither identical nor interchangeable.

Publishing to Share Ideas

The most principled reason for academics to publish is to share ideas and engage with the ideas of others, as part of a larger process of enriching the body of knowledge. At its best, producing scholarship means stepping out of individual isolation and into a public forum, where we test out new ideas, build on foundations offered by others, and challenge ways of thinking that conflict with our own point of view. By sharing ideas in our writing and by reflecting on and responding to the writing of others, we contribute to the creation of intellectual communities. The more widely ideas are shared, the better off we all are. Neither personal gain nor professional status is the primary motivation here. Instead, we publish to become part of something larger than ourselves.

While we aspire toward this noble goal in *Writing History in the Digital Age*, we also recognize the pressures for professional advancement faced particularly by newer scholars entering the field. At a conference workshop where we demonstrated our digital pilot project, we heard from many graduate students and junior faculty who were eager to share their historical writing online but who also needed affirmation that it would "count" in the eyes of future hiring and tenure committees. Could we find an established peer-reviewed journal or press whose role would lend sufficient status to enable them to fully participate in our collective effort? At the same time, we wondered whether we could find a journal or press that embraced our ideal of sharing our scholarship on the open web. Might there be a middle ground where all of these competing needs could be met?

One intriguing possibility was the University of Michigan Press. In 2009, the University of Michigan restructured its press to become part of its library, with a pioneering mission statement: "to use the best emerging digital technology to disseminate such information as freely and widely as possible while preserving the integrity of published scholarship."[24] The press maintains its editorial role and quality standards, but as a budgeted unit within the library, thereby reducing the pressure to recover costs through book sales revenue (though not alleviating it entirely). The boldest model of this library-press collaboration is its digitalculturebooks imprint, which disseminates peer-reviewed scholarship in two formats: print-on-demand books (for sale) and its open-access website (for free). At present, the press is still straddling old-world publishing and its new-world aspirations, with an increasing percentage of its books to be distributed in print and open-access formats, under Creative Commons licensing.[25] As we drafted our proposal for this edited volume, the University of Michigan's hybrid model—a reputable academic press combined with open-access digital publishing—offered the best means of accommodating our scholarly goals and realities.

Why Not Publish on the Open Web?

Two words that strike fear in the hearts of many historians are *blogs* and *wikis*. The problem is not simply that these web technologies may be new and unfamiliar but also that they challenge us to reconsider established norms about what counts as scholarly work in our colleges and universities. For instance, if the new history professor at the other end of the hall starts a blog, should that count as a publication? What if it is a long, expository blog essay with scholarly footnotes? If there are readers' comments on a blog, especially from other historians, should this count as peer review? Or must a publisher other than the author be involved in the process? If so, does that mean we should "count" an essay that a historian contributed to an online publication, such as *Wikipedia*? What if the *Wikipedia* entry was expanded on or modified by other contributors? Would that make it count more or count less? And what on earth does it mean to "publish" scholarly work in this digital age? Unsurprisingly, these questions make many historians nervous.

In fact, it is neither blogs nor wikis but, rather, another trend entirely that historians should fear: the creeping price of scholarly monographs. As authors, our worst nightmare is to toil away for years on a book that no one reads. Many of us are watching academic publishers issue hardcover-only editions and holding off on paperbacks in an effort to squeeze as much sales revenue as possible from libraries. Our jaws dropped over a year ago when a major publisher listed a colleague's hardcover historical monograph at $95. That copyrighted text is effectively locked inside a very expensive box that very few can afford, and the author has no legal recourse to let it out. Some of our academic libraries will refuse to buy it. When our books are priced this high, who really has access to our work? What happens to our noble goal of publishing to share and engage in the ideas of others?

Understandably, many historians still favor printed books as a familiar and reliable mode for sharing knowledge. Books offer a stable technology that does not rely on Internet access or operating systems. We enjoy the feel of books in the palms of our hands, the ease of reading wherever we choose to sit, and the ability to display our acquired knowledge on our bookshelves. We can purchase printed books from local booksellers and online vendors or borrow them from academic and public libraries (provided that these institutions continue to be supported by tuition and tax dollars). But one serious limitation of printed books is that they are built to provide only one-way scholarly communication of ideas, from author to audience. Information is disseminated to readers, who play no part in the knowledge-development process, unless they also happen to discuss it in a class or book group, send a letter to the author, write a book review, or incorporate it into their own scholarship. Certainly, readers can take the initiative to dialogue with the author or other readers, but printed books, by themselves, are not designed to promote a two-way exchange of ideas.

Despite the fanfare surrounding e-books, the current generation of this digital technology comes with limitations. The e-book formats currently found most commonly in academic libraries allow users to flip through images of book pages on our browsers, search the text, and copy passages into our notes, but they do not alter the one-way flow of scholarly communication from author to audience. Consumer-oriented e-books, such as those available for Amazon's Kindle, now permit readers to pay for an upgraded service to create highlights and notes on the text, which may be publicly shared online. However, Amazon's initial e-book licensing agreement was not library-friendly and did not legally permit the lending of content.[26] Only in September 2011 did the company appear to have shifted its policy by launching a beta program for selected public libraries to distribute e-books, but users are redirected from the public catalog to Amazon's commercial website with sales pitches. Moreover, critics have questioned the practice of using taxpayer-funded public libraries to boost Amazon's hardware sales (ranging from $80 to $200 per unit).[27] Whether proprietary e-books are a cost-effective means to expand public interaction with historical scholarship remains doubtful.

Our Web-Book Design

When proposing this volume, we sought a digital format that matched our scholarly values of sharing and engaging with ideas in public. Unlike most e-books (which emphasize one-way communication) or proprietary formats (which require subscription fees or the purchase of a new device), our solution was to create what we call a "web-book": built with open-source tools, it allows readers to freely access and respond to the text online, using a standard web browser. We believe that open-web scholarly publishing can merge the best of digital innovation and traditional practices. It should:

Look Like a Book

While not all digital history products are (or should be) book-like, we recognize that historians are skilled in writing in the traditional long-argument book format and comfortable in reading and evaluating others' works in that format. Our model uses a combination of open-source WordPress tools to deliver what historians seek: easily readable pages of text divided into chapters and sections, with clear attribution to individual authors or coauthors and *Chicago*-style footnotes. All of our software is freely available, and we were able to modify portions to fit our specific needs.

Protect Authors' Attribution Rights While Maximizing Public Access

Our text is shared under a Creative Commons Attribution-Noncommercial license, an extension of standard copyright that allows readers to freely share the essay content, with a citation to the author. Furthermore, our WordPress technology welcomes readers' comments in the margins while assuring authors that others cannot "rewrite" their original text (as wiki-style tools allow). As the book's editors, we also serve as website administrators, with the power to moderate any comments deemed inappropriate according to our editorial policy.

Integrate Narrative Text and Multimedia Source Materials

This quality strongly interests historians whose arguments rely on evidence not easily captured in conventional print. Visual historians can display images and video, social science historians can upload datasets, and spatial historians can walk us through maps. With open-web publishing, authors can link to any source that is freely available on the Internet. By contrast, Amazon's current best-selling historical e-books with audio and/or video clips provide only a limited selection of media content, packaged inside the proprietary book file, not on the public web.

Speed Up Distribution While Preserving Archival and Print Formats

Historians want it both ways: we desire instant access to the newest works in our field, while also demanding that the past be safely archived. We also insist on having the choice to read on screen or in print. While we acknowledge that this volume's publishing formats are imperfect, they do represent a step forward. At present, our web-book platform allows us to immediately distribute the latest version and maintain internal links to prior versions, with a basic archival copy, including comments, in PDF format. Although text links to external sites may break, our style guide requires a full citation and URL in the endnotes. In addition, our contract specifies that the University of Michigan Press will publish the book in two formats: a print-on-demand edition and an open-access online edition, which will be preserved by its Library.

Be Findable with Existing Library Search Tools

Currently, the *Writing History in the Digital Age* web-book is hosted on a server at Trinity College in Hartford, Connecticut, where librarians created a MARC record for the item and uploaded it to WorldCat, to increase its likelihood of being found by other scholars.[28]

Promote Peer Review with Two-Way Scholarly Communication

As authors, we cannot judge whether our own writing successfully communicates complex ideas without receiving some type of feedback from our intended audience. When publishing a scholarly print book or e-book, we generally have little idea how it is received unless a reader happens to contact us directly or an academic journal prints a review, typically a year or two later. By contrast, socially networked texts allow substantive communication between writers and readers. In the case of this volume, online commenting, combined with view data for the web pages, tells us exactly which passages readers praised, panned, or never even bothered to read.

Perhaps the scariest question of all is, do we really want to know what our readers think or how many readers we actually have? The risk of having our ideas openly criticized, on the very same digital pages that we labored over, is very real. But it also forces us to reflect on the central question—why do we publish?—and on whether we genuinely desire to share and engage with the ideas of others in public or prefer the traditional norms of writing in private and publishing in increasingly expensive and exclusive outlets.

Whether they prefer print, e-books, or web-books, all historians agree that the quality of the work is what truly matters. Yet we sometimes lack agreement on how scholarly work should be evaluated (particularly in the humanities) and at what stage(s) of the process it should happen. In the traditional publishing model, academic presses employ editors and external reviewers to filter their products prior to publication, to signal that books meet their selective standards and are deemed worth reading. Several models of digital publishing reverse this equation by placing content on the Internet and relying on the wisdom of the readership to sort out what is—and is not—worth reading. Both exercise a form of peer review, but at different stages in the scholarly communication process. Media studies scholar Kathleen Fitzpatrick elaborates on this point.

> In a self-multiplying scholarly commons, some kind of assessment of the material that has been published remains important, but not because of scarce resources; instead, what remains scarce are time and attention. For this reason, peer review needs to be put not in the service of gatekeeping, or determining what should be published for any scholar to see, but of filtering, or determining what of the vast amount of material that has been published is of interest or value to a particular scholar. As Clay Shirky has argued, "Filter-then-publish, whatever its advantages, rested on a scarcity of media that is a thing of the past. The expansion of social media means that the only working system is publish-then-filter."[29]

For many historians, our interest in the "publish-then-filter" concept arose independently of the Internet. Arguably the most widely discussed issue of the *Journal of American History* in recent decades was a controversial roundtable issue in 1997 titled "What We See and Can't See in the Past." Editor David Thelen published an article on the history of lynching submitted by Joel Williamson, followed by the reports of six reviewers. After receiving all of the reports, Thelen persuaded everyone to attach their names to the original documents, "to demystify our own practice," and openly published them in the journal alongside Williamson's article. In his introduction, Thelen justified this nonconventional approach, arguing, "We live in an age when historians are as interested in the doing of history as in the products of that doing."[30] As it happened, the reviewers sharply disagreed on the strengths and weaknesses of Williamson's historical analysis of race, and the numerous letters to the editor published in the subsequent issue of the journal revealed the need for a deeper discussion about how historians judge the quality of each other's scholarly writing.

Elsewhere in the humanities, we have been inspired more recently by innovative combinations of web technology and open peer review that invigorate scholarly communication. Some of the most prominent examples are hybrids—a mixture of invited and public reviewers—that retain an editorial board's sense of confidence in its appointed experts, while reaping the benefits of the crowd's wisdom. In 2009, under the auspices of MediaCommons Press, Kathleen Fitzpatrick released a full draft of her book manuscript *Planned Obsolescence: Publishing, Technology, and the Future of the Academy* for open peer review, in an agreement with her prospective publisher, NYU Press, which simultaneously sent it out for blind review and subsequently published the book two years later.[31] In 2010, Media-Commons Press hosted an open-review edition of a leading literary journal, *Shakespeare Quarterly*, where contributors' submissions received open-review commentary from designated and self-selected reviewers.[32] What is most striking about these hybrid models is their mixture of public space (for open commentary) and private space (for final editorial decisions).

Our Proposal

We propose *Writing History in the Digital Age* as one (but certainly not the only) model for rethinking publishing in ways that preserve our scholarly values. As you immerse yourself in the individual essays on history, technology, and our craft as authors, consider the argument embedded in this book's born-digital format, open-review editorial process, and open-access distribution. We have already asked, why not publish scholarship on the open web? Now it is time to flip the question and ask, why are we still holding onto proprietary print and e-book publishing if there are better ways to achieve our goals? As academic authors, our primary aim is to maximize the quality and distribution of ideas. Whether we are motivated more by individual status or by broader principles, the rising price of hardcover-only books and commercial databases should cause alarm and lead us to seriously consider alternatives. Is there any reason to limit peer review to a small number of readers, when hybrid open-review online models reap the dual benefits of invited experts and the public at large? Does it still make sense to lock our texts into proprietary digital formats, when open-web publishing can protect authors' rights and connect us with wider communities of readers?

We do not claim that the transition to open-web scholarly publishing is simple, and we have always seen this volume as a very public experiment, with its failure a distinct possibility. Several questions that have continually arisen in public conferences and private conversations reveal many tensions that historians feel about these issues. How do we create communities of authors, readers, and commenters to enhance the quality of born-digital works? Does the open peer-review process discourage candid criticism from commenters who may be reluctant to post negative remarks on the public web? Finally, is open-access scholarly publishing, as exemplified by the University of Michigan library-press partnership, a fiscally sustainable model for the future? We address these questions in our concluding reflections in this volume, drawing on our experience with this volume's development. But in large part, the discussion of whether to change what and how historians write is moot. Scholarship-as-usual no longer appears to be a sustainable model, as much for historians as for others. We hope *Writing History in the Digital Age* will inspire others to join in rethinking how and why and even what we publish, all in the service of improving both our scholarship and others' access to it.

Notes

1. Kathleen Fitzpatrick and Katherine Rowe, "Keywords for Open Peer Review," *Logos: The Journal of the World Book Community* 21, nos. 3–4 (2010): 133–41, http://www.ingentaconnect.com/content/brill/logo/2010/00000021/F0020003/art00015.

2. Roy Rosenzweig, "Should Historical Scholarship Be Free?," *Perspectives*, April 2005, http://www.historians.org/Perspectives/issues/2005/0504/0504vic1.cfm, reprinted in *Clio Wired: The Future of the Past in the Digital Age* (New York: Columbia University Press, 2011), 117–23; John Willinsky, *The Access Principle: The Case for Open Access to Research and Scholarship.* (Cambridge, MA: MIT Press, 2006), http://mitpress.mit.edu/catalog/item/default.asp?tid=10611&ttype=2.

3. "About the Licenses," Creative Commons, http://creativecommons.org/licenses/.

4. See, for example, the work of the scholar-led NINES (Networked Infrastructure for Nineteenth-Century Electronic Scholarship, http://www.nines.org); the pioneering Stanford Humanities Lab (http://humanitieslab.stanford.edu/Metamedia/9); and HASTAC (Humanities, Arts, Science, and Technology Collaboratory, http://hastac.org/).

5. Roy Rosenzweig Center for History and New Media, http://chnm.gmu.edu/.

6. See, for example, Edward L. Ayers, *The Valley of the Shadow: Two Communities in the American Civil War,* http://valley.lib.virginia.edu/; American Historical Association, "Intersections: History and New Media," *Perspectives Online* 47, no. 5 (2009), http://www.historians.org/perspectives/issues/2009/0905/.

7. Daniel J. Cohen and Roy Rosenzweig, *Digital History. A Guide to Gathering, Preserving, and Presenting the Past on the Web* (Fairfax, VA: Center for History and New Media, 2005), http://chnm.gmu.edu/digitalhistory/.

8. Robert B. Townsend, "How Is New Media Reshaping the Work of Historians?," *Perspectives Online* 48, no. 8 (2010), http://www.historians.org/Perspectives/issues/2010/1011/1011pro2.cfm; Diane Harley et al., *Assessing the Future Landscape of Scholarly Communication: An Exploration of Faculty Values and Needs in Seven Disciplines* (Berkeley: Center for Studies in Higher Education, University of California, Berkeley, 2010); Rebecca Griffiths, Michael Dawson, and Matthew Rascoff, *Scholarly Communications in the History Discipline* (New York: Ithaka Strategic Services for JStor, 2006).

9. Sean Takats, "Adoption of 'New' Media by Historians," *The Quintessence of Ham,* October 28, 2010, accessed August 14, 2011, http://quintessenceofham. org/2010/10/28/adoption-of-new-media-by-historians/#identifier_1_279.

10. See specifically Townsend, "How Is New Media Reshaping the Work of Historians?," fig. 5.

11. Christina Haas, *Writing Technology: Studies on the Materiality of Literacy* (Mahwah, NJ: Lawrence Erlbaum Associates, 1996), 26.

12. Ken Hyland, "Authority and Invisibility: Authorial Identity in Academic Writing," *Journal of Pragmatics* 34, no. 8 (2002): 1091.

13. John Updike, "The End of Authorship," *New York Times Sunday Book Review,* June 25, 2006, http://www.nytimes.com/2006/06/25/books/review/25updike.html; Ken Hyland, *Writing in the Academy: Reputation, Education, and Knowledge* (London: Institute of Education, University of London, 2007).

14. Donald Eugene Hall, *The Academic Self: An Owner's Manual* (Columbus: Ohio State University Press, 2002), xviii.

15. Sean Takats, "Time Shifting and Historical Research," *The Quintessence of Ham,* March 20, 2011, http://quintessenceofham.org/2010/10/28/adoption-of-new-media-by-historians/#identifier_1_279.

16. Townsend, "How Is New Media Reshaping the Work of Historians?"

17. E. Bell, "Barriers to Institutional Digital History," *Jefferson's Newspaper: A Blog about Information, Education, and the (Digital) Humanities,* May 17, 2009, accessed September 19, 2011, http://jeffersonsnewspaper.org/2009/barriers-to-institutional-digital-history/.

18. Dan Cohen, Stephen Ramsay, and Kathleen Fitzpatrick, "Open Access and Scholarly Values," in *Hacking the Academy,* ed. Dan Cohen and Tom Scheinfeldt (Ann Arbor: University of Michigan Press, 2013), http://www.digitalculture.org/hacking-the-academy/hacking-scholarship/#scholarship-cohen.

19. Griffiths, Dawson, and Rascoff, *Scholarly Communications in the History Discipline,* 11.

20. Harley et al., *Assessing the Future Landscape of Scholarly Communication,* 392.

21. Ibid., 452.

22. Deborah Tannen, "Agonism in the Academy," *Chronicle of Higher Education,* March 31, 2000, B7–B8.

23. Sam Wineburg, *Historical Thinking and Other Unnatural Acts: Charting the Future of Teaching the Past* (Philadelphia: Temple University Press, 2001).

24. Jennifer Howard, "U. of Michigan Press Reorganizes as a Unit of the Library," *Chronicle of Higher Education,* March 23, 2009, http://chronicle.com/article/U-of-Michigan-Press/47128.

25. Tom Dwyer, phone conversation with Jack Dougherty, January 31, 2012.

26. Barbara Fister, "Blog U.: Why There's No Kindle 'Freedom' in Libraries," *Inside Higher Ed,* September 24, 2010, http://www.insidehighered.com/blogs/library_babel_fish/why_there_s_no_kindle_freedom_in_libraries.

27. Brier Dudley, "Kindle Library Lending: Good Deal for Everyone?," *Seattle Times,* September 26, 2011, http://seattletimes.nwsource.com/html/technology-brierdudleysblog/2016323413_kindle_library_lending_questio.html.

28. *Writing History in the Digital Age,* web-book ed., Spring 2012 version, http://www.worldcat.org/title/writing-history-in-the-digital-age/oclc/756644249.

29. Kathleen Fitzpatrick, *Planned Obsolescence: Publishing, Technology, and the Future of the Academy* (New York: NYU Press, 2011), 46, quoting Clay Shirky, *Here Comes Everybody: The Power of Organizing without Organizations* (New York: Penguin, 2008), 98.

30. David Thelen, "What We See and Can't See in the Past: An Introduction," *Journal of American History* 83, no. 4 (1997): 1217, http://www.jstor.org/stable/2952898.

31. Fitzpatrick, *Planned Obsolescence* (New York: MediaCommons, 2009), http://mediacommons.futureofthebook.org/mcpress/plannedobsolescence/.

32. Jennifer Howard, "Leading Humanities Journal Debuts 'Open' Peer Review, and Likes It," *Chronicle of Higher Education*, July 26, 2010, http://chronicle.com/article/Leading-Humanities-Journal/123696.

PART I

Re-Visioning Historical Writing

In the first part of this volume, Sherman Dorn asks, "Is (digital) history more than an argument about the past?" He draws distinctions between thesis-driven scholarly monographs and digital history projects, with examples and ideas for evaluating the latter. In "Pasts in a Digital Age," Stefan Tanaka follows up by arguing that today's digital media revolution should remind us that our present-day conceptions of history did not arise until the late-eighteenth century, when people began writing about the past in a linear, chronological structure.

Is (Digital) History More than an Argument about the Past?

Sherman Dorn

Digital history is one more historiographical development since World War II that has challenged professional historians' definition of scholarship. While oral history and quantitative social history questioned the primacy of the written document and an elite focus, they and public history challenged the centrality of the researcher trained in academic history departments, and postmodernism undermined the authority of categories.[1] Of central concern is not whether the online world has infected humanities scholars in the United States with intellectual challenges (and status anxiety) but what new forms these are taking and the new professional and intellectual questions that digital history poses for historians.[2] As younger scholars worry about what "counts" as scholarship in an online universe, fearing that their senior colleagues will not respect anything other than monographs published by university presses, they partly replay previous waves of concern about professional legitimation.

Other chapters in this book illustrate the degree to which historians have continued to extend long-term changes in the discipline. The use of databases for notes is a more sophisticated version of electronic note taking that started with the first laptops. Mapping locations of community events and resources is an extension of quantitative social history's wrestling with data. Social history "from the bottom up" becomes more intense and more public when members of a community can more easily contribute to and discover work about their shared history. Creating video games out of history is in some ways a new version of the simulation role playing that teachers have used for decades.

Yet there are new opportunities and challenges that did not exist several decades ago. One is the ability to display primary sources and related data objects tied to those sources (tables, charts, and maps). As this volume's chapters by Stephen Robertson and John Theibault demonstrate, we are surrounded not just by the type of static images and data objects that historians have used to make arguments for years but by the ability to present audiences and interlocutors with manipulable objects, using software to allow readers to zoom in and move around, add or subtract data layers, change axes and variables, or set the data object in motion.[3]

The second feature that is new today is the spread of publishing platforms. One made *Wikipedia* possible. Another allowed this volume to have open peer review. At the same time, we have seen the erosion of the university press and subscription-based journal publishing as a viable commercial infrastructure for scholarship. The ease of disseminating gray literature and the growth of technological platforms for open-access publishing has undermined the case for continued reliance on subscription-based journals and university presses as gatekeepers with prepublication review. Intensified budget pressures on academic libraries have accelerated this discussion. The results have included more experimentation with alternative publishing pipelines and processes, as well as the challenges in intellectual authority captured by the chapters of this volume focusing on *Wikipedia*.[4]

The third development is an artifact of the production of history in the first few decades of the "digital age" in historical scholarship: historians' first-mover advantage. It arose from funders having a range of interests; from a few senior historians, such as Roy Rosenzweig and Edward Ayers, using funding to develop diverse projects; and from the development of digitization technology far in advance of electronic book publication. The first-mover advantage for CD-ROM and then web projects leveraged interest in digitizing a range of sources at a time when it was neither technologically realistic nor professionally advantageous to try to publish long-form arguments online. Into that gap stepped funders, institutions, and individual academics and teams of scholars who had different priorities. At the same time, two developments at a national level in the United States created educational audiences as well as funding streams for a range of projects: a push for state-level standards in traditional K–12 academic subjects, including history, and a dedicated funding stream in the Teaching American History grant program.[5]

As a result of funding, entrepreneurial academics, ready audiences, and technological developments that benefited other formats over electronic books, the early production of digital history thus emphasized infrastructure over electronic equivalents of monographs. This first-mover advantage for new formats existed even when an individual digital project (such as Ayers's *The Valley of the Shadow*) was rooted in more conventional questions of scholarship. It required building idiosyncratic infrastructures that we usually associate with wealthy private or flagship public universities, but less prestigious public institutions, such as the City University of New York and George Mason University, built long-term structures where the new digital scholarship has thrived.

These developments happened in an era of existential threats to humanities scholarship whose roots lie far from the influence of technological change on the mechanics of scholarship. Long before Amazon.com, scholars have seen declining state support for public universities, vocational rhetoric surrounding the politics of higher education, the growing use of contingent academic labor, and increased pressures for scholarship at institutions that had focused on teaching only a few short years before.[6] Yet despite these ominous signs, the growth of digital scholarship provides an opportunity to understand our field in a richer way, and this understanding can serve both pragmatic and philosophical needs.

In one pragmatic sense, scholars whose work goes beyond the long-form argument need a way to help peers and administrators understand their work. Ernest Boyer's *Scholarship Reconsidered* describes a general way of communicating for such understanding but is not sufficiently specific for each discipline.[7] Public historians have often struggled to communicate the meaning of their scholarship in research-oriented institutions, and the development of disciplinary support for their work and appropriate tenure and promotion standards has been relatively recent.[8]

In a second pragmatic sense, we need a better way to teach historical scholarship for undergraduates, not only for the ordinary reasons why history departments should be concerned about an undergraduate education, but also because we need better teaching of history in elementary and middle schools. Frequently, the second-to-last exposure to history for an elementary school teacher is her or his high school history classes, leaving the task of helping them understand history as a discipline to just one or two college courses. College history classes have little room for error in educating future teachers about what history is and can be.

But if we use digital history projects as an opportunity to explore the nature of historical scholarship, that opportunity stretches beyond the practical issues of tenure, promotion, and exposing future teachers to disciplinary conventions. We can use the best of digital history work to redraw the discipline's boundaries. In attempting to battle the perception of his-

Fig. 1. Detail from the poster *History Is an Argument about the Past* (National History Education Clearinghouse, 2010). The emphasis in the poster is on using primary sources, understanding multiple perspectives, and putting issues in historical context. Missing is the type of work that often dominates digital history projects, including the one that created this poster.

tory as a set of dates and names, or "just one damned thing after another," as Toynbee and Somervell put it, historians may have gone overboard in arguing that history is "an argument about the past," as a poster available to schoolteachers puts it (fig. 1).[9] The heterodox developments of the last few decades provide an opportunity to rethink the definition of historical scholarship. (See additional images for this essay at http://WritingHistory. trincoll.edu.)

Diverse Digital History

Digital history projects have a broad range of quality and scope. This section provides brief descriptions of several projects that were created by professional historians, public historians, and other scholars.[10] It describes projects with differing polish and scope, beginning with two projects originally distributed on CD-ROM.[11]

Who Built America? was an extension of a two-volume social history textbook of the same name, with two CD-ROMs constructed and published in the 1990s.[12] The CD-ROMs provided a digital expansion of the common textbook sidebar presentation of primary sources, including audio and video clips of speeches as well as photographs and text or facsimile primary documents. Creating such a compilation is a labor-intensive process, in part because of extensive licensure issues involved in using media.[13]

The Valley of the Shadow was also an extension of a book project, in this case Edward L. Ayers's comparison of lives in two counties (Franklin County, Pennsylvania, and Augusta County, Virginia) before, during, and after the Civil War.[14] The project had an early online life, which Michael O'Malley and Roy Rosenzweig described in 1997 as a guided exploration of primary sources: "It allows students to construct their own narratives of life in both towns in the years before the war, but it seems to encourage narratives that follow the framework of Ayers's planned book."[15] In the years since, it has had various versions, including the transformation of the materials to a website that now serves as an official "archive" of the project.[16]

The *American Memory* project displays both notable and little-known primary sources, photographs, and other artifacts in Library of Congress collections. Begun in the early 1990s with a pilot project and CD-ROMs, *American Memory* has continued as a sprawling online display of historical artifacts.[17] Individual items in the collection are displayed with archival metadata and can often be reached either as part of an organized presentation or through search tools.

The Papers of George Washington is a 43-year-old editing project that has produced more than 50 volumes of edited material (out of an anticipated 90). One digital version of the papers has public access. A more scholarly online version of the papers is available by individual or personal subscription as well as by purchase of individual printed volumes from the University of Virginia Press.[18] The general-access version contains a number of entrees to the primary sources, including chronological back/forward buttons that are akin to page turns.

Hypercities (http://hypercities.com or http://hypercities.ats.ucla.edu/) is a geographic display platform for layered maps built on Google Maps and the ability to geocode pictures and maps. While other platforms built on Google Maps focus on current events (for example, *Ushahidi*, originally created to map Kenyan election violence in early 2008), *Hypercities* focuses on the collection and curation of historical map information. It is the result of a 2008 MacArthur Foundation grant to Todd Presner of the University of California, Los Angeles, and Philip Ethington at the University of Southern California and has been used for a number of classes at various institutions as well as for scholarly research (such as Ethington's work on the history of Los Angeles).[19]

Europe, Interrupted is an online exhibit of the Inventing Europe project sponsored by the European Science Foundation and the Foundation for the History of Technology. It presents a structured path through collection items using the "exhibit" metaphor for presentation. It is an example of the type of exhibit produced using the open-source Omeka presentation software that public historians can customize for specific exhibits in museum collections.[20]

History Matters is a website originally created in the late 1990s by the same organizations that created *Who Built America?* (the American Social History Project at the City University of New York and the Roy Rosenzweig Center for History and New Media at George Mason University). The website supports survey courses in U.S. history at the high school and undergraduate levels (and is subtitled *The U.S. Survey Course on the Web*), with a range of materials from selected primary sources and historical links to sample syllabi, exemplary student work, and other resources for teachers.[21]

Digital History Undresses Scholarship

The scope of these and other projects illustrate their breadth of purpose and the varied extent to which individual projects make an explicit argument, ranging from what one might call demonstrative argumentation (*Europe, Interrupted* and the individual *Women and Social Movements* websites, as Kathryn Kish Sklar and Thomas Dublin's chapter explains) to arguments-in-process (see Erickson's chapter), evidence sets from projects that are either at the "messing around" level (*Hypercities*) or more carefully curated for the public (*The Valley of the Shadow*), edited collections with an implicit argument (*Who Built America?*), edited collections without a demonstrative focus (*American Memory* and *The Papers of George Washington*), and infrastructure (whether for research, such as software packages specially built for humanities projects or the Integrated Public Use Microdata Series database, or for teaching, such as *History Matters*).[22]

This range uncovers history as more than a polished argument about the past. Presentation of historical scholarship as an argument presumes a finished product. But most time spent on historical scholarship is messy, involving rooting through Hollinger boxes, begging someone for an oral history interview, coughing through a shelf of city reports or directories, rereading notes, drafting manuscripts, sorting through critical comments, revising, and so forth. A published work does not materialize from a vacuum, and all that preceded and underlays it is legitimately part of historical work. Public presentations of history in the digital age reveal the extent of that "preargument" work, often in an explicitly demonstrative fashion or allowing an audience to work with evidence that is less directly accessible in a fixed, bound presentation. Digital history thus undresses the historical argument, showing that all our professional garments are clothing, even those not usually seen in public. As reviewer William Thomas observed, the digital age also allows scholars to scale up the extent of explicit argumentation, either by redesigning a project's public face or by inviting open commentary (as this volume has done). This capacity is more than accessorizing; it allows explicit, public reworking of argument.[23]

Tools for Presentation of Artifacts and Events, Learning, and Argumentation

Recognizing the breadth of presentation is separate from having trustworthy evaluation practices. Projects described above have won a number of awards, and yet, of the collection listed here, only *Europe, Interrupted* (and none of the award-winning projects) focuses on the type of argument that historians value in monographs published by university presses. Can we attach evaluative criteria to nonargument scholarship? The fields at the margins of history departments provide a partial solution, as academic historians in the post–World War II era have recognized the value of nonargument activities and functions. Public history is valued in theory, even if only a few history departments have faculty who engage in public history projects (and fewer who have earned tenure on that basis). Archivists are essential to the work of historians, but they are usually trained in schools that teach library or information sciences.[24] History faculty whose primary tool is archaeology have the ability to write methodological papers for specialist journals. If this pattern extends to digital history, one should expect that a few departments will devote significant resources to the formal training of digital history technicians, those who have programming skills and some disciplinary history background, and that most departments will struggle to evaluate digital history projects except where professional awards clearly convey peer approval.

But there need not be significant difficulty in understanding the contributions of digital history projects. As demonstrated in the projects described in this chapter or in the rest of this volume, academic historians have little problem recognizing the value of outstanding digital history work. The question is how to articulate the contributions of digital history in a way that is conceptual rather than ad hoc. We may use the existing outstanding digital history scholarship to generate those concepts, and the rest of this section catalogs an initial classification.

Tools to Present Artifacts

There is a range of recognized professional presentations of historical artifacts, generally primary sources but also multimedia files. The Library of Congress *American Memory* project is the most extensive in North America, but both *The Papers of George Washington* and *The Valley of the Shadow* organize primary sources for an audience. The scope is different in each case: the Library of Congress (or a research library's special collections department) cares for and presents material from multiple collections in its custody, while an edited version of an individual's papers or a thematic collection is narrower in purpose as well as scope. The critical traits of an archival resource for historians include custodianship and proper sourcing, and the critical traits of an online presentation of historical artifacts parallel those: care of the digital resource and clear provenance. One can see similar parallels with edited collections of primary sources (a "Papers of . . ." project), though in the case of *The Papers of George Washington*, it is clear that while the editing quality is the same for the (identical) hard copy and online main text, the public digital version is missing critical traits of annotation that historians expect of scholarly edited collections of quality.[25]

Tools to Present Events

A second general use of tools for digital history is the presentation of "events," or, more generally, specifics of history bounded by time and place. A number of tools exist for creating online time lines such as the SIMILE tool that has been incorporated into Google Docs or the EasyTimeline markup format in MediaWiki software.[26] One does not need an online tool to create a time line. But complex time and space data require specialized tools for presentation. The construction of historical maps has been an art form for centuries, generally beyond the recognized skill set of academic historians.[27] *Hypercities* has attracted considerable attention in the few years of its development, because it allows the presentation of data in a form that is attractive, thought-provoking, and conceptually simple, with successive layers representing change over time. One does not need to be an artist to use *Hypercities*, though the required digitization and geocoding tasks require time and attention to detail. One could also argue that statistical presentation is an equally important activity in presenting "events," if one considers a datum bounded by time and place, with presentation of statistical data being a skill often neglected in history departments. Gapminder is currently the most generally known infrastructure for presenting historical data series online in an attractive and conceptually simple manner.[28]

Tools for Teaching and Learning

Classroom-focused digital history projects can encompass an expanded/ enriched textbook, a teaching portal with a range of resources, or other configurations. The construction of any website around learning is more than the appending of lesson plans to an existing website. It is the deliberate composition of resources that includes primary sources and support for activities that teachers might design or facilitate for students.

Tools for Argumentation

Tools for constructing arguments have begun to catch up with other digital technologies. Blogs have been a tool for short-form argumentation that has made self-publishing of short commentary accessible to individual scholars for more than a decade, but long-form or multimedia arguments have generally required specialized website construction until recently. Some blog tools, such as the WordPress plug-in Digress.it, now allow the publication of book-length projects with open commentary as the projects evolve (including the project that prompted this essay).[29] Omeka is a tool for online public history exhibits discussed earlier. Some of the more adventuresome university presses, such as the University of Michigan Press, have also explored different ways to extend the definition of the long-form argument beyond the hard-copy book.

As suggested earlier, historians will probably recognize the value of digital history in presentations of artifacts and sets of events and event representations when they contain the recognizable elements of quality work in offline parallels: care in custodianship and curation, tracking of provenance, match of organization with purpose, and accessibility of presentation. Such digital history projects may be viewed as inferior to long-form arguments unless they are adjuncts to scholarship that academic historians already recognize. But recognizing such projects as valuable scholarship does not require rethinking the fundamentals of historical work, since it matches up well to the traits of existing scholarly infrastructure for historians.

What requires more deliberate effort is the evaluation of scholarly work in creating tools and infrastructure. Here, an important consideration is the public visibility and use of the work. This is a pragmatic issue in terms of long-term impact as well as immediate value. Tools by themselves have little value as archived; because software quickly becomes outdated, a tool that is not used within a year or two will have no one providing feedback, no volunteers for further development, and no chance of support from potential funders. Yet, to gain users, most tools generally require a team that builds a community as well as creating a software package.

This requirement of effective team building makes collaboration an essential part of tool building, which may be the most difficult criteria for historians to assimilate in evaluation, more than use. Historical scholarship generally operates as solo projects or as the product of very small teams of scholars. In contrast with those small teams, a much larger community is required by the development, persistent use, and maintenance of software packages such as Omeka or Zotero.[30] A history department at a research university may give tenure to an assistant professor who writes a single-authored book on an obscure topic with fewer than 200 copies sold, based on a university press's prospective valuation of the manuscript and postpublication review by a small number of senior scholars. But if assistant professors continue to work on a software package they contributed to as graduate students, that collaboration risks their careers, even if the software is used extensively by museums and historical sites and has a broader professional impact than narrow monographs. I suspect many history departments would gladly value a scholar who headed such a project, but historians find the contribution of other project members difficult to evaluate.

Toward Bricolage or Narrative?

In addition to the difficulty they encounter in evaluating collaboration in infrastructure, historians find the value of long-form arguments easier to evaluate as scholarship because the long-form argument contributes to historiographical discourse. As we construct arguments, we patch together ideas of our peers, trained by the practices of graduate education ("What is the contribution of this week's book?") and the ethics of citation ("Where did I read about that theory?"). In this discourse community, a peer's polished argument is labile feedstock. Should digital history projects thus shape their public sides closer to argumentation, to be digested and recycled by the bricoleur historian?[31]

There is more long-term value in maintaining a range of presentation of history in digital form than in trying to match contemporary writing habits too closely. It is not utopian to trust that bricoleurs will find value in pieces of digital history not presented as argument. It is not utopian to understand that while the definition of historical scholarship is centered heavily on the argument, there is an older tradition of history as narrative. It is not utopian to trust that if 20th-century historians learned to become bricoleurs, 21st-century historians will use digital forms to modify both argument and narrative. This chapter addressed argument; the next addresses narrative.

Notes

1. For an example from oral history, see Alessandro Portelli, *The Death of Luigi Trastulli, and Other Stories* (Albany: SUNY Press, 1991). For the barest taste of more general historians' navel-gazing, see Roy Rosenzweig and David Thelen, *The Presence of the Past* (New York: Columbia University Press, 1998); Joyce Oldham Appleby, Lynn Hunt, and Margaret Jacob, *Telling the Truth about History* (New York: W. W. Norton, 1994); Peter Charles Hoffer, *Past Imperfect* (New York: PublicAffairs, 2007); Jon Wiener, *Historians in Trouble* (New York: New Press, 2005).

2. This chapter focuses on both the professional dynamics in the United States and websites in English, but the argument is more general: we should see the

diversity of successful digital projects everywhere as a way to talk about historical scholarship.

3. The access (and business) models chosen by scholars heading projects do not always allow public access. The website for *The Papers of George Washington*, described in this chapter, requires institutional subscriptions for scholarly details. Subscriptions are also required to access the *Women and Social Movements* collections (described in this volume by Kathryn Kish Sklar and Thomas Dublin) or the tables and figures of the online *Historical Statistics of the United States, Millennial Edition*, ed. Susan B. Carter et al. (New York: Cambridge University Press, 2006), available at http://hsus.cambridge.org.

4. Kathleen Fitzpatrick, *Planned Obsolescence* (New York: NYU Press, 2011).

5. Maris Vinovskis, *From a Nation at Risk to No Child Left Behind* (New York: Teachers College Press, 2008); Alex Stein, "The Teaching American History Program: An Introduction and Overview," *History Teacher* 36, no. 2 (2003): 178–85.

6. For a sample of the recent literature on such changes, see Derek Bok, *Universities in the Marketplace* (Princeton: Princeton University Press, 2004); David L. Kirp, *Shakespeare, Einstein, and the Bottom Line* (Cambridge, MA: Harvard University Press, 2004); Martha C. Nussbaum, *Not for Profit* (Princeton: Princeton University Press, 2010).

7. Ernest Boyer, *Scholarship Reconsidered*, 1st ed. (San Francisco: Jossey-Bass, 1997).

8. Working Group on Evaluating Public History Scholarship, "Tenure, Promotion, and the Publicly Engaged Academic Historian: A Report," *AHA Perspectives*, September 2010, http://www.historians.org/perspectives/issues/2010/1009/1009new3.cfm.

9. Arnold Toynbee and D. C. Somervell, *A Study of History* (New York: Dell, 1965), 295; National History Education Clearinghouse, "History Is an Argument about the Past" (poster), described in "Free Historical Thinking Poster!," August 17, 2010, http://teachinghistory.org/nhec-blog/24174/.

10. There are also creditable digital history projects by amateurs, such as Phil Gyford's presentation of a 17th-century London source, "The Diary of Samuel Pepys," as a series of blog entries, at http://www.pepysdiary.com. The Internet advances the blurring of boundaries between academic and other production of history, a topic this volume's chapters on *Wikipedia* explore further.

11. With some important exceptions, such as *The Papers of George Washington* and *Women and Social Movements*, digital history projects in the past decade have generally had publicly accessible online distribution. This essay does not discuss distinctions between public and subscription availability and related issues of ethics and business models.

12. Roy Rosenzweig, Steve Brier, and Joshua Brown, *Who Built America? From the Centennial Celebration of 1876 to the Great War of 1914* (Santa Monica: Learning Technologies Interactive/Voyager, 1995), CD-ROM; American Social History Productions, *Who Built America? From the Great War of 1914 to the Dawn of the Atomic Age in 1946* (New York: Worth, 2000), CD-ROM.

13. Daniel Jared Cohen and Roy Rosenzweig, *Digital History* (Philadelphia: University of Pennsylvania Press, 2006), chap. 7.

14. Edward L. Ayers, *In the Presence of Mine Enemies* (New York: W. W. Norton, 2003).

15. Michael O'Malley and Roy Rosenzweig, "Brave New World or Blind Alley? American History on the World Wide Web," *Journal of American History* 84, no. 1 (1997): 145.

16. Edward Ayers, *The Valley of the Shadow: Two Communities in the Civil War,* http://valley.lib.virginia.edu/. For this site, it is implied that the term *archives* refers to a static entity that will not be revised, rather than a living, curated collection of materials.

17. Library of Congress, "Mission and History," *American Memory,* http://memory.loc.gov/ammem/about/index.html.

18. *The Papers of George Washington,* http://gwpapers.virginia.edu; Mount Vernon guest version, http://rotunda.upress.virginia.edu/founders/GEWN.xqy; Rotunda scholarly edition by subscription, http://rotunda.upress.virginia.edu/founders/GEWN. The project has received considerable support over the decades from the National Endowment of the Humanities and the National Historical Publications and Records Commission.

19. *Hypercities,* http://hypercities.com or http://hypercities.ats.ucla.edu/; *Ushahidi,* http://www.ushahidi.com/; Philip Ethington, "Ghost Metropolis," *Hypercities,* 2011, available at http://hypercities.ats.ucla.edu.

20. *Europe, Interrupted,* http://www.inventingeurope.eu/invent/exhibits/show/europeinterrupted; Center for History and New Media, *Omeka,* http://omeka.org.

21. American Social History Project and Center for History and New Media, *History Matters,* http://historymatters.gmu.edu/.

22. An online exhibit such as *Europe, Interrupted* is a relatively straightforward translation of long-form historical arguments to a hyperlinked environment, akin to a conventional, curated public history exhibit with a strong focus.

23. Will Thomas, comment on Sherman Dorn, "Is (Digital) History More than an Argument about the Past?," in *Writing History in the Digital Age,* web-book ed., Fall 2011 version. This undressing also demonstrates how historians make choices as they fashion scholarship; for more on selection and silencing, see, for example, David William Cohen, *The Combing of History* (Chicago: University of Chicago Press, 1994); Michel-Rolph Trouillot, *Silencing the Past* (Boston: Beacon, 1995), especially chap. 1.

24. The *Directory of Archival Education* of the Society of American Archivists (http://www2.archivists.org/dae) lists seven archival degree programs located in history departments.

25. A separate issue is the organization of such artifacts, and I recognize that one could argue that an exhibit using Omeka is also a presentation of artifacts.

26. Semantic Interoperability of Metadata and Information in unLike Environments (SIMILE) project, SIMILE software (Massachusetts Institute of Technology), available at http://www.simile-widgets.org/timeline/; WikiMedia Foundation, EasyTimeline extension, http://www.mediawiki.org/wiki/Extension:EasyTimeline.

27. The classic is Charles Joseph Minard's display of Napoleon's march into and out of Moscow. See Edward R. Tufte, *The Visual Display of Quantitative Information,* 2nd ed. (Cheshire, CT: Graphics, 2001), 40–41. See also, more generally, Dan-

iel Rosenberg and Anthony Grafton, *Cartographies of Time* (New York: Princeton Architectural Press, 2010).

28. Gapminder Foundation, Gapminder software, available at http://gapminder.org.

29. WordPress Digress.it plugin, http://digress.it.

30. These software packages produced by the Rosenzweig Center for History and New Media are available at http://www.omeka.org and http://www.zotero.org, respectively.

31. See comments by William Thomas and Timothy Burke on Sherman Dorn, "Is (Digital) History More than an Argument about the Past?," in *Writing History in the Digital Age*, web-book ed., Fall 2011 version; James E. Porter, "Intertextuality and the Discourse Community," *Rhetoric Review* 5 (1986): 34–47.

Pasts in a Digital Age

Stefan Tanaka

> "Digital remembering erodes time."
>
> —Viktor Mayer-Schönberger[1]

> "My working hypothesis is that all views of history have been fundamentally shaped by the way records are duplicated, knowledge transmitted, and information stored and retrieved."
>
> —Elizabeth L. Eisenstein[2]

Digital media are altering our practice of history. The essays in this volume explore the many ways we have used and can use it to facilitate our research, aid and improve our teaching, and enhance scholarly communication. Others are also encountering a horizon of which Clay Shirky warns, "The communications tools we now have, which a mere decade ago seemed to offer an improvement to the twentieth-century media landscape, are now seen to be rapidly eroding it instead."[3] When applied to history, the preceding epigraph from Mayer-Schönberger suggests such erosion. Since the eighteenth century, chronological time has been foundational in how we conceive of and practice history. Erosion or not, a horizon of change also emerges when we line up his statement with the proliferation of digital information and the second epigraph, from Elizabeth Eisenstein.

These statements raise the question, to what extent does electronic media change our relation to the past and future? The Internet is the largest repository of data, ever. Today, information is more readily available, the Internet seemingly forgets nothing, and we see people and institutions confronting their future past. Individuals now have to prevent their past that might possibly haunt their future.[4] Indeed, we need to question to what extent the past is past and whether the distinction of past and present has ever been clear. Electronic data is ephemeral; digital information disappears, is erased, and is frequently modified. Our governments and corporations regularly shred hard drives. Regardless of one's position, the past is not just becoming larger, it remains varied and is changing.

History and how we write history will also change. But to negotiate this transformation and especially to use this as an opportunity to explore new modes of writing history, we must understand that some of the issues we are confronting are not as new as we might think; similar issues arose during the late eighteenth and nineteenth centuries, when history became the form of knowledge we know and practice today. For example, Zygmunt Bauman describes modernity today as passing from the "solid" to a "liquid" phase.[5] Yet while social forms of modernity might now be more fluid and ephemeral, we must ask how today stacks up to what Marx identified over 150 years ago when he wrote, "All that is solid melts into the air."

At this point, before we celebrate or lament the changes, it is important to recognize that the deep, chronological way of thinking about the past that pervades modern society is far from natural. Unless we are mindful of the conditions that produced this naturalized understanding of the past, we restrict our options to a return to a nineteenth-century mode of thinking (still practiced today in academia) or a valorized "new," as if new social forms are better simply because they are more recent.[6] Moreover, we might learn about different, "new" ways of interacting with the past from these earlier moments.

History as a Virtual Reality

History, as we understand it today, emerged during the late eighteenth century. By the early nineteenth century, a specific form of historical thinking emerged, where people began to separate past from present and to write about the past using a linear—that is, chronological—structure.[7] The iconic phrase that has been used to capture this shift is from Leopold von Ranke, who wrote in his first major work, *Histories of the Latin and Germanic Nations* (1824), "To history has been given the function of judging the past, of instructing men for the profit of future years. The present attempt does not aspire to such a lofty undertaking. It merely wants to show how, essentially, things happened."[8] This is the passage from which historians have extracted his most famous and misused phrase, *wie es eigentlich gewesen*, to claim scientific, neutral, and objective status.

The popularization of one phrase from this passage indicates that sound bites, excerpts distanced from context, are not new to the electronic age.

More important, this phrase that stands for the objectivity of history was only the last part of a passage that advocates for a new understanding of the past. Ranke is proposing a new reality: historical thinking. This historical thinking is the chaining of facts together into linear narratives where chronological time—not place, community, or environment—become central to understanding.[9] The purpose of the past is no longer something continually present in our lives through Ranke's sarcastic "lofty undertaking" that judges and instructs. The history that Ranke sought to replace was a practical past, *historia magistra vitae*.[10] It is a repository of moments, ideas, deeds, and events that guides life in the present. It is an ethical past.

The new, linear mode of understanding the past led Thomas Carlyle to complain in 1830, "Things done are in a group, not in a series." The historian Aron Gurevich described time during the ancient period as "spatialized," that is, dependent on space and environment: "Ancient man saw past and present stretching round him, in mutual penetration and clarification of each other." Locale, not time, then provided a different understanding of depth and connectivity. More recently, the psychologist Sam Wineberg argued that historical thinking "goes against the grain of how we ordinarily think."[11]

In the world of the early nineteenth century, the "common sense" of today's history was then a new "virtual reality." History became a technics, a science of describing that plotted facts according to the recently popularized Newtonian time, increasingly accepted as universal time.[12] Here, Michel de Certeau's sage reminder that chronology and time are not synonymous is pertinent: "Recast in the mold of a taxonomic ordering of things, chronology becomes the alibi of time, a way of making use of time without reflecting on it."[13] In contrast to the practical past, the historical past is separated from people. Data becomes a commodity—something dated, recorded, and verifiable, shorn from its immediate context. The subject shifts to the rise of some collectivity, usually the nation-state. Human activities—that is, social life, sensibility, the everyday, emotions, and culture—are de-emphasized and have often been excluded from the historical past.

This form of historical thinking is not going to disappear; nor should it. It serves as the basis of our liberal-internationalist world. For this reason, alone, it has purpose. This historical thinking emerged to deal with the new ideas (such as linear, progressive time) and forms (like the nation) that became increasingly common during the early nineteenth century. The new practices provided order for an expanded realm that now included the Americas and Asia and for the concomitant rise of new data that had to be defined, collected, and organized. Institutions—libraries, archives, universities, and publishers—were reordered and created to manage this new knowledge.[14] The practitioner of this form of historical thinking becomes the professional historian safely ensconced in the university. These are components of our academic and liberal-capitalist world. Carla Hesse calls it the modern literary system.[15]

This modern literary system is built on a notion of information scarcity. Its goal is to collect, categorize, and disseminate information to better understand this ever-expanding world (both geographically and scientifically). As the increasing specialization of academia indicates, it is an ever more complicated structure that has been more or less effective for rendering a complex world understandable. Here, drawing from complex adaptive systems, the terms *complex* and *complicated* are distinct.[16] Our current mode of accommodating increasing scale is to continue piling stuff into these categories (and create ever more subcategories) and building more complicated systems to handle them. History is one technology that gives form to and supports such complicated social forms. For example, throughout the late nineteenth and twentieth centuries, nascent nations struggled to find and write their own history. (It is amazing that places with several millennia of civilization, like China and Japan, learned, in their late nineteenth century encounter with the West, that they were without history). In these history-writing projects, the relegation of the past into chronological narratives of the nation-state and the subsequent forgetting of this act reinforced the new as "real." The proliferation of history departments throughout the world has helped to naturalize those social forms that seem decreasingly stable in the digital realm.

We must remember that the spread of this form of historical practice both synchronized the world and proselytized a certain kind of forgetting, a devaluation and even denigration of the multiplicity and heterogeneity of pasts. The parallel that I am drawing between nineteenth-century transformation of history and pasts in a digital age is in the historical condition of what we consider solid as well as the commodification of data that occurred to support that solidity. In short, our current understanding of history, the history that might be changing under pressure from digital media, has parallels in the commodification of data, the changing subject, and the new relation between past and present.

Toward Complex Pasts

We need to ask to what extent our current structure is still apposite. If modernity is indeed moving from some version of solid to liquid, then by its very connection to institutions and knowledge systems, the modern literary system is also shifting. Moreover, there is an important shift that makes Eisenstein's hypothesis worth serious consideration. Digital media no longer operate under the condition of information scarcity. Indeed, there is a proliferation of data, ease of access, and means of disseminating interpretation. Observers and scholars now recognize this shift. Bauman's recognition of this change is a different, perhaps radical, way of knowing: "A swift and thorough *forgetting* of outdated information and fast ageing habits can be more important for the next success than the memorization of past moves and the building of strategies on a foundation laid by previous *learning*."[17] Mayer-Schönberger, too, recognizes the reversal of this relationship between preservation and forgetting, where the former has become the default. In his book *delete*, he offers a concrete proposal that information contain user-set expiration dates. On the surface, for the historian, this proposal sounds preposterous. Yet it points to the massive amounts of data that are increasingly being saved. This does not make history and the past outmoded; it does alter how we value, access, and use pasts and histories.

Moreover, the use of the computer is a terrific aid to existing practices, but I (and, I believe, many others) have often wondered while adapting to digital media, "Why do we do xxx this way? " Of course, we have been taught/socialized/professionalized to these forms of historical thinking in high school, graduate school, and beyond. But at this point, I would like to introduce a simple but important observation from Jerome McGann: "The simplicity of the computer is merciless. It will expose every jot and tittle of your thought's imprecisions."[18] Interestingly, the more we integrate digital technologies into history, the more we confront practices that historians have naturalized to manage the past as "imprecisions." Digital technologies often bring out the peculiarity of inherited social forms; we begin to understand data differently, we have new ways to connect data, and we have more tools through which we can represent the past.

Before I continue, it is important to point out that the interpretations that I am offering are not created by or new to the digital media. As I hope my endnotes suggest, historians—often called intellectual historians or philosophers of history—have long written about the limitations of our current practices of history. It has been a recurrent theme. Indeed, a history of forgetting about the history of history might be in order here. But as McGann, Bauman, and others suggest, the digital does provide us with an important opportunity to explore the possibilities for reconsidering and reformulating the practice and value of history to contemporary society.

One way that I see history benefiting from the intervention of digital media is through an understanding that other forms of sociotemporal modes of organization did and do exist. I recognize that we operate in a modern temporality and that we cannot merely disavow or easily forsake it, even if doing so is a good idea. Yet it is different to operate within it and write history as if it is the only form of time. We have an opportunity to recognize that history has forsaken an important task that some might call practical, others ethical; we can also recognize that understanding is the accumulation not of data but of locus, relations, and connections. I extract the following discussion from a project, "1884," that seeks to write history using digital tools. I will not explain this project here,[19] but I draw from it to suggest some ways that digital technologies have helped me formulate history differently.

An image of temporality that I use to imagine complex and heterogeneous pasts comes from Michel Serres: "Time does not always flow according to a line . . . nor according to a plan but, rather, according to an extraordinarily complex mixture, as though it reflected stopping points, ruptures, deep wells, chimneys of thunderous acceleration, rendings, gaps—all sown at random, at least in a visible disorder."[20] Serres's turbulence recognizes the multiple ways in which time might be organized; yet there is still a dominant flow (that of liberal capitalist society). It accounts for multiplicity and heterogeneity in relation to a hegemonic process; it accounts for complex adaptation where one shift might reverberate broadly.

Once freed from the limitations of absolute, linear time, we are able to use the past much more differentially; we can think of different ways to structure more expansive and heterogeneous pasts that operate in the multiple temporalities of life. Data can record happenings, not just facts. For example, in 1883 and 1884 Meiji Japan, there was a spike in newspaper accounts of mysterious sightings. This is an example of how history fragments the past, by rendering these beliefs as the forgotten of history; today, these sightings are categorized as time forms of past or backward societies—superstitions and folklore, not facts. For example, the *Shizuoka daimu shinbun*, a regional paper, reported on May 18, 1884,

Chiyo (14 years old), one of the three daughters of the Fujimoto household, was routinely babysitting for a year at a shop in Gofuku. On the third of this month she did not return; her master inquired about her whereabouts, became suspicious, and began searching. Her parents became frantic. Five or six days later Chiyo returned in a daze. She said that she went with an unknown, old, white-haired man who said that he would show her interesting places.

Kidnapping, disappearance, running away might explain why Chiyo disappeared. Yet the notion that she was "spirited away," *kamikakushi* (the English title of a popular anime film by Miyazaki Hayao), was common. We could dismiss this incident as the antics of an imaginative, naughty teenage girl as interpreted through the backwardness of a rural society steeped in superstition. Yet when placed alongside a depression that began in 1881, the proliferation of stories of mysterious happenings also signals beliefs or anxieties of various people during a period of severe hardship and rapid change. We might also wonder if there is a connection to the rise of interest in the supernatural, folk, and ghostly in Japan today. Here, time need not designate one as old and the other new.

Decades ago, Georg Simmel argued that human society operates at a different temporal scale than technological society: "The things that determine and surround our lives, such as tools, means of transport, the products of science, technology and art, are extremely refined. Yet individual culture, at least in the higher strata, has not progressed at all to the same extent; indeed, it has even frequently declined."[21] Rather than pity the backward for their ignorance and misfortune, this notion of heterogeneous time gives us a different understanding of how individuals deal with an increasingly abstract, rational, and mechanical society. A survey conducted in 1946 Japan provides an example of such a coexistence of multiple time systems. That study showed that many communities still used the lunar calendar over 70 years after Japan adopted the solar calendar. Ninety-three percent of urban residents solely used the solar calendar, while only 8.8 percent of rural inhabitants solely used the solar calendar. Among rural residents, 37.6 percent only used the lunar calendar, and 48.8 percent used some combination of the two.[22] This heterogeneity existed amid an era of unprecedented unity within fascist Japan (at least, that is what the history books say).

From this recognition of heterogeneity, it is possible to think of a scalability within the nation that is simultaneously diverse but also contained. Here, I find the metaphor of wayfaring from Tim Ingold, in his recent book *Lines: A Brief History*, to be helpful in thinking of different ways that people, things, and institutions connect and interact. In wayfaring one moves *along*, taking in the surroundings, and inhabits that which she or he traverses. In contrast, in transport one moves *across*, from point to point, or from one predefined category to another.[23]

Ingold applies this formulation to narrative, and I would extend it to academic disciplines, including history. Travel becomes the effort to reach the destination, a modern liberal-capitalist nation-state; mapping is provided through the models and tools for achieving that goal, and textuality becomes the establishment of a history (building on the lessons from

Ranke) that synchronizes a Japanese history into the teleology of world history at that time. It is a complicated negotiation of different categories—Ingold's precomposed plots. The variability of the regions and of people's beliefs and anxieties is lost. Stories are replaced by "important" knowledge. Ingold argues for a storied, not classificatory, form of knowledge. The former is like the wayfarer who inhabits the specific "timespace," is embedded in practice and movement, and sees within the complex interplay of ideas, people, and events. At times, individuals connect, directly or indirectly, to the categories of the nation-state; at other moments, they do not. For me, this is not an exercise in bringing back individuals to history. It includes some of that, but it leads to a very different narrative of Japan's transformation in the nineteenth and twentieth centuries.

A second way that a different understanding of pasts might help us write deeper and, I believe, more accurate histories is to reconsider our understanding of change. We can describe quite well how societies have (and have not) become like the present. The default mode for ordering and connecting data has been from old to new. Such a structure is anything but neutral. It is a technological metric that establishes value, with recent or new being better than older.[24] It orients society toward production, not life. It presupposes mechanical, orderly causality. Yet through psychological and cognitive studies, we know that in individual learning, the mind is not a blank slate or a computer hard drive that merely needs to be filled with meaningful information. It is a complex process of biological organisms, acquired knowledge, external stimulus, and environment. Societies, too, have inherited practices and knowledge systems that affect how the new is understood and adapted. Sylvia Scribner uses the work of psychologist Lev Vygotsky to state what might seem obvious: "Societies and cultural groups participate in world history at different tempos and in different ways. Each has its own past history influencing the nature of current change."[25] Yet in our understanding of other cultures, we almost always locate them (as if they are singular, such as "the Japanese") in some temporal category of the "not yet."[26] We describe how they have made mistakes and failed (to be like our idealized selves), not how those processes are and are not appropriate, how they are understood, and how different places adapt those processes.

A different way to study change would be to adapt Lucian Hölscher's notion of a historical event as a "common reference point of many narratives told about it."[27] Such a concept recognizes that there are many stories told about an event, at that time, later, and even later, by historians. Ambiguity, insignificance, and conflicting views coexist. To return to my discussion of the non-West as the "not yet," Hölscher's new annalistic history enables us to write a much more layered history that sees the variability of process (such as modernization), place, event, and the way that a particular past impacts change. A simple example is the International Meridian Conference held in Washington, DC, in October 1884. Forty-five countries participated in this conference, which determined the prime meridian, international dateline, and beginning of the day. Each country had one vote; Japan and Hawaii were equals with the United States, France, and Great Britain. The conference is significant in that it moved us toward a universal world time; that is, it became possible to both standardize and synchronize world time with the decisions of the conference.

From this event, we can see that Japan officially adopted modern time before many European countries and the United States. Japan unified time around the 24-hour clock and adopted the Gregorian calendar in 1873; it synchronized its time with Greenwich time in 1889. The United States did not officially adopt Greenwich time and the time zones until 1918, although railroads adopted the time zones in 1883; France remained 9 minutes and 21 seconds ahead of Greenwich time until 1911; and Germany unified its time in 1893. In this case, Japan was not behind; indeed, it was often ahead. But the setting of the beginning of the day at roughly 180 degrees longitude geographically codified Asia as the East (Oriental), that is, the "not yet." Examining the move away from absolute time to a temporality that includes a multiplicity of time systems, tempos, and utility, as well as ignorance, gives both a history of our current knowledge system and a deeper, richer understanding of the past, of other cultures, and of how people either changed or did not.

Finally, while I am troubled by the "forgetting" of the past as well as the limited context and meaning that past events now contain, I am more worried about the limited recognition of the past that occurs under our existing historical practices.[28] We too often insist on a single, correct understanding of an event or of the past. A richer history would include a heterogeneity of interpretations, the diversity of practices, the contestations, and the processes and negotiations by which people have dealt with such differences—turbulence. Keith Sawyer points out that innovative change occurs in heterogeneous group settings; uniformity and certainty reinforce the status quo.[29] Digital media present us with an opportunity to use tools that facilitate more complex, not complicated, narratives and stories of the past and how they continue to operate in our present.

By bringing out such variability, we can show more of the operations of history, the stories embedded in primary data and the negotiations and decisions that lead to the structures, ideas, and social forms of our narratives. Constantin Fasolt quotes a rather casual but provocative statement by Thomas Kuhn: "In history, more than in any other discipline I know, the finished product of research disguises the nature of the work that produced it."[30] In the writing of history, we traditionally background our research, the management of a multitude of information, data, and social forms, for a more or less straightforward, unitary narrative. We limit our studies to book or article length, omit contradictions, and make decisions on conflicting views. This has considerable implications for the relation of past and present in history, but my hope is that if we bring stories together with the narratives of historical thinking, we might be able to regain the role of practicality that professional historians gave up over a century ago.[31] Moreover, the role of the historian shifts from expert who masters (and protects his or her) knowledge of a specific (increasingly narrow) area—an increasingly futile task—to that of a skilled and reliable organizer of the myriad data that helps us understand human experience. Here, it is worthwhile to consider (but not imbibe) Bauman's warning that knowledge for the future "is not *conformity* to rules . . . but *flexibility.*"[32]

My hope is that an expanded past can bring the diversity of human experiences back to history. That, of course, is an overstatement, but we need to return the practical aspect of pasts to history. Digital tools help us reformulate history so that we might recover some of the complexity of human activity.

Acknowledgments: This essay began as a talk delivered at the Center for Digital Research in the Humanities at the University of Nebraska. I would like to thank Kenneth Price, Katherine Walter, and William Thomas III for the invitation to speak and for the stimulating environment that received me.

Notes

1. Viktor Mayer-Schönberger, *delete: The Virtue of Forgetting in the Digital Age* (Princeton: Princeton University Press, 2009), 113.

2. Elizabeth L. Eisenstein, "Clio and Chronos: An Essay on the Making and Breaking of History-Book Time," *History and Theory* 6, no. 6 (1966): 36–64 (quotation from 40).

3. Clay Shirky, *Cognitive Surplus: Creativity and Generosity in a Connected Age* (New York: Penguin, 2010), 189.

4. Jeffrey Rosen, "The Web Means the End of Forgetting," *New York Times*, July 21, 2010.

5. Zygmunt Bauman, *Liquid Times: Living in an Age of Uncertainty* (Cambridge: Polity, 2007), 1.

6. See, for example, works in media archaeology, such as Lisa Gitelman and Geoffrey B. Pingree, eds., *New Media, 1740–1915* (Cambridge, MA: MIT Press, 2003), and Friedrich A. Kittler, *Gramophone, Film, Typewriter*, trans. Geoffrey Winthrop-Young and Michael Wutz (Palo Alto: Stanford University Press, 1999).

7. For excellent studies of the relation between absolute time and the formulation of history, see Reinhart Koselleck, *Futures Past: On the Semantics of Historical Time*, trans. Keith Tribe (Cambridge, MA: MIT Press, 1985), and Michel de Certeau, *The Writing of History*, trans. Tom Conley (New York: Columbia University Press, 1988).

8. Quoted in Leopold von Ranke, *The Theory and Practice of History*, ed. Georg G. Iggers and Konrad von Moltke (Indianapolis: Bobbs-Merrill, 1973), 137.

9. See, for example, Koselleck, *Futures Past*, 267–88.

10. See, for example, Koselleck, *Futures Past*, 21–38, and Michael Oakeshott, *On History, and Other Essays* (Totowa, NJ: Barnes and Noble Books, 1983), 1–44.

11. Thomas Carlyle, "On History," in *Historical Essays*, ed. Chris R. Vanden Bossche (Berkeley: University of California Press, 2002), 7; Aron J. Gurevich, *Categories of Medieval Culture*, trans. G. L. Campbell (London: Routledge and Kegan Paul, 1985), 29; Sam Wineberg, *Historical Thinking and Other Unnatural Acts* (Philadelphia: Temple University Press, 2001).

12. One of the best studies that describes this transformation of the reckoning of time in Europe is Donald J. Wilcox's *The Measure of Times Past: Pre-Newtonian Chronologies and the Rhetoric of Relative Time* (Chicago: University of Chicago Press, 1987). For an account of the transformation of time in Japan, see my *New Times in Modern Japan* (Princeton: Princeton University Press, 2004). Two fine overviews on the social constitution of time are Barbara Adam's *Time* (Cambridge: Polity, 2004) and Norbert Elias's *Time: An Essay* (Oxford: Blackwell, 1992).

13. Michel de Certeau, *Heterologies*, trans. Brian Massumi (Minneapolis: University of Minnesota Press, 1986), 216.

14. For two fine works that discuss the transformation of the knowledge system, see Thomas Richards, *Imperial Archives: Knowledge and the Fantasy of Empire* (London: Verso, 1993), and Mary Louise Pratt, *Imperial Eyes: Travel Writing and Transculturation* (London: Routledge, 1992).

15. Carla Hesse, "Books in Time," in *The Future of the Book*, ed. Geoffrey Nunberg (Berkeley: University of California Press, 1997).

16. For two rather different works on complex systems, see John H. Miller and Scott E. Page, *Complex Adaptive Systems: An Introduction to Computational Models of Social Life* (Princeton: Princeton University Press, 2007), and R. Keith Sawyer, *Social Emergence: Societies as Complex Systems* (Cambridge: Cambridge University Press, 2005).

17. Bauman, *Liquid Times*, 3.

18. Jerome McGann, *Radiant Textuality: Literature after the World Wide Web* (New York: Palgrave, 2001), 142.

19. For an overview of this project, see my essay "New Media and Historical Narrative: 1884 Japan," in *Performance Research* 11, no. 4 (2006): 95–104.

20. Michel Serres with Bruno Latour, *Conversations on Science, Culture, and Time*, trans. Roxanne Lapidus (Ann Arbor: University of Michigan Press, 1995), 57.

21. George Simmel, *The Philosophy of Money*, ed. David Frisby, trans. Tom Bottomore and David Frisby (London: Routledge, 1990), 448.

22. Okada Yoshirō, *Meiji kaireki: "Toki" no bunmei kaika* (Tokyo: Taishūkan shoten, 1994), 224–25.

23. Tim Ingold, *Lines: A Brief History* (London: Routledge, 2007), 75.

24. See David Edgerton, *The Shock of the Old* (Oxford: Oxford University Press, 2006).

25. Sylvia Scribner, "Vygotsky's Uses of History," in *Culture, Communication, and Cognition: Vygotskian Perspectives*, ed. James V. Wertsch (Cambridge: Cambridge University Press, 1985), 139.

26. See, for example, Dipesh Chakrabarty, *Provincializing Europe* (Princeton: Princeton University Press, 2000). I have written elsewhere that Asia is still in the place of the Orient. See "Time and the Paradox of the Orient," *Tōajia bunka kōshō kenkyu*, 2009 bessatsu (special issue) 4 (2009): 165–74.

27. Lucian Hölscher, "The New Annalistic: A Sketch of a Theory of History," *History and Theory* 36, no. 3 (1997): 317–35.

28. See, for example, Jean Comaroff's discussion of "ritual commemorations of the past" in "The End of History, Again: Pursuing the Past in the Postcolony," *Postcolonial Studies and Beyond*, ed. Ania Loomba et al. (Durham, NC: Duke University Press, 2005).

29. Keith Sawyer, *Group Genius: The Creative Power of Collaboration* (New York: Basic Books, 2007).

30. Constantin Fasolt, *The Limits of History* (Chicago: University of Chicago Press, 2004), 39.

31. I am indebted to Hayden White for suggesting ways to bring practicality back to history in "Politics, History, and the Practical Past," *Storia Della Storiografia* 61 (2012): 127–34.

32. Bauman, *Liquid Times*, 4.

PART 2

The Wisdom of Crowds(ourcing)

How does historical writing change when technology enables everyone to publish online? Leslie Madsen-Brooks opens up the conversation with her essay "'I Nevertheless Am a Historian': Digital Historical Practice and Malpractice around Black Confederate Soldiers," which investigates how false claims about U.S. Civil War history arose and have been combated on the Internet. Other contributors focus on the world's most popular crowd-sourced encyclopedia, *Wikipedia*. Over 30 million registered users have collectively contributed to this open-access knowledge platform, launched in 2001. Yet *Wikipedia* has generated controversy for its democratization of historical expertise and authorship, the practice of a so-called neutral point of view (NPOV) as its editorial stance, and conflict among educators on whether it should be referenced in or even considered as part of academic writing. Robert Wolff's essay "The Historian's Craft, Popular Memory, and *Wikipedia*" explores what we can learn from analyzing debates over editing Civil War history in the multiauthor *Wikipedia* platform. In "The Wikiblitz: A *Wikipedia* Editing Assignment in a First-Year Undergraduate Class," Shawn Graham recounts what he and his students learned while updating a single page on Canadian history. Martha Saxton at Amherst College describes challenges that she faced when confronting the NPOV editing standard, in "*Wikipedia* and Women's History: A Classroom Experience." (See also the essays by Adrea Lawrence and Amanda Seligman in part 3.)

"I Nevertheless Am a Historian"

Digital Historical Practice and Malpractice around Black Confederate Soldiers

Leslie Madsen-Brooks

I have a good deal of interest in how members of the public who are not academically trained historians "do history." For me, then, "public history" does not mean just projects, programs, and exhibits created by professional historians for the public but, rather, the very broad and complex intersection of "the public" with historical practice. When you provision those occupying this intersection with freely available digital tools and platforms, things become interesting quickly. Because setting up a blog, wiki, or discussion forum means only a few mouse clicks and because archival resources are increasingly digitized, we are seeing a burgeoning of sites that coalesce communities around historical topics of interest. Even those who have no interest in setting up their own websites can participate in history-specific Facebook groups, blogging communities, and genealogy sites.

Such digital spaces expand and blur considerably the spectrum of what counts as historical practice. For example, on Ancestry.com, users piece together family histories by synthesizing government records and crowd-sourced resources of varying origin and credibility. Professional historians might take an active interest, then, in how digital archival and communication resources affect the spread or containment of particular historical myths.[1] It is not clear, however, how these technologies aid academic historians in participating or impede them from intervening in these discussions. This essay uses discourses about black Confederate soldiers to explore how digital technologies are changing who researches and writes history—as well as what authorial roles scholars are playing in the fuzzy edges of historical practice where crowdsourcing and the lay public are creating new research resources and narratives. These digital tools and resources are not only democratizing historical practice but also providing professional historians with new opportunities and modes for expanding historical literacy.

The Origins of the Black Confederate Soldier

Historian Kevin Levin recently pointed out that discourse around "black Confederates" ramped up after the release of the 1989 film *Glory*, which showcased the sacrifices of the 54th Massachusetts Volunteer Infantry in the American Civil War. Viewers of that movie might reasonably have wondered whether there was a similar regiment fighting for the South, so it is not surprising that an Ngram search of Google Books reveals the use of the term *black Confederate* rose dramatically after the movie's release.[2] More surprising is the term's staying power over the ensuing two decades (see fig. 2). As we move through the four-year sesquicentennial of the Civil War, the term—its currency not yet graphable on Ngram because that tool does not search books published after 2000 or websites—seems to be enjoying a resurgence. A Google search for the exact phrase "black Confederate" (inside quotation marks) turns up 102,000 matches.

The typical discourse in support of the existence of black Confederates refers to them as "soldiers" or claims they served in vital support roles just behind the front lines; believers assert that all of these soldiers and supporters were "loyal" to the Confederate cause, even if they were enslaved. Take, for example, the following comment by Edward A. Bardill in an editorial from 2005:

> Deep devotion, love of homeland and strong Christian faith joined black with white Confederate soldiers in defense of their homes and families. A conservative estimate is that between 50,000 to 60,000 served in the Confederate units. Both slave and free black soldiers served as cooks, musicians and even combatants.[3]

Such effusive praise may confuse Civil War historians, as the historical record does not support claims that large numbers of slaves and former slaves volunteered. Quite the contrary: slaves who served the Confederate army were volunteered by their masters, and slaves on plantations collaborated actively with agents of the Union army to secure their freedom.[4] Some historians have asserted that some African Americans "passed" as

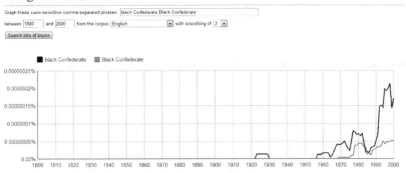

Fig. 2. Google Books Ngram view of the frequency of the term *black Confederate* from 1800 to 2000

white to enlist.[5] Others have acknowledged free and enslaved blacks' non-combatant contributions—as body servants, cooks, foundry workers, and nurses—to the Confederate war effort, but it appears that no academic historians have subscribed to the narrative that there were thousands of black Confederate soldiers.[6]

The rapid spread of black Confederate soldier narratives is a function not only of proponents' apparent desire to openly admire the Confederacy without appearing to favor a white supremacist society and government but also of the rise of inexpensive and easy-to-use digital tools.[7] Prior to the widespread adoption of the Internet, published discussion of the black Confederate soldier was contained to books like James Brewer's *The Confederate Negro*, which is careful to emphasize that blacks—free or enslaved—working on behalf of the Confederacy were "labor troops" and not soldiers; Ervin Jordan's *Black Confederates and Afro-Yankees in Civil War Virginia*, which does not always distinguish as carefully between volunteer soldiers and impressed or hired laborers; and Charles Barrow, Joe Segars, and Randall Rosenburg's *Black Confederates*, which relied on the Sons of Confederate Veterans to "submit information about blacks loyal to the South" and emphasizes "many instances" of "deep devotion and affection" that "transcended the master-slave relationship" and inspired blacks to "[take] up arms to defend Dixie."[8] Today, however, the digital footprint of people who maintain that there were significant numbers of black Confederate soldiers appears far larger than that of historians and others who attempt to refute the myth. (Alas, the 21st-century footprint is no longer merely digital; a textbook distributed to Virginia students in September 2010 stated that "thousands of Southern blacks fought in the Confederate ranks, including two black battalions under the command of Stonewall Jackson.")[9]

Proponents' Use of Digital Platforms and Sources

Sites focused on black Confederate soldiers and related "Southern heritage" sites seem to arise from both a desire to tell a history suppressed by Northern partisans—including the assertion that the war was fought over states' rights, not slavery—and an explicit goal of recognizing the service of African Americans in the military. Blogger Connie Ward writes, for example, "So they weren't on some official muster roll and they weren't handed a uniform and soldierly accouterments. So? What interests me is . . . did they pick up a gun and shoot at yankees? Then they need to be commemorated."[10]

These claims are grounded in shallow, often uninformed, and frequently decontextualized readings of primary source documents that have been digitized and made available online. Take "Royal Diadem's" (Ann Dewitt's) reading of a ledger digitized on Footnote.com:

> Captain P.P. Brotherson's Confederate Officers record states eleven (11) blacks served with the 1st Texas Heavy Artillery in the "Negro Cooks Regiment." This annotation can be viewed on footnote.com. See the third line on the left.[11]

Andy Hall of the Dead Confederates blog stepped up with an additional analysis of the document, noting first that the phrase "Negro Cooks Regiment" does not actually appear on the document. Hall provided and transcribed the digitized document: "Provision for Eleven Negroes Employed in the Quarter Masters department Cooks Regt Heavy Artillery at Galveston Texas for ten days commencing on the 11th day of May 1864 & Ending on the 20th of May 1864."[12] (In this case, "Cook" refers to the commanding officer, Col. Joseph Jarvis Cook.) In a comment on his post, Hall expands on his research methods.

> There are a number of cases of African American men being formally enrolled as cooks in the Confederate army and, so far as CSRs seem to indicate, formally enlisted as such. The researcher has been highlighting a number of these individual cases lately, always leaping straight from them to a universal assertion, *this proves all Confederate cooks were considered soldiers.* . . .

I took 20 Confederate regiments more or less at random, and went through their rosters as listed in the CWSSS, and in those 20 regiments . . . found a total of FIVE men with records of formal enlistment as cooks. . . . [C]learly the takeaway is that formal enlistment of cooks in the Confederate army was not only not common, it was exceedingly rare.

Here, Hall demonstrates an alternative and ultimately more persuasive reading of the document. He also illustrates how to place a source in a broader archival context.

This demonstration of contextualization and interpretation might be a sound response to another common sticking point on the black Confederate websites: the pensions awarded to African Americans following the war. Mississippi, Tennessee, South Carolina, Virginia, and North Carolina all eventually provided pensions to African Americans who served as noncombatants in the Confederate war effort, including soldiers' personal servants, many of whom had been slaves.[13] They were not enlisted soldiers, as it was only in March 1865 that the Confederate Congress passed and Jefferson Davis signed into law a bill that allowed the recruitment of blacks.[14]

Black Confederate websites, however, frequently cite these pension records as evidence that African Americans served as soldiers in the Confederate armed forces. Sometimes the writers imply this elision of noncombatant and soldier; Ann DeWitt makes it explicit.

Over the course of history, these men have become known as Black Confederates. Because their names appear on Confederate Soldier Service Records, we now call them Black Confederate Soldiers.[15]

At the blog *Atrueconfederate*, David Tatum blurs the line between cook and soldier, writing that a cook named William Dove appears on a muster roll that includes the term *enlisted* followed by a date.[16] The digitization of documents opens opportunities for more people to delve into the arcana of the past, but Tatum's and DeWitt's misinterpretations suggest one important role for historians at this cultural and digital moment is helping people gain the skills to interpret an era's documents, photographs, and material culture.

Kevin Levin has provided the most extensive and substantive critiques of the black Confederate myth, including analyses of the major websites dedicated to the topic. On his blog *Civil War Memory*, Levin carefully dissects the failures of Ann DeWitt's *Black Confederate Soldiers* site to distinguish between soldiers and slaves on the front line. Levin highlights the site's utter lack of realistic context for the experience of African Americans laboring on behalf of the Confederates. For example, DeWitt's site assumes that parallels can be drawn between "body servants"—a term she uses to denote slaves who accompanied their owners into the field—and pink- or white-collar administrative employment today: "In 21st century vernacular the role is analogous to a position known as an executive assistant—a position today that requires a college Bachelors [sic] Degree or equivalent level experience."[17] Public audiences may find history more lively if they can draw parallels with their own era, but this particular comparison effaces the deprivations faced by slaves and wartime laborers.

Another case of black Confederate proponents misinterpreting a primary source—or, rather, trusting a manipulated photographic scene—involves a photograph of a "black Confederate corpse." The website *Black Confederate Soldiers of Petersburg* published a photo of one white and one black corpse lying on the ground, stating that the "original caption" referred to them as "rebel artillery soldiers." However, the version of the image at the Library of Congress website, as well as those I located elsewhere, is titled "Confederate and Union dead side by side in the trenches at Fort Mahone." Further complicating website author Ashleigh Moody's presentation of the image, the Library of Congress summarizes photographic detective work by David Lowe and Philip Shiman: "Photo shows a body lying in the background that is actually the photographer's teamster posing for the scene. The live model appears in the same clothes in negative LC-B811-3231." While Moody likely posted her photo prior to the discovery of photographer Thomas Roche's duplicity, she has not removed the photo from her website since its fraudulence was brought to the black Confederate proponents' attention by Andy Hall and Kevin Levin.[18] This is not the only case of this kind; the proponents' credulity is echoed in their acceptance of a photo that is purported to be of a gray-coated "Louisiana Native Guard" in 1861 but is actually an 1864 photo of a company of the 25th United States Colored Troops unit wearing pale blue winter overcoats—with the dark-coated unit commander cropped out of the image.[19]

Conspiracies and Credentials

Many black Confederate proponents invoke conspiracies as the reason more people have not heard of these soldiers. For example, H. K. Edgerton calls the black Confederate narrative "a perspective of Southern Heritage not taught in our public schools or seen in our politically correct media."[20] The implication is that Edgerton's and others' websites provide a valuable public service in highlighting primary source documents and interpreting them for an Internet audience—though a brief survey of their sites often reveals conservative and even reactionary ideologies—while at the same time occasionally calling out as white supremacists those historians who seek to debunk the black Confederate soldier narrative.[21]

Such charges highlight one significant way in which digital tools have changed the way people do history: there has been an increase in the speed with which they exchange information or, more likely in the case of proponents and dissidents of the black Confederate soldier narrative, barbs. Prior to the age of easy digital publishing tools, such unpleasant exchanges might have been kept private, perhaps e-mailed among colleagues and partisans; they would have been unlikely to see print, and they certainly would not have been found as easily as they now are by Google's indexing. This war of words flared up tremendously in the summer of 2011, when the exchanges devolved into name-calling, with each side accusing the other of revisionism motivated by racism.[22]

Milder ad hominem attacks take the form of a questioning of credentials and a disagreement about what constitutes a historian. In one weeks-long iteration of this rhetorical dance, Connie Ward takes issue with some bloggers' insistence that *real* historians do history *for a living:* "I'm as much a historian as Corey [Meyer], [Kevin] Levin, [Andy] Hall and [Brooks] Simpson. I'm a writer of history; I work with history. No, I'm not employed to do that, but I nevertheless am a historian." She then turns the tables, claiming that these men are teachers more than they are historians: "With the possible exception of Andy [Hall], . . . what these gentlemen do for a living . . . is teach. That makes them teachers."[23] She voices a common charge of black Confederate soldier proponents: historians are only willing to share certain facts and are suppressing some big truth.

> To be a historian at an institution of learning just means you have to show some papers that presumably verify that you've studied and learned. Most people so credentialed get their papers from institutes of higher learning, which as we know, have changed over the last fifty or sixty years from places of free thought and inquiry— a setting for acquiring knowledge—to centers of indoctrination.

Corey Meyer calls Ward "an amateur historian" and points out to Ward:

> I nor the other blogger claim no more authority than you. . . . You and yours have repeatedly shown that you do not have a grasp of the original source material that you present. However, the other blogger and I have

history degrees which is not the be-all-to-end-all on the situation, but it does help us when we are working with source materials. . . . [W]e have a background understanding of how to work with those items.[24]

This exchange raises three related questions, one of which lies at the heart of this volume: what constitutes real historical practice, how are digital research and publishing tools changing that practice, and what ought to be the role of professional historians in a space where authorship has been democratized? On the Internet, nobody knows you are a dog[25]—and they cannot be sure, either, that you are a credentialed historian.

Interventions by Professional Historians

The most vocal opponents of the black Confederate soldier narrative in the digital realm are not employed by universities, museums, or other organizations as public historians. Corey Meyer teaches U.S. government and history; Kevin Levin was a high school teacher until 2011 and now bills himself as a "history educator" and "independent historian" who publishes in academic publications and has a book forthcoming from a university press; and Andy Hall does not disclose his profession.[26] Brooks Simpson appears to be the only regular commenter employed as a historian outside of K–12 education.

Why have academically employed historians been reticent to engage in such debates? "Eddieinman" suggests that participation is pointless: "Seems to me about like space scientists devoting themselves to the Roswell incident."[27] Similarly, Matthew Robert Isham writes that countering the black Confederate soldier narrative distracts historians from more significant and rewarding varieties of public engagement during the sesquicentennial.[28] Marshall Poe offers a more substantial reason for historians' absence: such online engagement "doesn't really count toward hiring, tenure, and promotion."[29] Furthermore, he points out, while "amateurs" have written books, authored screenplays, and created historically themed TV programs, academic historians have tended to write for an audience of other academics. The result of historians' and their institutions' reluctance to embrace digital media and public engagement means that, in Poe's words, "'users'—uncritical, poorly informed, and with axes to grind—are now writing 'our' history. Some of that history may be good. But the overwhelming majority of it is and will be bad." He maintains that crowdsourcing history via the "wisdom of the crowds" fails because "the crowds are not wise."[30]

My outlook on how the public "does history" online is less cataclysmic than Poe's. I have seen enthusiasts produce interesting and useful historiography, and the ease of sharing digitized primary sources makes it easier than ever to determine the strength of the evidence presented in those narratives. Even when a narrative is on shaky factual ground, we can learn about the writer's—and possibly the audience's—beliefs, habits, and values, which can also be useful to historians seeking to understand a cultural moment. That said, there is much at stake in the case of black Confederates. John Gillis has written that the people and places of our imagined past give meaning to present-day people and places.[31] Furthermore, Michel-Rolph Trouillot argues that the production and dissemination of historical narratives consolidate power in much the same way as do firearms, property, and political crusades.[32] The black Confederate myth does have political currency in this era where partisans seek to weaken the federal government and consolidate power with the states: the existence of black Confederate soldiers has been cited as proof that the Civil War was fought over a regional disagreement about states' rights, not slavery. In this case, the attempt to historicize states' rights as a deeply rooted political tradition while effacing its history as a tool of racist subjugation is troubling. This neo-Confederate narrative has real political consequences, as throughout U.S. history, some states have repeatedly tried to curtail civil rights gains made by women and minority groups elsewhere in the country.

So where do we go from here? Levin suggests that a better sense of mission and audience would help historians determine when to become involved in discussions of black Confederate soldiers. He writes that persuading the Sons of Confederate Veterans to adopt a different perspective is a lost cause but that mainstream audiences might be highly responsive to historians' critiques of the black Confederate soldier narrative. In that sense, Levin points out, the effort to debunk this narrative is about digital literacy, as professional historians can provide alternative and ultimately more convincing interpretations of primary sources.[33] This approach makes sense; it is in line, after all, with what historians already do: help the public make sense of primary sources. It may be time for us to bring more of those efforts into the highly democratized digital realm.

Beyond increasing digital literacy, each such interaction provides an opportunity to educate people about historical context. High school and college students often take multiple-choice tests that focus on textbook *content* rather than historical *context*, on political players and events more than on the diverse everyday realities and allegiances of, in this example, nineteenth-century black men, enslaved or free, literate or illiterate, throughout the United States. Brooks Simpson emphasizes the importance of sharing not only the quotidian experiences of blacks living in the Confederacy but also what these people's experiences, mundane and extraordinary, meant in the bigger picture. He tells historians that, in best practice, "you are going to make sure that, for all this talk about memory, . . . we remember that the Civil War destroyed slavery in the reUnited States, and that black people, free and enslaved, played a large role in that process and in the defeat of the Confederacy. Tell that story, and tell it time and time again."[34]

The same digital resources that allow for the spread of the black Confederate soldier myth may provide for its reconsideration and revision. Deployed thoughtfully, digital technologies allow public historians to focus on details that, were they merely in print, might seem abstruse or patronizingly didactic. The annotation feature on Flickr, for example, which lets enthusiasts highlight and comment on the smallest details of a photograph, could allow for nearly pixel-level analysis and discussion of Civil War photos. "Black Confederate soldier" photos could provide a rich location for pixel-scale interpretation of much larger issues. Take Thomas Roche's photo of the dead artilleryman and his own not-so-dead assistant (fig. 3); historians could unpack elements of the photo in ways that prove useful to students, and in many cases, Civil War enthusiasts might recognize important details that escaped the historian.[35] Similarly, audio annotation of visuals, as on VoiceThread.com, might provide both the lively polyvocality many netizens desire and a venue for the historian's expertise, without descending into unbridled relativism.

Considering the low opinion some reference librarians and historians have of genealogists, historians might be surprised to find genealogy forums to be self-regulating regarding the black Confederate myth.[36] For example, multiple threads on the *Afrigeneas Military Research Forum* open with a question about black Confederate soldiers and then turn immediately to a debunking of the myth. Sharon Heist there offered the following counternarrative in response to a post:

> I'm sorry, but I have to tell you there were no Black Confederate soldiers. There has been a lot of confusion about this, but they were illegal until the very end of the war (General Order # 14, passed two weeks before Appomatox [sic].)

> There were thousands who served as servants, teamsters, laborers, cooks, etc. but the fact is they were not there willingly, and to fight for the Confederate cause.[37]

Fig. 3. Flickr photo annotation of Civil War dead—posed photo, original from Library of Congress.

As these examples make clear, digital technologies allow a broader spectrum of people to research the past and write about it for a large audience. Previously, one needed the time and money to travel to archives and, in some cases, the academic credentials to study particular primary source documents. Once the research had been transformed into an article or book, gatekeepers—publishing houses, editors, and peer reviewers—ensured academic rigor. More historians need to explore new roles in the digital realm, assuming whatever responsibilities appeal to us as individuals. For some, this might mean starting a blog or podcast on an area of research; for others, it might mean publishing an e-book on how to interpret primary sources from a particular era and geographic region. Others will relish a more assertive or even combative role as debunkers of myths on forums or *Wikipedia*.

That said, our best role is perhaps not that of an authoritative figure or the "sage on the stage"; the "guide on the side" role makes more sense in the digital space. There are tremendous possibilities for collaboration with the lay public, amateur historians, and other professionals. This digital revolution is making ever-larger pools of primary source materials accessible and opening avenues for exciting and sometimes challenging interpretations of those sources. Our role as historians—whether we hold academic degrees in history or learned to practice public history on the job—ought to be encouraging greater, more thoughtful participation in historiography regardless of medium. Citizen science—collaborations between the lay public and trained scientists on projects that are meaningful to specific communities—provides one model for the intersection of rigorous research, lay and amateur engagement, and the increased public understanding of complex subjects. We ought to look for others. At a moment of multiple social, economic, and environmental crises, citizens would benefit from employing the critical and creative thinking required by historical practice. Despite my own dissatisfaction with some of Connie Ward's assertions about black Confederate soldiers, I would like more members of the public to share her interest in historical interpretation; I would like to hear more people say, despite their lack of academic credentials, "I nevertheless am a historian."

Notes

1. The ethics of digital data collection are much debated—especially reading, analyzing, and citing postings on blogs and forums. My stance is that blogs and static websites are analogous to any serialized print publication; they are published online and, if indexed by major search engines, are discoverable by any Internet user. I did not post, comment, or otherwise influence the discussions. I cite posts only from public forums that do not require membership approval. See Heidi McKee and James E. Porter, "The Ethics of Digital Writing Research: A Rhetorical Approach," *College Composition and Communication* 59, no. 4 (2008): 711–49.

2. Kevin Levin, "Ngram Tracks *Black Confederates* and *black Confederates*," *Civil War Memory*, 20 December 2010, http://cwmemory.com/2010/12/20/ngram-tracks-black-confederates-and-black-confederate/. I also searched for terms that may have been used to describe black soldiers prior to 1989 and particularly during the nineteenth century, including *Negro soldier, black soldier,* and *nigger soldier.* None of these terms, of course, isolates Confederate soldiers from Union troops. Not surprisingly, the term *negro soldier* spiked (in books) in the 1860s. Searches for these terms in digitized periodicals from the era proved unsuccessful.

3. Edward A. Bardill, "Black Confederate Soldiers Overlooked during Black

History Month," *Knoxville News-Sentinel*, 27 February 2005, http://www.freerepublic.com/focus/f-news/1351948/posts.

4. Stephanie McCurry, *Confederate Reckoning: Power and Politics in the Civil War South* (Cambridge, MA: Harvard University Press, 2010), 265–66; 288–300.

5. Ervin L. Jordan Jr., *Black Confederates and Afro-Yankees in Civil War Virginia* (Charlottesville: University Press of Virginia, 1995), 217.

6. For more on African Americans' contributions to the Confederate war effort, see James Hollandsworth Jr., "Looking for Bob: Black Confederate Pensioners after the Civil War," *Journal of Mississippi History* 69, no. 4 (2007): 295–324, and Bruce Levine, *Confederate Emancipation: Southern Plans to Free and Arm Slaves during the Civil War* (Oxford: Oxford University Press, 2006).

7. For more on this shift in discourse and the growing acceptance of the black Confederate soldier myth by Southern heritage enthusiasts, see Bruce Levine, "In Search of a Usable Past: Neo-Confederates and Black Confederates," in *Slavery and Public History: The Tough Stuff of American Memory*, ed. James Oliver Horton and Lois E. Horton (Chapel Hill: University of North Carolina Press, 2006), 189–91.

8. James Brewer, *The Confederate Negro: Virginia's Craftsmen and Military Laborers, 1861–1865* (Tuscaloosa: University of Alabama Press, 2007), 7–8, 135–36; Jordan, *Black Confederates and Afro-Yankees*; Charles Barrow, Joe Segars, and Randall Rosenburg, eds., *Black Confederates* (Gretna, LA: Pelican, 2001), 2, 4, 8.

9. Kevin Sieff, "Virginia 4th-Grade Textbook Criticized over Claims on Black Confederate Soldiers," *Washington Post*, 20 October 2010, http://www.washingtonpost.com/wp-dyn/content/article/2010/10/19/AR2010101907974.html.

10. Connie Ward (aka Chastain), "The Black Confederates Controversy," *180 Degrees True South*, 8 June 2011, http://one80dts.blogspot.com/2011/06/black-confederates-controversy.html.

11. Royal Diadem, posting to Southern Heritage Preservation Group on Facebook, 7 August 2011, https://www.facebook.com/groups/shpg1/?view=permalink&id=271184879563396, accessed in May 2012 but has since been removed. For the identification of "Royal Diadem" as a pseudonym used by Ann DeWitt, see Corey Meyer, "The Leap . . . ," *The Blood of My Kindred*, 14 April 2011, http://kindred-blood.wordpress.com/2011/04/14/the-leap/.

12. Andy Hall, "Famous 'Negro Cooks Regiment' Found—in My Own Backyard!" *Dead Confederates*, 8 August 2011, http://deadconfederates.wordpress.com/2011/08/08/famous-negro-cooks-regiment-found-in-my-own-backyard/.

13. Hollandsworth, "Looking for Bob," 304–5.

14. Levine, *Confederate Emancipation*, chap. 5, Kindle location 1795.

15. Ann DeWitt, "Confederate Soldier Service Records," *Black Confederate Soldiers*, n.d., http://www.blackconfederatesoldiers.com/soldier_records_for_black_confederates_50.html.

16. David Tatum, "Myth Buster!" *Atrueconfederate*, 2 July 2011, http://atrueconfederate.blogspot.com/2011/07/myth-buster.html.

17. Ann DeWitt, "Civil War Body Servants," *Black Confederate Soldiers*, 1 May 2010, http://www.blackconfederatesoldiers.com/body_servants_17.html, accessed in May 2012 but has since been removed.

18. "[Confederate and Union dead side by side in the trenches at Fort Mahone]," photo by Thomas C. Roche, 3 April 1865, Selected Civil War Photographs, 1861–

1865, Library of Congress, http://www.loc.gov/pictures/item/cwp2003000602/PP/; David Lowe and Philip Shiman, "Substitute for a Corpse," *Civil War Times* 49, no. 6 (2010): 40–41; Kevin Levin, "Scratch Off Another Black Confederate," *Civil War Memory*, 10 August 2011, http://cwmemory.com/2011/08/10/scratch-off-another-black-confederate/.

19. Jerome Handler and Michael Tuite, "The Modern Falsification of a Civil War Photograph," *Retouching History*, March 2007, http://web.archive.org/web/20080908190524/http://www.retouchinghistory.org/. My search on 14 August 2011 for the original version of this photo at TinEye.com turned up more instances of the cropped photo than the one with the officer.

20. H. K. Edgerton, "Southern Heritage 411," n.d., http://www.southernheritage411.com/index.shtml.

21. See, for example, Edgerton's publication on his site of the article "Isn't the Southern Poverty Law Center the Real Hate Group?" by Michael Brown, 28 July 2011, http://www.southernheritage411.com/newsarticle.php?nw=2270. See also Carl Roden's comments, as reprinted on Andy Hall's site: "The Self-Appointed Defenders of Southern Heritage," *Dead Confederates*, 3 August 2011, http://dead-confederates.wordpress.com/2011/08/03/the-defenders-of-southern-heritage/.

22. For some examples of the vitriol, see David Tatum's posts at *Atrueconfederate*, http://atrueconfederate.blogspot.com/2011/08/anti-southern-society.html (11 August 2011) and http://atrueconfederate.blogspot.com/2011/08/research-is-like-box-of-chocolates.html (10 August 2011), as well as Connie Ward's post "The Civil War Thought Police," *180 Degrees True South*, 10 August 2011, http://one80dts.blogspot.com/2011/08/civil-war-thought-police.html.

23. Connie Ward (aka Chastain), "Corey's Back for More," *180 Degrees True South*, 8 August 2011, http://one80dts.blogspot.com/2011/08/coreys-back-for-more.html.

24. Corey Meyer, "Connie (Chastain) Ward Responds Again" and "Connie (Chastain) Ward Admits: 'History & Heritage Are Not Synonymous,'" *The Blood of My Kindred*, 8 August 2011, accessed 13 August 2011, http://kindredblood.wordpress.com/2011/08/08/connie-chastain-ward-responds-again/, and 22 July 2011, accessed 13 August 2011, http://kindredblood.wordpress.com/2011/07/22/connie-chastain-ward-admits-history-heritage-are-not-synonymous/.

25. See Peter Steiner's cartoon for the *New Yorker* 69, no. 20 (1993): 61.

26. Corey Meyer, comment on "Ponderings on American Exceptionalism," *The Blood of My Kindred*, 25 September 2009, http://kindredblood.wordpress.com/2009/09/25/ponderings-on-american-exceptionalism/#comment-147; Kevin Levin, "Welcome" and "Resume," *Civil War Memory*, n.d., http://cwmemory.com/about/ and http://cwmemory.com/cv/.

27. Eddieinman, "Re: Simpson—Prof. Historians and the Black Confederate Myth," 19 June 2011, http://groups.yahoo.com/group/civilwarhistory2/message/173491.

28. Matthew Robert Isham, "What Will Become of the Black Confederate Controversy? A Follow Up," *A People's Contest*, 13 May 2011, http://www.psu.edu/dept/richardscenter/2011/05/what-will-become-of-the-black-confederate-controversy---a-follow-up.html.

29. Marshall Poe, "Fighting Bad History with Good; or, Why Historians Must Get on the Web Now," *Historically Speaking* 10, no. 2 (2009): 23.

30. Poe, "Fighting Bad History," 22.

31. John Gillis, *A World of Their Own Making* (New York: Basic Books, 1996), xvi.

32. Michel-Rolph Trouillot, *Silencing the Past* (Boston: Beacon, 1995), xix.

33. Kevin Levin, "What Will Become of the Black Confederate Controversy? A Response," *Civil War Memory*, 8 May 2011, http://cwmemory.com/2011/05/08/what-will-become-of-the-black-confederate-controversy-a-response/.

34. Brooks Simpson, "Professional Historians and the Black Confederate Myth: Part Two," *Crossroads*, 20 June 2011, https://cwcrossroads.wordpress.com/2011/06/20/professional-historians-and-the-black-confederate-myth-part-two/.

35. Leslie Madsen-Brooks, "Civil War dead—posed photo," Flickr photo annotation, 21 September 2011, http://www.flickr.com/photos/trillwing/6169777283/, based on original 1865 photo, available at the Library of Congress, http://www.loc.gov/pictures/item/cwp2003000602/PP/. For more about this photo, and how it is posed, see David Lowe and Philip Shiman, "Substitute for a Corpse," *Civil War Times* 49, no. 6 (2010): 40–41.

36. For librarians' stereotypes of genealogists, see Katherine Scott Sturdevant, *Bringing Your Family History to Life through Social History* (Cincinnati: Betterway Books, 2000), 166–70.

37. Sharon Heist, "Re: AA Confederate Solider (*sic*) Info," *Afrigeneas Military Research Forum*, 24 October 2004, http://www.afrigeneas.com/forum-militaryarchive/index.cgi/md/read/id/1553/sbj/aa-confederate-solider-info/.

The Historian's Craft, Popular Memory, and *Wikipedia*

Robert S. Wolff

How has the digital revolution transformed the writing of history? If asked, I suspect most historians would point to the tremendous advantages of electronic access to published scholarship and primary sources. In this view, the digital revolution has served primarily to enhance scholarly productivity, much as other once-new technologies, such as online card catalogs and word processing software, facilitated research and writing. Yet, as the essays in this volume demonstrate, digital spaces offer platforms for entirely new kinds of research, while "digital-first" publishing simultaneously accelerates the propagation of ideas. As Dan Cohen observes, this nascent transformation in the historian's craft challenges the academic status quo assumption that scholarly success and intellectual credibility stem from a PhD and a published monograph. Even as radically new forms of publication emerge, print-first journals and books continue to reign over the profession. It is no wonder that despite a willingness to explore new media, few historians take the plunge and immerse themselves in the digital world. Concerned that online scholarship will be found wanting by their peers and institutions, most shy away.[1] Open-source knowledge generated through transparent drafting and review procedures does not yet resonate with the norms of the historical profession, nor does the notion that quality scholarship might be freely available.[2] Beyond the ivory tower, however, purportedly authoritative histories proliferate throughout the Internet, accessible to all. Herein lies an important challenge for professional historians as they confront the digital age.

Underlying much of the trepidation with digital-first scholarship may be the realization that on the web, professional historians are not the sole arbiters of what constitutes "history." As academic scholarship (with some exceptions) lies on library shelves or behind electronic subscription pay-walls, vast swaths of historical information and analysis can be found readily on the open web. For the experienced scholar, the riches there seem endless. In moments, I can choose class material from *Documenting the American South,* browse the *Perry-Castañeda Library Map Collection,* and peruse the criminal records of the Old Bailey. I can read about 18th-century funeral broadsides at *Common-Place* or download articles from the latest *African Diaspora Archaeology Newsletter.*[3] Yet the exponential growth of historical discourse on the Internet draws on the labors of not professional historians but, rather, the wider public that edits entries on *Wikipedia,* contributes to genealogical discussions on Ancestry.com, posts photos of historic sites to Flickr.com, and invokes the Founding Fathers or scripture in the comment pages of the *Washington Post.*

People with little or no formal training in the discipline have embraced the writing of history on the web, which raises the question, whose histories will prove authoritative in the digital age? Since the professionalization of history in the last decades of the 19th century, college and university professors have worn the mantle of authority. Through creation of such professional associations as the American Historical Association (founded in 1884) and through editorial control of academic journals and book presses, they have determined which narratives meet their standards of scholarly rigor.[4] At first, the emergence of the digital age did little to dilute the authority of disciplinary experts in history, but that has begun to change. Although Dan Cohen and Roy Rosenzweig rightly observed that "the Internet allows historians to speak to vastly more people in widely dispersed places," it can just as easily be said that the Internet allows vastly more people to speak about history without professional historians.[5] The popular understanding of the past differs greatly from that of academic historians; it often reflects an effort to muster the past in service of a particular worldview. As such, it may tell us as much about memory—how events are remembered—as it tells about history.

Ordinarily, historians see history and memory as distinct ways of understanding the past, the former governed by professional imperatives, the latter by cultural and familial expectations. David Blight summarizes this distinction as follows: "History—what trained historians do—is a reasoned reconstruction of the past rooted in research; critical and skeptical of human motive and action. . . . Memory, however, is often treated as a sacred set of potentially absolute meanings and stories, possessed as the heritage or identity of a community. Memory is often owned; history, interpreted. Memory is passed down through generations; history is revised."[6] Writing history in the digital age will force professional historians to share a space (i.e., the Internet) with others whose narratives draw on the "sacred set of potentially absolute meanings" that characterize popular memory. Nowhere is this characteristic of the web more apparent than in *Wikipedia*, which, for good or ill, provides more historical information to the public than any other site on the web. When you type any historical topic into the search engine of your choice, chances are excellent that the first hit will be *Wikipedia*. Its extensive entries demonstrate the ways in which popular understandings shape digital narratives about the past.

Why explore writing history through *Wikipedia*? Simply put, because it allows any reader to peel away layers of narrative to explore how entries have changed over time, juxtaposing revisions for comparison. In keeping with its self-fashioned identity as a community of writers, *Wikipedia* also maintains discussion pages for each entry that permit even the casual visitor—as well as the scholar bent on digital history—to follow the give and take between different contributors. In short, *Wikipedia* invites readers to peer behind the curtain and, if interested, take a place at the controls. This open-source quality has troubled many observers, who question the accuracy of *Wikipedia*'s entries and/or deny that it has any utility as a reference source for students and the wider public. Rather than discuss its accuracy, however, I wish to explore the process by which *Wikipedia* contributors craft entries about the past. Despite protestations that its entries may not serve as either a "soapbox" or "memorial site," *Wikipedia* is not simply an online encyclopedia.[7] Its historical entries serve as virtual "sites of memory" (to borrow from Pierre Nora), places at which people attempt to codify the meaning of past events.[8] Moreover, as they discuss and debate the language used to narrate the past, *Wikipedia* contributors may strive for a "neutral point of view" (NPOV), but in practice, they judge new entries and revisions via a moral economy of crowdsourcing.[9]

How does *Wikipedia* depict past events? How do contributors resolve debates about history? What happens when popular understandings (memory) clash with academic discourse (history)? To answer these questions, I traced a single entry for the "Origins of the American Civil War" (OACW) beginning with its first appearance in December 2003, when anonymous "User 172" posted a dense, 9,700-word essay accompanied by two images. Since then, more than 900 other users (some of them automated) have updated the page,[10] which now consists of roughly 19,000 words, 14 images, four maps, copious notes and bibliography. Because debates about the war's

Origins of the American Civil War

From Wikipedia, the free encyclopedia

For events following South Carolina's declaration of secession from the Union, see Battle of Fort Sumter and American Civil War.

Historians debating the **origins of the** American **Civil War** focus on the reasons seven states declared their secession from the U.S. and joined to form the Confederate States of America (the "Confederacy"). The main explanation is slavery, especially Southern anger at the attempts by Northern antislavery political forces to block the expansion of slavery into the western territories. Southern slave owners held that such a restriction on slavery would violate the principle of states' rights.

Abraham Lincoln won the 1860 presidential

The Battle of Fort Sumter was the opening battle in a conflict that had been brewing for decades.

Fig. 4. Locating "Talk" and "View History" tabs in *Wikipedia*

origins have often served as proxies for other struggles, such as the 20th-century civil rights movement, the OACW seemed likely to show traces of contestation. Depending on region and background, as a sizable literature demonstrates, the popular understanding of the American Civil War varies tremendously.[11] I paid particular attention to skirmishes in the OACW's discussion and history pages (see fig. 4). Most editorial changes elicited no controversy whatsoever; they either added new information or tackled the perennial problems of organization that plague longer *Wikipedia* entries. I also ignored minor acts of vandalism. For example, for nearly five days in 2004, the phrase "Michael Cox is the coolest kid at CMS" appeared in the OACW; perhaps for those days he was.[12] Excepting these pages, considerable discussion about the "Origins of the American Civil War" occurred behind the scenes as contributors challenged one another over terminology, imagery, and context. (See the images in the web version of this essay at http://WritingHistory.trincoll.edu.)

Wikipedia currently provides a plausible, if somewhat rambling, essay on the origins of the American Civil War. It opens with a statement with which many academics will agree: "The main explanation for the origins of the American Civil War is slavery, especially Southern anger at the attempts by Northern antislavery political forces to block the expansion of slavery into the western territories. Southern slave owners held that such a restriction on slavery would violate the principle of states' rights."[13] On this essential point, the OACW shares the broad consensus in the historical profession. User 172's narrative of the events leading up to the American Civil War resembles that of many American history textbooks; it covers the rise of the Republican Party, the Kansas-Nebraska Act, "Bleeding Kansas," and the collapse of the Whig Party as a national alternative to the Democrats. It further places that narrative within the context of a significant historiographic divide between scholars who have viewed the Civil War as irrepressible (i.e., as the inevitable consequence of the regional differentiation between an agrarian, slave-labor South and an increasingly industrial, free-labor North) and those who have argued that the conflict was repressible (i.e., the result of blundering politicians and/or reckless agitators in both regions). To be sure, the original narrative did not address events that professional Civil War historians today see as essential to our understanding of secession and the outbreak of hostilities, such as the Compromise of 1850, the Fugitive Slave Act, and John Brown's raid on Harper's Ferry. User 172 relied on much-dated historical works, which explains the original narrative's narrow emphasis chronologically (the 1850s) and thematically (politics).[14]

Beyond this, the OACW offers an unruly congeries of information reflecting its crowdsourced roots. Not only is every Wikipedian his or her own historian, but for each, the past possesses different meanings. User 172's narrative strongly suggested that white Southerners bore more responsibility for the outbreak of war than their Northern counterparts. User 172 wrote that the "vitriolic response" of the "Reactionary South" to Northern concerns about slavery in the Western territories exacerbated sectional tensions and that Southerners, "increasingly committed to a way of life that much of the rest of the nation considered obsolete," therefore responded to the election of Abraham Lincoln in 1860 by seceding from the Union.[15] In January 2005, a contributor with the evocative name "Rangerdude" challenged "anti-southern biases" in the OACW, objecting to the header "The Reactionary South" as "pejorative" and deleting a reference to the South's "hysterical racism."[16] Underlying Rangerdude's criticisms lay a preoccupation with the OACW's depiction of nonslaveholding whites in the South as racist: "The term is a modern one and is not neutral for a historical article."[17] Not surprisingly, Rangerdude's editorial changes provoked a response several hours later from User 172, who insisted that the underlying causes of the Civil War could not be addressed without discussing racism: "To claim that all references to racism should be removed from the article is patently absurd. It would leave us with no way to address how white people came to believe that Africans should be kept in bondage. That's why the relationship between slavery and racism has inspired a rich tradition in scholarly literature."[18] In an "edit war," the two contributors fought back and forth, taking turns deleting the other's revisions and substituting his own text. At one point, Rangerdude exclaimed, "Please do not revert edits because they remove bias that you happen to like."[19] User 172 asserted the importance of authoritative secondary sources, while Rangerdude challenged User 172 through demands for neutrality. Perhaps because both invoked the moral economy of *Wikipedia,* if in different ways, revisions to OACW sought a middle ground. The header "The Reactionary South" gave way to "The Southern Response." A reference to Southern whites so poor that they "resorted at times to eating clay" disappeared. References to Southern racism, supported by User 172's references to secondary sources, remained.

But what happened when one person's interpretation clashed with the collective narrative? In August 2004, user "H2O" insisted that OACW include African American slaveholders in its description of the antebellum South.[20] "The article," H2O complained, "implies that [slavery] was about the rich white people suppressing the poor black people, when it was really about the powerful (white or black) using the powerless (white or black) for their own gain, as evidenced by the fact that there were free black slaveowners who took advantage of the system as well." This is, of course, a nonsensical position, as there were no instances of powerful blacks owning white slaves. For H2O, slavery was simply an exploitative economic system in which whites and blacks participated equally according to their ability. H2O must have seen as incidental the fact that all slaves were of African descent. Elsewhere H2O makes the claim that slaveholders "treated their slaves kindly, and wanted to see an end to slavery, and believed that it eventually would die out, but did not see a simple way to end the practice."[21] Another contributor proposed that the OACW be rewritten to reflect that Northern aggression led to hostilities, driven by people "wholly opposed to the regular order of living and more into experimentation, the counterculture."[22] Neither of these proposals led to changes in the OACW, because other contributors judged them baseless. In other words, they failed to meet the community's standard for authoritative information. These examples, from both the OACW page and its talk history, suggest that the *Wikipedia* community does effectively gauge basic historical knowledge and can exclude claims that lack a factual basis.

Authoritativeness in *Wikipedia,* however, is not simply an imperfect version of scholarly authority. In other words, although it is tempting to see

Wikipedia as a space in which the expertise of professional historians is not yet (or not always) recognized, the popular understanding of the past that informs *Wikipedia*'s moral economy has never accepted PhD academics as definitive experts. Of course, some contributors do acknowledge the influence of professional scholarship. When challenged by Rangerdude to defend the argument that Southern society entwined slavery and racism, User 172 cited a battery of prizewinning scholars—Oscar and Mary Handlin, Winthrop Jordan, David Brion Davis, Peter Wood, and Edmund Morgan.[23] Others reject scholarly expertise altogether, positing that only original sources can reveal true history. For example, User 138.32.32.166 lambasted other contributors for their "repugnant bias," meaning by this that instead of presenting just the facts, they "editorialized." First-person perspectives are authoritative, User 138.32.32.166 seemed to say, but everything else is opinion: "Remember in you[r] search for history, do read memoirs, diaries and other accounts. Old newspapers articles are always interesting. You can always corroborate the memoirs etc. . . . for accuracy against accounted for events." For this person, history can only be accurate if it chronicles the past in the words of those who experienced it.[24] Across this spectrum, contributors share a belief that known facts form the foundation of historical narrative. A willingness to see professional scholarship as a source of factual information separates User 172 from User 138.22.32.166, but not even User 172 acknowledges that historians interpret past events. Intriguingly, although OACW contributors accept that slavery was a cause of the Civil War and that racism was a fundamental aspect of antebellum Southern society, Martha Saxton demonstrates, later in this volume, that *Wikipedia* editors consistently obscure American women's history through "suppression, exclusion, and marginalization." As she argues, American exceptionalism—the desire for a unitary, triumphalist historical narrative—frames the worldview that many contributors bring to *Wikipedia*.[25]

Although impossible to specify for any one entry, the demographics of *Wikipedia* contributors must also play a role in shaping their perspectives on the past. According to its own research, *Wikipedia* contributors are 26 years old on average. Roughly half hold a bachelor's or more advanced degree. Surprisingly, 34 percent have completed high school only, 11 percent not even that.[26] If the profile of OACW contributors resembles this overall picture, most have studied history—in high school or college—but few will have studied it in depth. Perhaps this explains the stunning omission of Edward Ayers's prizewinning *In the Presence of Mine Enemies* and its companion website, *The Valley of the Shadow*, from the OACW.[27]

If, according to Roy Rosenzweig and David Thelen, "millions of Americans regularly document, preserve, research, narrate, discuss, and study the past," it should not be surprising that they are drawn to *Wikipedia*.[28] More than just an encyclopedia, *Wikipedia* serves as a people's museum of knowledge, a living repository of all that matters, where the exhibits are written by ordinary folk, with nary an academic historian in sight. On the 150th anniversary of the firing on Fort Sumter, South Carolina (the event that began the American Civil War), more than 28,000 people visited the fort's *Wikipedia* entry. In 2011, when presidential aspirant Sarah Palin provided her own take on Paul Revere's famous ride, people turned to the relevant *Wikipedia* page in droves—peaking at 140,000 visitors in a single day.[29]

As the digital revolution spreads popular historical narratives, academic and public historians have an unprecedented opportunity to make our expertise available and relevant to an audience that, whatever its assumptions, possesses a deep, abiding investment in the importance of the past. This is not a plea for all PhD scholars to rush out and edit *Wikipedia* pages—far from it—but it is a call to greater engagement with those digital spaces that "document, preserve, research, narrate, discuss, and study the past." That engagement can take many forms but must begin with an acknowledgment that popular audiences understand and have always understood history without the scholarly norms familiar to professional historians. Digital technology may transform the production and performance of historical narratives, but it will not necessarily change the relationship between the public and the academy. That said, open discussions of NPOV, targeted "wikiblitzes" (such as the one described in this volume by Shawn Graham)[30] and sustained efforts to better integrate academic insight into popular narratives (see again Saxton's discussion of Women and *Wikipedia*) can all be part of a larger strategy to reconcile history and memory. Indeed, this is essential, because the momentum of the digital age can only further blur the line between scholarly and popular narratives of the past, a line first drawn in the late 19th century with the professionalization of history. Before that moment, published histories were but one form of memory. In the 21st century, the discipline of history seems likely to come full circle as all history and memory become digital. This does not mean that monuments, museums, historical reenactments, and print scholarship will disappear. But the normative form of access to the past will be electronic, and the line between history and memory will be difficult to discern.

Notes

1. Dan Cohen, "The Ivory Tower and the Open Web: Introduction: Burritos, Browsers, and Books (Draft)." *Dan Cohen's Digital Humanities Blog*, 26 July

2011, http://www.dancohen.org/2011/07/26/the-ivory-tower-and-the-open-web-introduction-burritos-browsers-and-books-draft/; Robert Townsend, "How Is New Media Reshaping the Work of Historians?," *Perspectives on History*, November 2010, http://www.historians.org/perspectives/issues/2010/1011/1011pro2.cfm.

2. In addition to this volume, see, for example, Kathleen Fitzpatrick, *Planned Obsolescence: Publishing, Technology, and the Future of the Academy* (New York: NYU Press, 2011), which first emerged online at http://mediacommons.futureofthebook.org/mcpress/plannedobsolescence/.

3. *Documenting the American South*, University of North Carolina at Chapel Hill Library, http://docsouth.unc.edu/;*Perry-Castañeda Library Map Collection*, University of Texas Libraries, http://www.lib.utexas.edu/maps/; *The Proceedings of the Old Bailey, 1674–1913*, University of Sheffield, http://www.oldbaileyonline.org/; Joanne van der Woude, "Puritan Scrabble: Games of Grief in Early New England," *Common-Place* 11, no. 4 (2011), http://www.common-place.org/vol-11/no-04/van-der-woude/; *African Diaspora Archaeology Newsletter*, University of Illinois at Urbana-Champaign, http://www.diaspora.uiuc.edu/newsletter.html.

4. American Historical Association, http://www.historians.org; Peter Novick, *That Noble Dream: Tthe "Objectivity Question" and the American Historical Profession* (Cambridge: Cambridge University Press, 1993).

5. Daniel J. Cohen and Roy Rozenzweig, *Digital History: A Guide to Gathering, Preserving, and Presenting the Past on the Web* (Philadelphia: University of Pennsylvania Press, 2006), 5.

6. David W. Blight, *Beyond the Battlefield: Race, Memory, and the American Civil War* (Amherst: University of Massachusetts Press, 2002), 2.

7. See Roy Rosenzweig, "Can History Be Open Source? *Wikipedia* and the Future of the Past," *Journal of American History* 93, no. 1 (2006): 117–46; "Key Policies and Guidelines" and "What Wikipedia Is Not," *Wikipedia*, http://en.wikipedia.org/wiki/Wikipedia:Key_policies_and_guidelines and http://en.wikipedia.org/wiki/Wikipedia:What_Wikipedia_is_not.

8. Pierre Nora, "Between Memory and History: *Lex Lieux de Mémoire*," *Representations* 26 (Spring 1989): 7–24.

9. "Neutral Point of View," *Wikipedia*, http://en.wikipedia.org/wiki/Wikipedia: Neutral_point_of_view. By "moral economy," I mean a set of normative beliefs and expectations collectively held.

10. For more on automated editing, see R. Stuart Geiger, "The Lives of Bots," in *Critical Point of View: A Wikipedia Reader*, ed. Geert Lovink and Nathaniel Tkacz, Institute of Network Cultures Reader 7 (Amsterdam: Institute of Network Cultures, 2011), 78–93.

11. This particular topic lies close to my own expertise—I teach a graduate course on the Civil War and Reconstruction—and is also the subject of many volumes. See, for example, Kirk Savage, *Standing Soldiers, Kneeling Slaves: Race, War, and Monument in Nineteenth-Century America* (Princeton: Princeton University Press, 1997); David W. Blight, *Race and Reunion: The Civil War in American Memory* (Cambridge, MA: Belknap Press of Harvard University Press, 2001); David W. Blight, ed., *Beyond the Battlefield* (Amherst: University of Massachusetts Press, 2002); Gaines M. Foster, *Ghosts of the Confederacy: Defeat, the Lost Cause, and the Emergence of the New South, 1865–1913* (New York: Oxford University Press, 1988).

12. OACW, 16:39, 12 May 2004, http://en.wikipedia.org/w/index. php?title=Origins_of_the_American_Civil_War&oldid=3550913. With so many citations to the same *Wikipedia* page, I developed this shortened form for use in the notes. Unless otherwise noted, access to all *Wikipedia* URLs was verified in March 2012.

13. OACW, 23:20, 11 August 2011, http://en.wikipedia.org/w/index.php?title= Origins_of_the_American_Civil_War&oldid=444350362. This is a permanent link to the page current when this chapter was completed.

14. OACW, 9:12, 20 December 2003, http://en.wikipedia.org/w/index.php?title =Origins_of_the_American_Civil_War&oldid=2005512.

15. OACW, 11:39, 21 December 2003, http://en.wikipedia.org/w/index.php? title=Origins_of_the_American_Civil_War&oldid=2014509.

16. *Wikipedia* user Rangerdude, http://en.wikipedia.org/w/index.php?title=Use r:Rangerdude&action=history.

17. Talk: OACW, 07:07, 8 January 2005, http://en.wikipedia.org/w/index. php?title=Talk:Origins_of_the_American_Civil_War&diff=prev&oldid=9198574. Talk: OACW citations are references to the OACW discussion page, not the *Wikipedia* entry itself.

18. Talk: OACW, 12:49, 8 January 2005, http://en.wikipedia.org/w/index. php?title=Talk:Origins_of_the_American_Civil_War&diff=next&oldid=9201516.

19. OACW, 6:48, 8 January 2005, http://en.wikipedia.org/w/index.php?title= Origins_of_the_American_Civil_War&diff=next&oldid=9197400.

20. *Wikipedia* user H2o, http://en.wikipedia.org/w/index.php?title=User:H2O &action=history.

21. OACW, 7:43, 16 August 2004, http://en.wikipedia.org/w/index.php? title=Origins_of_the_American_Civil_War&oldid=5234557; Talk: OACW, 9:17, 16 August 2004, http://en.wikipedia.org/w/index.php?title=Talk:Origins_of_the_ American_Civil_War&diff=next&oldid=5235613.

22. Talk: OACW, 2:51, 23 December 2008, http://en.wikipedia.org/w/ index.php?title=Talk:Origins_of_the_American_Civil_War&diff=prev&oldid =259648581.

23. OACW, 12:49, 8 January 2005, http://en.wikipedia.org/w/index. php?title=Talk:Origins_of_the_American_Civil_War&oldid=9201556.

24. Talk: OACW, 08:34, 28 June 2010, http://en.wikipedia.org/w/index.php? title=Talk:Origins_of_the_American_Civil_War&oldid=370560458.

25. Martha Saxton, "*Wikipedia* and Women's History," in this volume, p. 92.

26. Ruediger Glott, Philipp Schmidt, and Rishab Ghosh, *Wikipedia Survey— Overview of Results*, Collaborative Creativity Group, UNU-MERIT, United Nations University, March 2010, http://www.wikipediastudy.org. The data also show that the vast majority of *Wikipedia* contributors are men; fewer than 13 percent are women.

27. Edward L. Ayers, *In the Presence of Mine Enemies: War in the Heart of America, 1859–1863* (New York: W. W. Norton, 2003); *The Valley of the Shadow: Two Communities in the American Civil War*, Virginia Center for Digital History and the University of Virginia Libraries, 1997–2003, http://valley.lib.virginia.edu/.

28. Roy Rosenzweig and David Thelen, *The Presence of the Past: Popular Uses of History in American Life* (New York: Columbia University Press, 1998), 24.

29. "Wikipedia article traffic statistics," *Wikipedia*, http://stats.grok.se/en/201104/Fort Sumter; Chris Beneke, "Revere, Revisited," *The Historical Society; A Blog Devoted to History for the Academy and Beyond*, June 13, 2011, http://histsociety.blogspot.com/2011/06/revere-revisited.html.

30. Shawn Graham, "The Wikiblitz: A *Wikipedia* Editing Assignment in a First-Year Undergraduate Class," in this volume.

The Wikiblitz

A Wikipedia *Editing Assignment in a First-Year Undergraduate Class*

Shawn Graham

In this essay, I describe an experiment conducted in the 2010 academic year at Carleton University, in my first-year seminar class on digital history. This experiment was designed to explore how knowledge is created and represented on *Wikipedia*, by working to improve a single article. The overall objective of the class was to give students an understanding of how historians can create "signal" in the "noise" of the Internet and how historians create knowledge using digital media tools. Given that doing "research" online often involves selecting a resource suggested by Google (generally one within the first three to five results),[1] this class had larger media literacy goals as well. The students were drawn from all areas of the university, with the only stipulation being that they had to be in their first year.

The positive feedback loops inherent in the World Wide Web's structure greatly influence the way history is consumed, disseminated, and created online. Google's algorithms will retrieve an article from *Wikipedia*, typically displaying it as one of the first links on the results page. Someone somewhere will decide that the information is "wrong," and he (it is typically a *he*)[2] will "fix" the information, clicking on the "edit" button to make the change. To Google's algorithms, this is one of many signals that the web page featuring this article is more valuable, more relevant, and thus worth a higher ranking. In this way, *Wikipedia* and Google feed one another, and the loop is strengthened.[3]

We as historians need to teach our students to understand how all this works and how it creates historical knowledge. Digital media make all history public history (whether we like it or not),[4] and we need to get our research into that positive feedback loop. While Google is a closed service, its workings only dimly perceived through its effects, we can at least engage with the other part of that positive feedback loop, *Wikipedia*.

Using *Wikipedia* in teaching is not a new idea; Roy Rosenzweig made that argument in 2006.[5] *Wikipedia* itself now has a page for "School and University Projects" that lists over 50 formal collaborations with *Wikipedia*.[6] This experiment was my first foray into using *Wikipedia* editing as a formative assessment exercise. While it was by and large a successful experiment, it did have one unexpected element: push back and resistance from one significant element in the class, my declared history majors.

FYSM1405a, Digital History

We took some time to get to *Wikipedia* in this course. The first section of the course looked at the sheer mass of historical materials available on the Internet, asking: How do we find our way through all of this? How do we identify what is important? The structured readings during this module were reflections by the seminal author Roy Rosenzweig (founder of the Center for History and New Media at George Mason University).

We also looked at how the "doing" of history was itself an "unnatural act," in Sam Wineburg's felicitous phrase.[7] This led to a second module where the students explored the idea that we never observe the past directly; we must build models to fit what we "know" into a system of explanation. In digital work, these models are explicitly written in computer code. Understanding how the code forces a particular worldview on the user is a key portion of becoming a "digital historian." Computer games are another kind of model of the world; historical computer games are some of the best-selling games on the market today. A consideration of gaming and "playing" with history led to a module focused on crowdsourcing history and to the Wikiblitz assignment. *Wikipedia* can be thought of as a kind of game where competing visions of common knowledge vie for dominance.[8] I introduced the related idea that since *Wikipedia* involved complex interactions between hundreds of thousands of autonomous individuals who interacted according to a small set of rules, it could be considered a kind of complex system. In this way, a coherent *Wikipedia* entry is an emergent property of decentralized, undirected cooperation and competition.[9] Before the Wikiblitz, we spent two sessions looking at crowdsourcing and ways that small changes/additions can add up to substantial revisions.[10] We discussed *Wikipedia*'s "neutral point of view" (NPOV) provisions by looking at political blogs and contrasting them with other resources.[11] We looked at the history of wikis more generally and that of *Wikipedia* itself specifically.[12]

The assignment prompt follows:

At your computer, examine the article at http://en.wikipedia.org/wiki/ Ottawa_Valley (the *Wikipedia* entry for Ottawa Valley).[13] Identify areas that are logically weak or poorly written, or areas (especially related to its history) that are otherwise incomplete. Using a pseudonym, log into *Wikipedia* and make a substantial improvement to the article. Email me with your pseudonym and a brief description of the changes you made. All changes are to be made within class time.[14]

During a subsequent class, you will review how the article evolved during your blitzing of it, and the subsequent changes made by the wider Wikipedian community. You will be asked to reflect on how much of your contribution survived the interval. Why did those parts survive? Why did some parts get reverted or deleted? How does the Wikipedian community deal with citations and points of view? Your reflection will be written before the class, taking the form of a short paragraph, and will form the starting point for the class discussion.

Part 1 of this assignment, the Wikiblitz itself, was conducted on November 26, 2010. Part 2, the reflection and discussion, took place on December 1, 2010. On December 1, the students were shown a time-lapsed video illustrating how the *Wikipedia* page changed over the course of the blitz and the subsequent week. They shared their observations with their classmates to either side, before sharing with the class as a whole. Their written reflections were taken in for grading per the rubric in table 1 (noting that the majority of the points concerned their actual engagement with the *Wikipedia* page).

My desired outcome was that the students should see how knowledge creation on *Wikipedia* is as much about style as it is about substance. I wanted them to see that writing for *Wikipedia* constitutes a kind of peer review. Finally, I hoped that they would perceive how the NPOV provisions could lead to particular kinds of rhetoric and judgments regarding knowledge credibility and suitability (and could thus situate this kind of writing firmly within the continuum of historiographic writing).[15] In preparing for this exercise, I did not engage in any explicit debate over whether wiki writ-

TABLE 1. Rubric for the Wikiblitz Exercise

	Criterion	3	2	1
Blitz	Editing	Major contribution made	Minor contribution with several corrections made throughout the text	Minor edits only
	Wiki Style	Observed *Wikipedia*'s house style	English is generally correct, but NPOV is not observed	English is problematic
	Sources	Cited appropriately	Citations problematic	No citations
Reflection	Knowledge creation	Reflection shows deep thought on how knowledge is negotiated in a wiki	Reflection shows some awareness of how knowledge is created	Reflection shows little awareness beyond the student's own point of view

Total points: 1/2

ing was an appropriate activity for a historian. Given the trajectory of the class content and conversation, I assumed that the rationale encapsulated in the opening to this essay was by this point self-evident. In hindsight, making that assumption was perhaps an error.

Resistance and Surprise

I had made it clear to my students that I felt that *Wikipedia* was a valuable resource, when students understood how it worked and used it appropriately. Curiously, however, there was push back from an unexpected quarter: my actual history students. As a first-year seminar at my institution, the majority of the students come from other majors. My history students themselves were actually in the minority. In conversation, it became apparent that these students already had quite clear ideas about authority, authorship, and intellectual property, ideas that fit in quite well with established ways of writing history.[16] They had internalized the main strength of a wiki, that it may be edited by anyone, as a challenge to "their" work and thus something to be avoided: "I did the work. I don't want somebody screwing it up." Others have noted this phenomenon.[17]

Clay Shirky wrote in 2003,

> And this [the speed with which changes can be reverted], *mirabile dictu*,
> is why wikis can have so little protective armor and yet be so resistant to

damage. It takes longer to set fire to the building than put it out, it takes longer to graffiti the wall than clean it, it takes longer to damage the page than restore it. If nearly two hours of work spent trying to subtly undermine a site can be erased in minutes, that's a lousy place to hang out, if your goal is to get people's goat.[18]

The idea that one has to *monitor* a site also produced push back in my core group of history students. It seems to me that trained by years of launch and forget—according to which a paper or assignment is written, graded, and then never revisited—has made it difficult for students to entertain the idea that scholarship is conversation, that what you write can have an impact and that you should respond to that impact.[19]

We discussed these issues in class, and I felt that I was making progress. However, when the day arrived to do the *Wikipedia* assignment in class, a large proportion of that minority of students were "sick."

The Day of the Wikiblitz

While the students were making their edits to the page, I observed the edits page and commented on what I was seeing via instant messaging to the class as a whole.[20] The class period was 1 hour and 15 minutes. Many of my comments concerned the intricacies of editing and formatting the page and guiding the secondary research going on in the background (or at least trying to guide it). Below are certain key observations:

> Great to see some changes being made already. But a question for you— many of the recent changes are focusing on the City of Ottawa itself: is that appropriate for an article on "the Ottawa Valley"? Shouldn't the focus be elsewhere? Perhaps this is a change that needs [to] be made . . . ? (n.b. You can of course make edits to somebody else's edits, from this class!)

> [some time later:] Folks, this is an article about the Ottawa Valley, not the city of Ottawa!

> [some time later again:] Seems to be a lot of energy focused on the tourism aspect . . . has anybody corrected any obvious errors in the text yet? What about the fact that a valley has two sides . . . ? where's the info on the Quebec side?

Perhaps one of the hardest lessons for the students to absorb was that *Wikipedia* articles are "spare" in the sense that they contain no fat. If an article loses its focus, other users will either delete that fat or remove it to its own wiki page. In the subsequent discussion of the exercise, the students were evenly split on whether or not I should have intervened during the exercise to remind them about scope. Was a paragraph on the Ottawa Valley's largest city warranted? By and large, the class ultimately decided that it was not, since the city is now culturally (at least in the students' point of view) and legally distinct from the other jurisdictions in the region. We explored the pattern of links that did or did not connect these two articles, noting that a person who landed on the "Ottawa (City of)" page or even the "Ottawa (disambiguation)" page would not be directed to the "Ottawa Valley" page, nor would a visitor to the "Ottawa Valley" page be directed to the "Ottawa (City of)" page.[21] As in life, so in art: the two concepts were distinct, and their treatment reflected and reinforced that distinction. It is important to remember and to make clear to students that what matters in *Wikipedia* is not just the content of a given page but also the network structure of links that connect pages together.[22] (Perhaps a few rounds of Six Degrees of Wikipedia could be useful to make that point.)[23]

The energy that the students expended on the tourism industry was interesting. In the discussion, it transpired that this was because it was the "easiest" subject. Aside from the *Wikipedia* link, a basic Google search for "Ottawa Valley" returns nearly nine million results, the first few pages of which are tourism related. We were on campus and had full access to library resources while we did this blitz, and we had already had numerous discussions about best practices in research. That it became apparent quite quickly and was publicly demonstrable that the students were not even approaching basic expectations for research was an important outcome.[24]

One event was a great surprise to the entire class, me included. I observed,

> [A student] has just made some edits to the site . . . but a wikipedia automated vandalism 'bot has reverted them!

We did not realize that these bots even existed. *Wikipedia* has a page explaining how wiki bots work.[25] Much of the tedious work of editing *Wikipedia* pages (correcting link formatting for instance) can be automated within the wiki framework. Currently, there are well over 1,000 distinct tasks that are approved for bots. Some of the earliest bots were created to upload massive amounts of material into *Wikipedia* quickly (apparently, this is how major portions of the 1911 *Encyclopedia Britannica* on the Project Gutenberg site were uploaded into *Wikipedia*).[26]

As we discussed this incident, we surmised that our small class's activities, a concentrated stream of edits, all from more or less the same place at the same time, must have triggered the bot to revert our changes. The student whose edit finally triggered the bot was greatly upset by this. How could a bot decide that *her* work was somehow malicious? It was a prime teachable moment on the way humans and computers interact.

My final comment during the Wikiblast follows:

> Hi everyone—in the space of a class, we've made 30 substantial edits to the page (and many minor ones); increasing its size from 13.8 kb to 23.4 kb—that's the equivalent of about four pages of text. Now—until Wednesday [the following week's class], keep an eye on the page. Let's see how long this version lasts; don't make any more edits.

A year after this class ended in 2010, there have been about 40 edits to the page. Clearly, this page is not one that attracts a lot of attention from the contributors to *Wikipedia*. But our burst of activity did attract others to the site, and some changes and reversions were made by other users. *Wikipedia* users and editors might often operate under pseudonyms, but activity draws attention. Many of the students were quite surprised by this, since it undermined the idea of the anonymous troll making malicious changes undetected.

The following week, I put together a time-lapsed video of the edits to the page from its one-line birth in 2005 to the end of November 2010, following the example of Jon Udell's "Heavy Metal Umlaut" video.[27] Visualizing the evolution of a *Wikipedia* page is very instructive. The interests and early structure that emerged in the article's first few months seem to set the skeleton for all subsequent revisions. Once a structure emerges, it seems that it takes a lot of energy to overrule it or otherwise make substantial changes. For instance, the political history of the Ottawa Valley was quickly expunged, but a section on First Nations land claims in the area resisted all efforts to remove it (by other *Wikipedia* authors that were not part of my class).

The exercise was mostly successful. In the students' written feedback, I was particularly heartened to read the following:

> The fact that many of the changes made by the class were reverted [by other Wikipedians] means that even an "any one can edit" site like Wikipedia is in fact conservative and resistant to change. Why is that? Perhaps it's because people take ownership of particular pages . . . I also thought it was quite amazing how the anti-vandalism bot reversed some

TABLE 2. Summary of Student Feedback on Wikiblitz Exercise

Gist of Comment	Number of Mentions by Students
Ease of use	1
The way *Wikipedia* "self heals"	3
Lack of professionalism	3
Content is contested by other Wikipedians	5
Fact that it is "in public" compels professionalism	1
Authority lacking—these people could be just like us!	2
Futility of trying to improve articles	2
Where do Wikipedians get their sources?	1

of our changes . . . this feature[,] designed to preserve the presentation of fact[,] has the effect of preserving misinformation as well . . .

The fact that the people writing and editing Wikipedia pages could in fact be just like us—first years with little in-depth knowledge—is actually rather frightening.

I tabulated the content of my students' feedback in table 2.

That students need to understand how knowledge can be crowdsourced, produced, and disseminated on the web is, I think, not a radical conclusion. What this small exercise demonstrates for writing history in the digital age is one small way of confronting the more important issue: that our history students can be reluctant to engage with this mode, this way of writing. There will be push back, and we need to explore it, understand where it comes from, and think carefully about how to address it. If we want to raise the quality of public discourse about history, we have to begin with our students and show them how what they do can have immediate impact, given the feedback loop that exists between Google and *Wikipedia*. My experiment failed in some ways, in that I did not achieve the buy-in of all of my "official" history students; but it succeeded in other ways, in that I reached my other students who did not normally (as a part of their regular course of study) have to confront the ways in which knowledge is socially constructed. For one brief moment, they were digital humanists.

Acknowledgments: The Wikiblitz was part of the course work for FYSM1405a (Digital History), and a brief reflection on this assignment was first posted on Graham's blog *Electric Archaeology: Digital Media for Learning and Research* (http://electricarchaeologist.wordpress.com).

Notes

1. This is a generalized pattern; see, for instance, Bernard Jansen and Amanda Spink, "How Are We Searching the World Wide Web? A Comparison of Nine Search Engine Transaction Logs," *Information Processing and Management* 42, no. 1 (2006): 248–63. Google currently has around two-thirds of the U.S. search market, according to comScore, a digital marketing research firm (comScore, "comScore Releases May 2011 U.S. Search Engine Rankings," company press release, June 10, 2011, http://www.comscore.com/Press_Events/Press_Releases/2011/6/). This pattern of shallow searching is also evident for more traditional sources; see Barbara Rockenbach, comment on Shawn Graham, "The Wikiblitz," in *Writing History in the Digital Age*, web-book ed., Fall 2011 version.

2. Ruediger Glott and Rishab Ghosh, *Analysis of Wikipedia Survey Data: Topic: Age and Gender Differences*, Collaborative Creativity Group, Wikimedia Foundation, United Nations University MERIT, Maastricht University, March 2010, 6, http://www.wikipediasurvey.org/docs/Wikipedia_Age_Gender_30March 2010-FINAL-3.pdf.

3. Shawn Graham, "Signal versus Noise: Why Academic Blogging Matters; A Structural Argument," *Electric Archaeology*, April 2, 2011, http://electricarchae-ologist.wordpress.com/2011/04/02/signal-versus-noise-why-academic-blogging-matters-a-structural-argument-saa-2011/; Roy Rosenzweig, "Can History Be Open Source? *Wikipedia* and the Future of the Past," *Journal of American History* 93, no. 1 (2006): 117–46. Google+ is a recent facet to this feedback loop. It is too early to say what its impact will be, but it seems designed to keep users in thrall to Google's services. See Stephen Levy, "Inside Google+—How the Search Giant Plans to Go Social," *Wired*, June 28, 2011, http://www.wired.com/epicenter/2011/06/inside-google-plus-social/. For how Google Scholar is affecting knowledge creation, see Jose van Dijck, "Search Engines and the Production of Academic Knowledge," *International Journal of Cultural Studies* 13 (2010): 574–92.

4. Neither paywalls nor logins ultimately keep materials hidden. See, for instance, on the Swartz affair, Ben Goldacre, "Academic Publishers Run a Guarded Knowledge Economy," *Guardian*, 2 September 2011, http://www.guardian.co.uk/commentisfree/2011/sep/02/bad-science-academic-publishing; see also http://youropenbook.org, on the porosity of Facebook. (This site was shut down for legal reasons in July 2012, "Openbook," *Wikipedia*, http://en.wikipedia.org/wiki/Openbook_%28website%29.)

5. Rosenzweig, "Can History Be Open Source?"

6. "School and University Projects," *Wikipedia*, http://en.wikipedia.org/wiki/Wikipedia:School_and_university_projects.

7. Sam Wineburg, *Historical Thinking and Other Unnatural Acts: Charting the Future of Teaching the Past* (Philadelphia: Temple University Press, 2001).

8. Jane McGonigal, *Reality Is Broken: Why Games Make Us Better and How They Change the World* (New York: Penguin, 2011), 228–31.

9. Cf. Melanie Mitchell, *Complexity: A Guided Tour* (Oxford: Oxford University Press, 2009), 215–20.

10. A useful source for this was Robert E. Cummings and Matt Barton, eds., *Wiki Writing: Collaborative Learning in the College Classroom* (Ann Arbor: University of Michigan Press, 2008), http://www.digitalculture.org/books/wiki-writing. See also, Jon Udell, "Heavy Metal Umlaut," January 21, 2005, http://jonudell.net/udell/gems/umlaut/umlaut.html.

11. See Robert Wolff, "The Historian's Craft, Popular Memory, and *Wikipedia*," in this volume.

12. Cummings and Barton, *Wiki Writing*; Rosenzweig, "Can History Be Open Source?"

13. Carleton University is based in Ottawa, in the heart of the Ottawa Valley, so I chose this particular article to connect the exercise with the students' personal backgrounds.

14. The time frame is why I named the assignment "The Wikiblitz."

15. Amanda Seligman deals explicitly with these issues in her essay in this volume, "Teaching *Wikipedia* without Apologies."

16. Cf. Stephanie Vie and Jennifer de Winter, "Disrupting Intellectual Property: Collaboration and Resistance in Wikis," in Cummings and Barton, *Wiki Writing*, 109–10, on the challenge wikis present to established patterns.

17. Brian Lamb, "Wide Open Spaces: Wikis, Ready or Not," *Educause Review*, 39, no. 5 (2004): 37–48, http://www.educause.edu/EDUCAUSE+Review/EDUCAUSEReviewMagazineVolume39/WideOpenSpacesWikisReadyorNot/157925; Cathlena Martin and Lisa Dusenberry, "Wiki Lore and Politics in the Classroom," in Cummings and Barton, *Wiki Writing*, 213–14. Blau and Caspi noted a similar mood in collaborative writing spaces like Google Docs, where students reported that their own edits improved the draft but that edits by others made it worse: see Ina Blau and Avner Caspi, "Sharing and Collaborating with Google Docs: The Influence of Psychological Ownership, Responsibility, and Student's Attitudes on Outcome Quality," in *Proceedings of the E-Learn 2009 World Conference on E-Learning in Corporate, Government, Healthcare, & Higher Education*, Vancouver, Canada (Chesapeake, VA: AACE, 2009), 3329–35, http://www.openac.il/research_center/download/Sharing_collaborating_Google_Docs.pdf.

18. Clay Shirkey, "Wikis, Graffiti, and Process," *Corante*, August 26, 2003, http://many.corante.com/20030801.shtml.

19. Cf. Martha Saxton, "*Wikipedia* and Women's History: A Classroom Experience," in this volume.

20. For the page history, see "Ottawa Valley: Revision History," *Wikipedia*, http://en.wikipedia.org/w/index.php?title=Ottawa_Valley&action=history.

21. While true at the time of the exercise, this was no longer the case in 2011, see "Ottawa," *Wikipedia*, http://en.wikipedia.org/wiki/Ottawa.

22. A. Capocci et al., "Preferential Attachment in the Growth of Social Networks: The Internet Encyclopedia Wikipedia," *Physical Review E* 74.3 036116, accessed January 13, 2012, www.inf.ufrgs.br/~buriol/papers/Physical_Review_E_06.pdf. The network structure to the patterning of author collaboration on *Wikipedia* should also be scrutinized. See Ulrik Brandes et al., "Network Analysis of Collaboration Structure in Wikipedia," in *Proceedings of the 18th International Conference on World Wide Web, Madrid, Spain*, ed. Juan Quemada et al. (New York: Association for Computing Machinery, 2009), 731–40.

23. *Wikipedia* can also serve as a platform for casual games of "racing" to find the shortest paths between random articles. See Alex Clemesha, *The Wikigame*, http://thewikigame.com/.

24. It is an outcome that Gabriel Bodard noted when using *Wikipedia* in classics courses ("Wikipedia as Teaching Tool," March 25, 2007, http://www.stoa.org/archives/600).

25. "Bots," *Wikipedia*, http://en.wikipedia.org/wiki/Wikipedia:Bots.

26. "History of Wikipedia," *Wikipedia*, http://en.wikipedia.org/wiki/Wikipedia:History_of_Wikipedia_bots.

27. Udell, "Heavy Metal Umlaut."

Wikipedia and Women's History

A Classroom Experience

Martha Saxton

In 2007, I began assigning my women's history students the task of researching a new *Wikipedia* article or making a significant editorial intervention in an existing essay on women. My colleague, Scott Payne, director of academic technology, had suggested I survey *Wikipedia*'s women's history content, and I was, as he anticipated, very distressed by its absence and by its superficiality and inaccuracies when present. A *New York Times*[1] article at the beginning of 2011 noting that only 13 percent of contributors to *Wikipedia* were women offered a partial explanation. Nonetheless, to explain the slowdown in entries about the United States, Jimmy Wales, founder of *Wikipedia,* said in a recent interview, "There aren't that many obvious topics left to write about."[2] A little checking for women's topics still reveals a great shortage of material on women. Historical material is confined to some profiles of the famous, and there is very little of substance on women in the more comprehensive articles. Therefore, my purpose initially was twofold: to increase the representation of women in this global source of information and to use a relatively new tool to teach students some not-so-new methods for evaluating and writing responsible history.

Many educators have expressed strong misgivings about *Wikipedia*'s role in education, due to its fast-changing content, the uneven level of research and writing, and its reliance, particularly in the humanities and social sciences, on the work of amateurs. (Robert Wolff's deeper criticism is significant but could be said to apply to all encyclopedia-like projects: "[P]rofessional norms of interpretation, discourse, and debate cannot be readily applied and may be unwelcome.")[3] Nevertheless, according to the "School and University Projects" page in *Wikipedia*, there are almost 200 documented college and university courses involving the encyclopedia, many of them ongoing.[4] Roy Rosenzweig's influential 2006 article expressing careful enthusiasm for *Wikipedia*'s accomplishments and potential and calling for academics to become involved helped increase faculty recognition that *Wikipedia* merits classroom time.[5] The present essay, written with contributions by Scott Payne and two students, Melissa Greenberg and Leah Cerf, will sketch in some of my and my colleagues' experiences and discoveries in trying to add women's content to *Wikipedia*.

Working with Scott Payne, I asked students first to analyze an entry, evaluating its content and sources for accuracy and significance. Their major assignment was to intervene in an existing article that they thought needed content on women or to draft one of their own on a new topic. They used the library to find articles and books to prepare them to compare accounts and sources. Unusually for a course requiring research, they did not use primary sources, as *Wikipedia* prohibits them as "unverifiable." But they did learn the technical skills and politesse required to intervene in *Wikipedia*.

Payne introduced students to the hierarchy of *Wikipedia* articles and its implications for how and what kinds of changes may be made. For example, articles that achieve the status of "featured" or that are successfully nominated as "good articles" are starred, and *Wikipedia* editors judge them to be well written, broad, stable, neutral in point of view, informative, and "verifiable." Former contributors and other interested people (as well as "bots" or automatic devices alerting concerned people to changes) keep track of these articles—including those titled "American Revolution," "Vietnam War," and "California Gold Rush," as well as numerous others—protecting their content.[6] Payne fine-tuned the best approach to editing articles on a case-by-case basis, inviting students to look at a topic's revision history and talk page to judge the activity, the types of changes being made (e.g., minor wording or more substantial edits where an ideological tug-of-war can sometimes be apparent), and who the main contributors are. The talk page gives a sense of how excited the back-and-forth has been. Payne's judgment also depended on the nature of the planned changes. If a student proposed a major rewrite, it was usually a good idea to run the proposal by the other contributors. Adding a section and/or and making some minor edits was normally less controversial. Payne sometimes recommended that students first explain their revision plans on the talk page; for quasi-dormant pages, he suggested that they revise immediately. These preparations were helpful, and some editors responded welcomingly, but students also encountered such criticisms as "irrelevance" or "inappropriate tone." An author may upload, of course, whatever she or he wishes, but the editors can and do remove material as they see fit.

While practicing the art of *Wikipedia* diplomacy, students also learned, as Shawn Graham describes in this volume, "how knowledge can be crowdsourced, produced, and disseminated on the web."[7] They also got a lesson in how little women's history has penetrated mainstream culture. A review of our activities and the lives and half-lives of the essays that students have posted suggests that this project teaches useful lessons about the protocol and mechanics of writing crowdsourced history in a digital format. But it also suggests that to the extent that popular judgment determines what history gets produced in this format, the significance of women's role in it and of gender as a discourse or a method of analysis are likely to be devalued.

Writing for *Wikipedia* is not the customary closed dialogue between student and instructor; it is, as Shawn Graham says, a conversation,[8] sometimes with many participants, and it may make unusual demands on students' social and intellectual abilities. When students propose changes to an active article's talk page, they can receive challenging feedback in a matter of minutes. During a workshop, one student posted her proposed revisions to the talk page for the article "Vietnam War."[9] The student's proposal was slightly ambiguous, prompting several fast responses, ranging from a call for clarification to sarcastic objections. (Ideologically charged conversations routinely take place in that space, despite instructions to discussants to "be welcoming" and "engage in no personal attacks.") Within a few minutes, a "reviewer" for the article responded with several substantive questions about the student's proposed modifications. A reviewer is an experienced and reliable contributor[10] qualified to evaluate possible changes to essays with "semi-protection" status (controversial articles can be "protected" to discourage vandalism and "edit wars"). The student huddled with a number of classmates, Scott Payne, and me to think through her response. What would have been an exchange between student and teacher became a less predictable conversation among some students of U.S. women's history and the *Wikipedia* community that had coalesced around its interest in the Vietnam War. Although several respondents were active, the reviewer seems to have had (at least as of this writing) the final word. Students had the experience of defending the inclusion of material on women to critics with little interest or knowledge in the subject, some of whom were hostile toward it.

Thus, writing for *Wikipedia* lets fledgling historians directly engage in the conflicts and debates over who gets to tell which stories about our past. Writing in the wake of the culture wars of the 1990s, Eric Foner, in a 2002 collection of essays entitled *Who Owns History?*, called for historians not to shy away from engaging in debate over history with the "larger public."[11] Learning *Wikipedia*'s evolving rules equips students to join the fight digitally. The struggle, unlike debates in print, occurs very publicly, is likely to be multivocal, and is often very fast-paced. It is not for the faint of heart.

Contributing to *Wikipedia* is a continuing, sometimes confusing and heated conversation that also blurs the boundary between author and reader. In *Wikipedia*, as cultural critic Dubravka Ugresic writes, "the balance of power formerly dominated by Author and Work, has been flipped in favor of the Recipient. . . . transforming perception, comprehension, and taste."[12] Students may not be aware of all these transformations, but they certainly feel the loss of ownership of their work when they click *Wikipedia*'s "Submit" button. Many have invested considerable work and time into formulating well-researched, cogent content, only to see it challenged, condensed, paraphrased, moved to a different location, or deleted altogether. Jimmy Wales, aware of the problem of potentially unreliable material, said in a recent interview, "Now there is an increasing focus on quality and referencing."[13] But unreliability and what seem to be arbitrary revisions of well-researched material remain particularly problematic when alterations appear to be motivated by sexism (in one instance, a kind of reverse sexism) and/or American exceptionalist bias. This notion will be explored in greater depth below.

Elsewhere in this volume, Robert Wolff found that in his study of discussions of the causes of the Civil War, the "*Wikipedia* community does effectively gauge basic historical knowledge and can exclude claims that lack a factual basis."[14] We learned, however, that crowdsourced judgments on women's history were more problematic. Some editors regard the insistence that women's historical experience is sometimes distinct from men's as a priori "inappropriate" and/or "irrelevant." Others find that discussing discrimination that has accompanied many of women's efforts to be included in mainstream activities does not pass muster because it is anachronistic or not neutral in point of view.

Students encountered acceptance, mild resistance, and vigorous opposition to women's content in *Wikipedia*. I recommended that students consider integrating women's experience into broad subjects, on the theory that this is both more challenging intellectually and, ultimately, more to the point of the overall project of bringing women into our acknowledged history. Adding a section that can be easily overlooked and that seems, by its separateness, to be incidental to central events of our past helps to confirm a view of women's participation in history as peripheral, precisely the view that our interventions are trying to challenge. Some students introduced women into the *Wikipedia* articles titled "American Revolution," "Vietnam War," "Reconstruction Era," "Prohibition," "Screen Actors Guild," and "Social Security Act," while others preferred the more manageable canvas of biographical profile. Students added entries on women's participation and experience to the articles titled "California Gold Rush," "Indentured Servant," "Incarceration of Women," "Elizabeth Cady Stanton," and "Women's Suffrage".[15]

Melissa Greenberg contributed to "Reconstruction Era" and found that her work was well received.[16] In her preliminary critique of the article, she observed that it was heavy on military and political history and light on "social history [altogether], including women's history." She was particularly struck by the absence of information on legalizing slave unions, which was "particularly important . . . [for] the ability of freed people to have control over their families."[17] Her contributions stand, although the preponderance of the article still concerns the military and formal politics, despite the widespread findings of African American women's remarkably active participation in Reconstruction politics.

Leah Cerf substantially revised "Eugenics in the United States," finding that the previous editor had never used the word *woman* in the text.[18] Cerf therefore anticipated that "[the editor] viewed women's contributions to the U.S. eugenics movement as 'inconsequential' and that her contributions, too, would be seen as 'inconsequential to the overall history.'" Nevertheless, she uploaded material on "how Native American and Black women were often sterilized without their consent," as well as other examples of "women's unique roles as victims of the eugenics movement." She also wrote about such women as "Margaret Sanger and members of several other women's associations," who "promoted the eugenic agenda and advocated for eugenic legislation." Leah writes,

> I was astonished! The editor . . . fully support[ed] my references to women as . . . victims but thought it was "anti-woman" and "biased" to write about their role as promoters of this dark pseudoscience. . . . To ignore women's historical role as champions of this now discredited movement not only fails to show the complete historical record, but it also ignores the political clout women had even before they were able to vote. To ignore that women were key players in this movement . . . is to say that men alone defined the political and social playing field. For me the article's [previous] editor was the one being "anti-woman."[19]

Repressing women's role in our darker chapters falsely removes them from participation, for better or worse, in many of our national debates, programs, and policies, and it just as falsely revives the fading myth that women are "better" than men.

As of this writing, much of the content on women that was created by my students has been removed and/or moved elsewhere. A 2007 student edited the article "Indentured Servant" to include the particular experience of women and the punitive lengthening of their terms if they became pregnant before their service ended. This material has disappeared. The article "California Gold Rush" was deemed "finished" by editors at the time that a student proposed an intervention in 2007. Editors permitted the student to upload quite a small amount of the material she had prepared, and a fraction of that material has persisted. In the article "American Revolutionary War," students entered material on the contributions of various groups of women to the war effort. Now there is a brief subcategory entitled "Sex, Race, Class," although sex, gender, and women are not mentioned. (The word *family is* used.)[20] There is room for confusion here, because there is also an article titled "American Revolution," with a brief but informative section on women's roles. But the material that my students uploaded appears in a new essay entitled "Women in the American Revolution."[21] It is unclear who thought to make this transfer, as the WikiProject Women's History, presumably a group that would be overseeing these kinds of articles, articulates its central goal as "incorporat[ing] the perspective of women's history in overview articles of historical periods . . . which may currently lack such coverage."[22] Meanwhile, the WikiProject editors as a whole, who describe themselves as [wanting] "to work together as a team to improve Wikipedia," rated "Women in the American Revolution" as having "low importance" for the WikiProject United States but "high importance" for the WikiProject Women's History. Herein lies the paradox that underlies and undermines my classes' work. As a separate and unequal field, women's history has the highest significance for itself, but it apparently has little when the goal is understanding the United States.[23]

At the moment, material that is segregated under such headings as "Women's Roles" or "Women's Experience" often has a better chance of surviving in featured *Wikipedia* articles than more integrated material. Women's content is easily criticized on grounds of organization, length, relevance, and lack of neutrality, even if the substance itself seems to be the problem. Introducing the experience of disadvantaged groups into narratives that are closely guarded by editors committed to American exceptionalism is difficult, and the notion of "separate but equal" offers an easy solution but fails to advance the cause of locating women's history—and all minority history—in our national development in all its complexity. Perhaps WikiProject Women's History will alter these tendencies of suppression, exclusion, and marginalization. Certainly, having women serve as more than 13 percent (or 18 percent, for that matter) of the contributors should make some difference. But for now, as Melissa Greenberg concludes, "I find it especially ironic given the . . . collectivism of Wikipedia . . . that contributors who wish to include women's history find it so difficult. One would think that Wikipedia should provide a more open platform for incorporating historical narratives that are traditionally excluded."[24]

Acknowledgments: The author credits three individuals who contributed to this essay: J. Scott Payne, director of Academic Technology Services at Amherst College; Leah Cerf, history major, class of 2013, Amherst College; Melissa Greenberg, history major, class of 2012, Amherst College.

Notes

1. Noam Cohen, "Define Gender Gap: Look up Wikipedia's Contributor List," *New York Times*, January 30, 2011, http://www.nytimes.com/2011/01/31/business/media/31link.html; see also Judd Antin, Raymond Yee, Coye Cheshire, "Gender Differences in Wikipedia Editing" (paper presented at WikiSym 11, Mountain View, CA, October 3–5, 2011), which revises the 13 percent to a possible 18 percent and argues that while women edit infrequently, they make more significant edits.

2. "Jimmy Wales Interview: Wikipedia is Focusing on Accuracy," *Telegraph*, August 15, 2011, http://www.telegraph.co.uk/technology/wikipedia/6589487/Jimmy-Wales-interview-Wikipedia-is-focusing-on-accuracy.html.

3. Robert Wolff, "Essay Idea Discussion" (#21), in *Writing History in the Digital Age*, web-book ed., May–August 2011.

4. "School and University Projects," *Wikipedia*, http://en.wikipedia.org/wiki/Schools_and_universities_project.

5. Roy Rosenzweig, "Can History Be Open Source? *Wikipedia* and the Future of the Past," *Journal of American History* 93, no. 1 (2006): 117–46.

6. See John Broughton, *Wikipedia: The Missing Manual* (Sebastopol, CA: O'Reilly Media / Pogue), 220–22, freely available online at http://en.wikipedia.org/wiki/Help:Wikipedia:_The_Missing_Manual.

7. Shawn Graham, "The Wikiblitz," in this volume.

8. Ibid.

9. "Vietnam War," *Wikipedia*, http://en.wikipedia.org/wiki/Vietnam_War.

10. See Broughton, *Wikipedia: The Missing Manual*, 219–20, for becoming a reviewer.

11. Eric Foner, *Who Owns History?* (New York: Hill and Wang, 2002), xviii.

12. Dubravka Ugresic, *Karaoke Culture* (Rochester, NY: Open Letter, 2011), 10.

13. "Jimmy Wales Interview."

14. Robert Wolff, "The Historian's Craft, Popular Memory, and *Wikipedia*," in this volume.

15. All articles listed are in *Wikipedia*, http://en.wikipedia.org.

16. "Reconstruction Era," *Wikipedia*, http://en.wikipedia.org/wiki/Reconstruction_Era_of_the_United_States.

17. Melissa Greenberg, e-mail message to Martha Saxton, August 11, 2011.

18. "Eugenics in the United States," *Wikipedia*, http://en.wikipedia.org/wiki/Eugenics_in_the_United_States.

19. Leah Cerf, e-mail message to Martha Saxton, August 29, 2011.

20. "American Revolutionary War," *Wikipedia*, http://en.wikipedia.org/wiki/American_Revolutionary_War.

21. "American Revolution," *Wikipedia*, http://en.wikipedia.org/wiki/American_Revolution; "Women in the American Revolution," *Wikipedia*, http://en.wikipedia.org/wiki/Women_in_the_American_Revolution.

22. "WikiProject Women's History," *Wikipedia*, http://en.wikipedia.org/wiki/Wikipedia:WikiProject_Women%27s_History.

23. "WikiProject," *Wikipedia*, http://en.wikipedia.org/wiki/Wikiproject; "Wiki Project United States," *Wikipedia*, http://en.wikipedia.org/wiki/Wikipedia: Wiki Project_United_States.

24. Melissa Greenberg, e-mail message to Martha Saxton, August 11, 2011.

PART 3

Practice What You Teach
(and teach what you practice)

When we initially proposed this book on our website, the first comments we received came from readers who demanded that we pay more attention to the teaching of historical writing. We listened and intentionally revised the scope of the volume to include essays on ways that new technologies affect how historians "think, *teach*, author, and publish." Several contributors leaped at the opportunity to share insights on digital writing from their history classrooms, often with richly detailed class assignments and examples of student writing. Collaborators Thomas Harbison and Luke Waltzer explore tensions between content coverage and "doing history" more deeply with their students in a media-rich curriculum, in "Toward Teaching the Introductory History Course, Digitally." Adrea Lawrence takes us into her graduate classroom in "Learning How to Write Analog and Digital History," to compare how students' authorship and understanding varied as they worked with both old and new media. Finally, Amanda Seligman explains why she is "Teaching *Wikipedia* without Apologies." She challenges educators who oppose it, by integrating her expertise in historical encyclopedia writing into her undergraduate history class.

Toward Teaching the Introductory History Course, Digitally

Thomas Harbison and Luke Waltzer

Introductory history courses regularly aim to meet a specific set of learning goals: introduce students to broad historical themes in an area, expose students to the importance of the historical project, and sharpen students' critical thinking skills around evidence gathering and argumentation. The last of these goals has been difficult for many instructors to achieve. Most survey courses have large class sizes and prioritize covering a vast range of material, and instructors lack the time and interactive space for all students to genuinely practice historical methods. Practical training is pushed to smaller, upper-level history courses where time can be spent discussing, researching, and writing about a set of topics drawn from a particular sub-field.

This approach accepts that nonmajors—the large majority of students in introductory courses—can do without significant exposure to the skills at the center of the historical trade. Although thorough development of skills in historical methods and extensive expertise requires the time afforded by upper-level courses, all students can benefit from hands-on experience with critical historical inquiry and the effort to produce scholarship. The writing and thinking skills at the core of historical practice are transferable across the curriculum, and they help prepare students for a range of careers.

Rarely are introductory history courses built around the development of such skills, usually as a result of tension around coverage. Most of these courses are surveys, and they begin in a moment and promise to end in a moment. Schedules require quick and steady forward progress whether or not students have mastered a period's complexity. Faculty members, especially new ones acclimating to the vocation (who teach a significant portion of the introductory courses offered at our college), are regularly plagued with guilt about oversimplification, leaving loose threads, and moving too fast. Students in these courses traditionally write a few research or synthetic papers, participate in class discussions, and prepare for exams. The reading load is heavy, and less time is usually devoted to written work.

Models other than the introductory history survey course do exist. For instance, at our college, students may elect to meet general education distribution requirements via a "themes" course, which is focused on a set of ideas, circumstances, or a period. Most of these courses still proceed chronologically, but students may linger on a particular subject for weeks at a time and explore it more deeply, reducing the coverage pressure so embedded in the survey.

Over the past three years, we have been exploring an approach to the introductory history course that we feel makes it a more immersive and, ultimately, a more valuable experience. Throughout the semester, students complete brief assignments that expose them to a range of research and analytical skills. Our goal is for students to emerge from the course not only familiar with the broad strokes of American history but also with a hands-on introduction to the skills necessary for uncovering, exploring, and understanding that history.

Such skills are valuable to students well beyond their study of history. Gardner Campbell has argued that general education curricula should focus on "generalizable education" and should provide "experience that stresses the kind of learning that stimulates persistent cross-domain thinking and imagining."[1] Our approach treats historical knowledge as valuable in its own right, but it also accentuates what is generalizable in historical methodology. Students conduct research with primary sources to deepen their comprehension of particular topics, learning about discovery, sourcing, and competing modes of interpretation. They enter into dialogues with existing analyses, to synthesize their own understandings and to practice integrating their perspectives and authority with others'. They revise conclusions in the face of new evidence and arguments, better grasping the contested nature of knowledge. They do this work on a small scale repeatedly and reflectively during the course. Ultimately, these experiences are valuable for both future historians being introduced to the field and students who will never study history again.

Given the increasing availability of digital tools, students in introductory history classes are able to engage with history in ever more intensive and dynamic ways. Over the past two decades, the Internet has made it easier to integrate additional goals into introductory courses. The combination of a scholarly "pictorial turn" and the explosion of primary sources on the web have injected introductory history courses with a more rigorous exploration of visual and aural resources.[2] Readily available datasets and archival materials allow for sophisticated lesson plans that help students better comprehend the vivid and contested density of many pasts. Introductory courses, in addition to their traditional roles, can now more directly address the increasingly important information and media literacy components of a general education curriculum.

Our approach synthesizes four specific and related pedagogical processes. The methods of Writing across the Curriculum/Writing in the Disciplines programs (WAC/WID) have helped us develop a wide variety of writing assignments that create a deep, sustained, and multimodal engagement with course materials. The Visible Knowledge Project has taught us that by engaging with course material publicly, students have the opportunity to see how their classmates make knowledge. Making knowledge visible also gives instructors more chances to intervene in the students' learning processes and to produce data that they can use to redirect their teaching.[3] The Open Educational Resources (OER) movement has expanded the source material we draw on in our teaching, moving us beyond a textbook, and has helped us play with the traditional definitions and boundaries of a "course." The principles of networked learning tie the other approaches together, emphasizing for students that doing history is a collaborative and dialogic process. Together, these ideas have encouraged us to teach history in an open digital space that prioritizes writing-intensive, project-based learning.

Before delving into additional detail about the courses in question, we would like to share a bit about our collaboration. Since 2006, we have worked together at the Bernard L. Schwartz Communication Institute at Baruch College at the City University of New York (CUNY), Tom first as a fellow for instructional technology and now as interim assistant director for educational technology, and Luke first as a CUNY writing fellow and now as the director of the Center for Teaching and Learning. We both earned our doctorates in history from the CUNY Graduate Center, and we each worked with the American Social History Project as graduate students. Luke has taught history at Baruch and Montclair State University; Tom has taught history at Baruch. The courses that prompted this essay were Tom's, and each was taught using Blogs@Baruch, with Luke as a sounding board, adviser, and occasional participant both in class and on the course sites.

In the fall of 2008, Tom taught his first class at Baruch, an introductory U.S. history course. For nearly all of the students, this was their first class in history and was likely to be their last.[4] Tom devoted roughly one-third of class time to historical methodology. Students used most of this time to work in groups to analyze photocopied primary source documents. Most students participated enthusiastically in these exercises, but their work was highly compartmentalized and constrained within small groups during the allotted class time. Students gained some experience practicing history, but not in the immersive, interconnected manner that Tom was seeking. Communication between instructor and students was limited to feedback transferred in a shuffle of paper; students were not seeing and learning from one another's successes and failures in reading, interpreting, and writing about history.

In an effort to expand and extend the sharing process, Tom turned to digital technology. At first, this meant the college's course management system, Blackboard. It provided students with a space to carry on discussions outside of class, where they could share conclusions from one day and pose related questions going into the next. Yet the system replicated many of the divisions encountered in the classroom and failed to break the call-and-response pattern in which students answered narrowly defined questions posed by the instructor. Because of its design, architecture, and the barrier between it and the open web, the system was hostile to student-published multimedia and student voices. Student work could not be shared beyond the class, and even within the class, it was difficult to create a web of knowledge that could be referenced, reorganized, and built on.

In the summer of 2010, Tom taught the survey again. This time, he made use of the college's open publishing platform, Blogs@Baruch, which Luke runs and organizes faculty development around.[5] During the first couple weeks of class, when student contributions to the blog were limited, students referred to the course site as a resource. They expected that it would spit out information that they needed or desired: the syllabus, readings, lecture slides, and, ultimately, a grade. Over the course of the semester, there were indeed many times that the site operated as a tool for the transmission of such information, and it did so effectively. But after about three weeks, students began to see the site as more than that. They recognized that it was, above all, an active workspace that both encapsulated and propelled the majority of the work for the course. During the semester, it became clear that using an open publishing platform expanded the opportunities for a range of student work and created conditions for pedagogical experimentation that simply were not present in a more traditionally structured introductory course.

In the following paragraphs, we detail some of the pedagogical opportunities that emerged during our integration of Blogs@Baruch into seven introductory history course sections taught in 2010–11. We highlight six characteristics of our sites that explain why they propelled us toward our pedagogical goals. We aim to retain these attributes in future online learning spaces, and we believe that the methods and skills they nurture in students should be in the forefront of any college's general education curriculum.[6]

1. Active

To challenge students' preconceptions that successful history equals memorizing content, we require them to constantly engage with a range of sources and write in a variety of modes. Students are required to visit the site between every class meeting and to contribute something new in response to a writing prompt. The prompts encourage students to specialize their knowledge in narrow topics of their choosing, positioning them to challenge historical treatment of that topic in the textbook, lectures, and discussions. This prepares students to teach their classmates about their topic and to field questions about the turf with which they have just familiarized themselves. There is not enough time for students to exhaustively research topics, but they get a strong taste of what it means to develop expertise and of the process by which a community of learners strives for this goal.[7]

The degree to which students develop deeper understanding is made visible via a series of "micromonographs," three- to four-paragraph essays that elaborate on very narrow topics. We find that many students, once they begin such investigations, thrive in the role of detective, particularly when assessing the accuracy of information. For instance, when students were asked to fact-check Martin Scorsese's *Gangs of New York* using a series of digital archives, most were able to effectively offer narratives that replaced and corrected those conveyed by the movie, expounding on their findings with embedded images, videos, and texts from both primary and secondary sources.[8]

Such activities set up reflective conversations in class about the processes in academia and commercial publishing by which monographic works are produced, interpreted, and synthesized. In this context, students began to evaluate their own work as a secondary source. This prepared them to practice modifying their historical narratives and conclusions as they answered their peers' questions and gathered new information. Assignments immersed students in the process that is so common to the work of humanists: constructing an argument and adjusting it recursively in the face of questions and new evidence. By doing so, they experienced firsthand the evolving and contested nature of historical understanding.

Through these types of activities, which range from flurries of informal discussion to synthesized research subject to revision, students constantly grapple with competing sets of ideas. This type of exploratory learning is closely in line with our belief that students learn best and acquire generalizable skills when they are producing knowledge.

2. Social

In the open environment of the course site, students routinely view and respond to classmates' historical arguments. In class, we review model critiques, guiding students toward the practice of constructive criticism. Students' quick access to new information from digital archives across the Internet enriches our online conversations. In addition to helping classmates by asking questions and offering critiques of blog posts, students often voluntarily share sources with one another. The course sites extend and tie together our face-to-face meetings: sometimes work on a site helps set up in-class conversations by establishing questions and lines of argument; at other times, it serves as an extension of debates and investigations that germinated while we met.

The social dimension of Blogs@Baruch became more pronounced when we incorporated BuddyPress in the fall of 2010. This WordPress plugin allows students to build profile pages, track their work across the system over their career at the college, and interact with other students on the platform. The simple act of linking their account to a profile picture gives students a stronger attachment to the course site, as their picture shows up every time they leave a comment in the system. The front page of Blogs@Baruch shows an activity stream of recent publicly posted work, increasing the likelihood of serendipitous connections within and beyond the system.

During the fall of 2010 and spring of 2011, Tom had students from two simultaneous course sections share a single web space. Many of the most probing questions and constructive criticisms were launched across sections. The extra social and physical distance between the students worked as an advantage more often than not, with shy students more likely to speak freely from a somewhat more anonymous position. The additional voices in the conversation intensified the rate at which ideas were exchanged and gave each class more material to consider.

Students at Baruch are introduced to Blogs@Baruch in their Freshman Seminar courses, and more and more students are using the system in their classes. We are exploring ways to develop curricula that take fuller advantage of the networked nature of this publishing. We have seen what can happen when we link a couple of sections of a class that share a professor and a syllabus; we would like to explore how the curriculum of the college can be impacted by experiments around interdisciplinary exchanges and co-teaching across departments, with the expectation that such a learning community has great potential to teach students the value of collaborative and cross-disciplinary production.

3. Open

Blogs@Baruch has granular privacy control: sites can be open and indexed by search engines, open and not indexed, open only to Blogs@Baruch users, open only to users added by the individual site administrator, or open only to administrators. Beyond that, individual posts and pages may be password protected, and an author may publish under an alias. Much of the faculty development and instruction done around the system is oriented to equip users to best navigate these options given their needs, and such instruction regularly extends to the classroom. The default setting on all course sites on the system is open, a choice we have made to urge members of the community to think through the possibilities of openness.

Everything the students contribute to our sites, unless they themselves choose otherwise, instantly becomes visible across the web. On a few occasions, students have received comments on their posts from professional historians. In one case, a photo archivist from a presidential library asked a student about the provenance of an image he had posted. Apparently, the image the student had used was pervasive on the Internet, but the original source information had been lost. The student did not have the answer to the archivist's puzzle, but the situation prompted a series of valuable teaching moments about the implications of open publishing, the work of the archivist and the historian, and the complex issues that surround questions of intellectual property in the digital age. Such conversations help students better comprehend both the power and ethical implications of researching information on the Internet, as well as the evolving nature of historical knowledge.

A learning environment as open as this also profoundly improves students' ability to imagine audiences for their writing. Before using an open publishing platform in the survey course, students wrote primarily for us as the instructors, with some peer review sprinkled in. When students publish to an open platform, indexed by Google, the stakes are immediately raised. We spend significant time in class discussing the implications of openness on writing and review processes. Such diversity of audiences and intensive peer review—core WAC/WID principles—sharpen students' writing and their historical thinking.

Institutions and instructors doing coursework on the open web should be aware of but not hamstrung by concerns about FERPA (the Family Educational Rights and Privacy Act). Though FERPA has not adapted to new communication realities, such pedagogical experiments do require thought and ethical consideration. FERPA alone is an inadequate guide to such consideration. Sharing student work publicly is not a violation of FERPA, but students need to know that this is happening and need to have control over their work, including the ability to remove or restrict its viewing if they so choose.

Though users should be aware of the risks, we believe that the pedagogical benefits of open learning far outweigh any potential downside. Using an open system for student production makes learning processes more transparent, promotes dialogue between students and source materials across the web, and drives home to students the reality that they are engaged in making actual knowledge.

4. Media Rich

In addition to linking to a vast network of media, students on Blogs@Baruch can easily combine video, audio, and images with their text composition. WordPress enables them to elegantly combine multiple media forms. Many assignments call on students to present and interpret evidence represented in a variety of formats, introducing students to the power of multimedia to represent (or misrepresent) historical ideas. This brings them face to face with particular methodological challenges that accompany the use of visual and aural sources, and it offers them a sandbox in which they can practice distinctive techniques for reading such sources. As they embed images, students consult online tutorials for analyzing visual evidence (such as those provided on *History Matters*) and write up their findings.[9]

The aesthetic richness of the site is achieved primarily through the work of the students. They use multimedia to illuminate points in their own writing. At times, they are given an opportunity to contribute to site design. For example, in one assignment early in the semester, they uploaded images that they deemed representative of important turning points in U.S. history. For the remainder of the semester, their images rotated in the course site's header. This encouraged students to see themselves as producers with a significant degree of control over their learning space. Students have remarked that seeing their work profiled prominently on the site gives them a sense of ownership over the space.

As students work through the challenges of reproducing and interpreting visual and aural evidence in support of their arguments, the past becomes more vibrant and recognizable, and they learn valuable and broadly applicable media literacy skills.

5. Metacognitive

Our writing assignments regularly encourage students to categorize and prioritize their arguments. When we drafted the general architecture of the web space, we structured the space with a flexible categorization system that brought order to the content as it accrued over time. We created two types of categories: major themes of the course and out-of-class assignments. We intentionally left the taxonomy loose, leaving much of the classification work to the students.

Before adding any text or media to the site, students must think about the most appropriate placement of their new information, deciding whether to write a new post, respond with a comment to an existing post, or reply to a comment in a threaded conversation. Students also gain experience classifying knowledge after they have finished composing a post. When they tag a post, students must extract the three or four key ideas present in their discussion, implicitly defining their work relative to the larger themes of the course. Their choices contribute to the building of a folksonomy of the content of the course. Tagging organizes the roughly five hundred posts authored by each class during the semester in archives using WordPress's built-in taxonomical structure. This eases assessment and review, as students and instructors can review a portfolio of contributions arranged by theme, and the dominant tropes of the course emerge.

As the class brings order to an increasingly complex web of information over the course of the semester, we reflect on the process together. Students witness how new ideas and concepts emerge as layers of meaning develop. The abilities to manage and create taxonomies and regroup, rearrange, and reinterpret knowledge are valuable skills both within and beyond the discipline of history.

6. Immersive

Many existing history teaching modules that employ technology punctuate single units alone. Our course sites on Blogs@Baruch build over time and reveal to students major themes and connections across a course in a way they can easily grasp, engage with, and revisit. The publishing environment enriches the class as a laboratory does in the hard sciences. It gives students hands-on experience with the skills of the historical trade, especially analyzing primary documents. Thanks to digital archives and such projects as *The Lost Museum, Picturing U.S. History,* and *The September 11 Digital Archive,* we witness students grappling with historical questions while navigating a sea of sources.[10] During assignments that require them to engage with these types of complex datasets, students visualize the tension between breadth and depth in the study of history, engage a range of methodologies, and develop a sharper awareness of historical perspective.

The Blogs@Baruch space also immerses the teacher deeply in the pedagogical experience. As the Visible Knowledge Project (VKP) has demonstrated, digital tools can foster transparency of processes that allow teachers to better assess not only their students' learning but also their own teaching strategies. Documentation of student learning in an open publishing space on the web forces important questions about teaching to surface. Some of those questions follow:

- How can student work outside of class be seamlessly integrated with face-to-face experiences in the classroom?
- On what types of writing should students spend their time?
- How tightly should instructors scaffold research and writing assignments?
- How frequently and bluntly should instructors redirect communication from and between students?
- To what degree should larger research and writing projects be assigned across the semester, relative to smaller, daily tasks?
- How often should students practice and reflect on methodology and historiography, as opposed to historical content?

- What factors determine whether students should work independently or in groups?

These pedagogical puzzles do not disappear with the implementation of an open publishing environment, but they are more routinely foregrounded in the preparatory process, and in order to make the space an effective one, the instructor must grapple with them. While projects like VKP have exposed the "intermediate thinking process" in particular projects and course units, publishing platforms like WordPress now make it possible across not only an entire course but multiple iterations of the course. Both students and faculty can navigate the sites conducting the type of "socially situated learning" promoted and prized by VKP as "intrinsic to the development of expert-like abilities and dispositions in novice learners."[11]

Assessment and Moving Forward

When Luke asked Tom's students how they felt about their course blog, one student responded, "I don't like it because it keeps the class always on my mind." To a faculty member, this is praise with faint damnation. We all want our students to be absorbed in our course, even if we would prefer they be less resistant to such absorption than this student. We have not yet designed a formal assessment to measure student learning within this type of course, though it is something we would like to find the time and resources to implement. Students in these classes are certainly writing more frequently and voluminously than they have in previous courses that we have each taught. In earlier iterations, students wrote on average three five- to seven- page papers, or roughly four thousand words, over the course of the semester. In these recent courses, students are writing about twice that, just in shorter and much more varied bursts.

The course sites are highly effective assessment tools. They paint a more complete, richer picture of student performance and understanding than does a traditional midterm/essay/final exam model. A significant portion of the final grades (at least 30 percent) is determined by the quality of students' work on the course website, where they are judged on creativity, effort, attention to instructions, and the timeliness of contributions. Instructors can respond to students as frequently as they wish, although we found it to be most manageable and effective to concentrate on redirecting student writing with general advice aimed at guiding revisions. If we detected historical inaccuracies or improper sourcing, we intervened immediately with a detailed response, but we otherwise tried to judge student contributions generally and in the context of the broader conversations in which they were engaged.

Some faculty members may fear increased workload and thus refrain from implementing a course site like that outlined here. Yet such concerns are often overblown. After the additional labor of reconceptualizing a traditional syllabus and crafting the writing prompts, the workload during the semester was similar to what we faced when teaching with minimal technology. As we read student posts in advance of class meetings, we were aided in both assessment and preparation, since the material enabled us to hone in on struggles students were having with certain concepts.

Questions of scale and efficiency inevitably arise around teaching with digital tools. Like most public universities, ours is under significant pressure to cut costs. Two methods that are being explored are dramatically increasing class size to save money on labor and offering online instruction to save money on space. Technology is necessarily implicated in both of these processes, and we have been insistent that Blogs@Baruch and the services of the Schwartz Institute not become regarded as "efficiency" tools at the college. But faculty members are increasingly caught in a situation where they are forced to teach courses much larger or different in structure than what they would prefer, and the experimentation around questions of pedagogy and curriculum development that we are doing can provide guidance and models through this transition. Small introductory history courses at large public universities are simply not on the horizon anytime soon. This context increases pressure on faculty to stress coverage, because assigning reading and delivering lectures appears to be more manageable and measurable than having students produce a significant amount of work in their own words.

We have not yet attempted this model in a class with more than fifty students, but we feel as though it could be adapted, with some modifications toward group work and co-creation, to a course of any scale. We are eager to try such an approach. Our experiments suggest that courses that embrace and build on the idea of "the student as producer" can invigorate introductory history instruction, as well as introductory courses in other disciplines, while pushing back against the passivity and anonymity that prevail in larger courses.[12] It is important that we not eschew factual knowledge, but we need not be limited by concerns about coverage. At their best, these courses not only provide a baseline for our students to know about the past but also teach our students what is to be gained by doing history.

Acknowledgments: We would like to thank Mikhail Gershovich, the Bernard L. Schwartz Communication Institute, and the Baruch Computing and Technology Center for their support of Blogs@Baruch. We would also like to thank all those who commented on our essay during the open-review process, particularly William Caraher, Jonathan Jarrett, Andrea Nichols, Bethany Nowviskie, Charlotte D. Rochez, Amanda Seligman, and William G. Thomas.

Notes

1. Gardner Campbell, "Integrative Learning and the Gift of New Media: General Education for the 21st Century," *Gardner Writes*, August 29, 2010, http://www.gardnercampbell.net/blog1/?p=1394.

2. Michael Coventry et al., "Ways of Seeing: Evidence and Learning in the History Classroom," *Journal of American History* 92, no. 4 (2006), http://www.journalofamericanhistory.org/textbooks/2006/introduction.html.

3. Visible Knowledge Project, Georgetown University, 2009, https://commons.georgetown.edu/blogs/vkp/.

4. According to a 2010 fact sheet, 78.2 percent of Baruch undergraduate students intend to study a field within the Zicklin School of Business (http://www.baruch.cuny.edu/about/factsheet.htm).

5. Blogs@Baruch, http://blsciblogs.baruch.cuny.edu.

6. See illustrations in the web version of this essay, at http://WritingHistory.trincoll.edu.

7. Sam Wineburg has shown that students of history process new information in a more sophisticated and productive way as their expertise in a field deepens. See Samuel S. Wineburg, "The Cognitive Representation of Historical Texts," in *Teaching and Learning in History*, ed. Gaea Leinhardt, Isabel L. Beck, and Catherine Stainton (Hillsdale, NJ: Lawrence Erlbaum Associates, 1994), 85–135.

8. *Gangs of New York*, directed by Martin Scorsese (2002; Burbank, CA: Miramax Films, 2003), DVD.

9. See "Making Sense of Evidence," *History Matters*, http://historymatters.gmu.edu/browse/makesense/.

10. American Social History Project/Center for Media and Learning, CUNY Graduate Center, *The Lost Museum*, http://www.lostmuseum.cuny.edu/home.html; *Picturing U.S. History*, http://picturinghistory.gc.cuny.edu/; Roy Rosenzweig Center for History and New Media, *The September 11 Digital Archive*, http://911digitalarchive.org/.

11. See Visible Knowledge Project, https://commons.georgetown.edu/blogs/vkp/themes-findings/.

12. For more on "the student as producer," see the project website of Mike Neary and Joss Winn at the University of Lincoln, http://studentasproducer.lincoln.ac.uk/.

Learning How to Write Analog
and Digital History

Adrea Lawrence

Creating a robust historical work has long been an exercise in extensive
research, careful interpretation, and the crafting of arguments with tight
prose and a solid evidentiary base. Cast as an objective enterprise in the
nineteenth century, doing history has since become infused with research
approaches and theories of scholarship that span the humanities and social
science disciplines.[1] Yet historians have largely remained solitary researchers and writers, often developing idiosyncratic but fruitful methods of
research, analysis, and writing in their production of knowledge.[2] Learning
how to "do history" can feel like learning through osmosis. The training is
often oblique with little direct instruction but with multiple opportunities
to practice archival research, "document analysis," historical conversation,
and writing. One eventually figures it out, but until one has read enough of
the secondary literature and spent scores of hours doing archival research
and written mini-monographs that peers read and critique, the history
experience is frequently one of consumption. Even when one transforms
from a knowledge consumer to a knowledge producer, the exposure of
one's work to the outside world is quite limited, except when burgeoning
historians publish their work digitally in public spaces, such as on blogs, on
Wikipedia, or on their own websites. With this in mind, I set out to develop
a course on the histories of education that featured student work in old and
new media.

Design of the Course and the History Signature Pedagogy

In the fall of 2010 at American University, I taught, for the first time, a graduate seminar entitled EDU/HIST 596: Histories of Education.[3] Though this course attempted to survey the histories of education in North America over the last five hundred years, the primary emphases of the course were to evaluate the historiography of education history and experiment with different historical research and writing methods and formats.

With the goal of helping students learn how to think historically[4] by sourcing evidence, developing inquiry questions, weaving context, and evaluating historical significance, I designed my Histories of Education course around two questions: when did education begin in the Americas,[5] and how have historians of education framed the field of study? The readings were selected to jar students' preconceptions about who constructed education and how they went about it, beginning with a close reading of Urban and Wagoner's survey text: *American Education: A History.*[6] The final segment of the course was devoted to reading autobiographical accounts of individuals' educations.

Though reading and discussion were a large part of the course, this essay focuses on the written work students created. They experimented with three different platforms of historical writing. First, students produced an analytical critical review of two scholarly articles or books against the backdrop of a common question or theme. Students were to look in academic journals and the *New York Review of Books* for examples of compelling reviews. Second, students created a brief contribution to *Wikipedia* to situate themselves as knowledge producers in order to publicly share what they learned with the world and to evaluate *Wikipedia* as a source of information.[7] Third, students produced an online, publicly available digital history on a topic of interest that they began researching with their *Wikipedia* contribution. Unlike their *Wikipedia* contributions, though, students did original research for the digital history project and had to develop not only the textual history but also its online environment.

This study examines the written work of five out of the nine students in the class. After students submitted each piece, the class debriefed the research, writing, and revision process, articulating challenges and breakthroughs. In every class meeting throughout the semester, students reported on the status of their long-term digital history projects and offered each other ideas for possible source material or ways of analyzing what they had found. By the time class members presented their digital histories at the end of the semester, the degree of familiarity they had with each other's interests and research afforded a hearty discussion about the construction of each digital history project. An anonymous follow-up survey was sent out to participants via Google Docs several months later to gather more information about each student's writing and revision process. Though this sample is small and should not be taken as representative, it does reveal practices, considerations, and points of confoundedness that other historians, student or professional, might well experience as they move from analog to digital platforms and audiences.

The Critical Review

The critical book or article review is a staple not only in the history profession, as numerous academic journals illustrate, but also in the graduate training of future historians. Learning how to write an analytical, pithy review hones one's ability to evaluate texts in terms of their argument and use of evidence and to place a text in relation to the broader field of study. In crafting an analog critical review for the class, students evaluated two texts that we had read or that they had found on their own, appraising the significance of each piece within the history of education or another subfield of history. Students submitted their reviews (twelve hundred to fifteen hundred words) in standard essay format through Google Docs, and several published their reviews on the course website after revision.

Students reported that writing the critical review was a very familiar process. Analyzing texts was almost automatic for them, and they were also comfortable taking a comparative approach. Most spent two to four hours initially drafting the review, and most revised their reviews twice before submission, with a day's lag time in between each revision. The speed of the initial drafting and the structure of students' reviews bears out their stated familiarity. (See a visualization of Student 5's critical review structure in the web version of this essay at http://WritingHistory.trincoll.edu.) Students typically introduced the authors and central arguments of the secondary sources examined within the first two paragraphs of their reviews. The structure of the reviews then oscillated between descriptions of the authors' arguments and use of evidence, each student's own analysis, and citations referencing specific ideas or phrases in each source. The sequence of each student's analysis varied, but each critiqued the two sources in relation to one another, identifying commonalities, gaps, and shared or disparate evidence. Students also explained each author's research and/or reporting methodologies, many of which could only be uncovered through an extremely close inferential reading. Students closed their critical reviews with statements about the significance of each author's contribution.

Though the structure of the students' reviews follows convention, crafting such reviews is no easy task. To contextualize a piece, assess its significance, or identify gaps in a study, it is necessary to have read widely and to engage a synthetic understanding of a research area. It is not surprising that most students aligned their critical reviews with their digital history project topics and *Wikipedia* contributions, opting to search for and select articles for review rather than to examine those already read for class, so that they could build a body of factual and interpretive knowledge source by source throughout the semester. Through this process, students were thinking historically by sourcing the materials they examined, developing a complex set of questions to further probe each source, and weaving together a contextual backdrop based on authors' normative and descriptive assumptions as well as students' own positionalities.[8]

The *Wikipedia* Contribution

Unlike the critical review, contributions to *Wikipedia*, the online, crowd-sourced encyclopedia, are not (yet) staples in the professional training of historians. Over the last decade, *Wikipedia* has grown to include nearly four million articles in English. For many, it has become the default source and starting point for learning about something. In his 2004 study of *Wikipedia* as a secondary source, historian Roy Rosenzweig noted that this reference tool confounds many of the assumed trademarks of historical scholarship, such as singly authored, detailed works; individual recognition for scholarly work; and cogent narrative analysis that evaluates a subject's historical significance. Original research and presenting a particular point of view—practices that are valued among historians—are eschewed on *Wikipedia*, which promotes, instead, secondary research and descriptions of others' arguments. Even with these practices, *Wikipedia* is widely visited and widely edited, offering transparent discussions between editors about why particular sources were chosen and presented in a particular sequence or manner.[9] Working with *Wikipedia* from the inside as a contributor can thus expose students to debates over source material and their interpretations.

The "*Wikipedia* Article and Tracking Report" assignment in my Histories of Education course is modeled on the one that Jeremy Boggs created for his students. I assigned the *Wikipedia* contribution to my students for two reasons: to demonstrate that students could be and were knowledge producers and to have students critically examine *Wikipedia* as a secondary source that purports to publish descriptive, fact-only material.[10] Students in my class had to conduct research, including finding a topic that ideally corresponded to their digital history project and was a desired article on *Wikipedia* as noted on the education stubs page, which lists articles that the editors wish to see expanded.[11] Like Boggs, I asked my students to write a five-hundred-word article or contribution that included footnoted references to two books or scholarly articles, two external websites, and two internal *Wikipedia* pages. Once they had posted their contribution, students were to share the URL with me and do everything possible to prevent their contributions from being deleted. After a month, they were to describe their experience through a tracking report, detailing how many edits the post received, what types of edits they were, discussions they had with other editors, and efforts they made to prevent their article from being deleted. Students also reflected on what they learned, from an insider perspective, about *Wikipedia* as a source.

Of the five student contributions examined here, three students created their own unique articles on *Wikipedia*, while two students added content to existing pages. As with their critical reviews, students structured their *Wikipedia* articles in a manner that toggles between the presentation of another's idea, argument, or set of facts, on the one hand, and citations to supporting secondary sources, on the other. Rather than provide their own analysis, however, students described the debates or arguments that others had on a given topic.

Acutely aware of their own limitations as emerging scholars in a discipline that has idealized the lone historian researching and writing exhaustively on a subject, the thought of historical collaboration and intellectual ownership of historical writing with other anonymous contributors felt unnatural to seasoned history students. Students were surprised that people looked at and presumably read their contributions. Students' doubts about anyone reading their work were unfounded, as shown in table 3. Even the most modest number of total views since the article posting—925—reflects a readership that is much more extensive than what students could expect to receive in a classroom setting. In general, the number of edits to a page since students posted in October 2010, suggests a sustained interest in the page topic. So, too, does the fact that all but one of the articles were flagged for further development, with editor requests for additional citations and revisions that attend to *Wikipedia's policy of maintaining a* neutral point of view. All told, the number of page views of *Wikipedia* articles students created or contributed to totaled 70,244 between October 2010, when students made their posts, and August 5, 2011, when this essay was drafted. Though these data are limited and should not be considered representative, they confirm Rosenzweig's contention that *Wikipedia* is an important source for people who want to learn more about a topic and share their research with others, despite the elements that run counter to the practice of professional historians.

When debriefing this assignment, students reported not only that they viewed *Wikipedia* as a secondary source worth consulting but also that they began viewing secondary sources altogether more critically. Most students began fact-checking other pages on topics about which they considered themselves to be proficient, and well after the assignment for class was due, students made concerted efforts to present material in a convincing and verifiable way to avoid having their posts deleted. Contributing to *Wikipedia* became, effectively, a series of self-sustaining, creative intellectual acts.

TABLE 3. *Wikipedia* Page Views and Revisions for Five Sample Student Articles, 2010–11. See Additional Images on the Web Version at http://WritingHistory.trincoll.edu

	Our Movie Made Children	Urban Teacher Residency	Living History	Federal Involvement in U.S. Education	Dame Schools
URL	http://en.wikipedia.org/wiki/Our_Movie_Made_Children	http://en.wikipedia.org/wiki/Urban_Teacher_Residency	http://en.wikipedia.org/wii/Living_history#Living_history_in_education	http://en.wikipedia.org/wiki/Federal_Involvement_in_US_Education	http://en.wikipedia.org/wiki/Dame_school
Date page	20 Oct. 2010	21 Oct. 2010	13 Nov. 2002	21 Oct. 2010	13 Jan. 2005
Number of editors	7	5	98	6	59
Total number of page views since student edit	925	2050	38,694	1879	26,696
Average page views *per month* since student edit	84	186	2251	171	1651
Total number of revisions since student edit	16	7	171	98	

The Digital History Project

Building on students' experiences writing conventional critical reviews and more unconventional *Wikipedia* articles and posts, the digital history projects that my Histories of Education students undertook sought to explore whether the medium did, in fact, become the message[12] or if the message itself might help a creator construct the medium. As students reported weekly on the development of their digital history projects and continued to build their research expertise, the shape each project took was formed inductively from the research content. Indeed, one of the primary concerns that emerged was how to capture and present their research in ways that were true to their inquiry experiences and methods.

For most students, creating a project in an online, public environment was new and intimidating; only one student had taken the graduate-level digital history course offered at American University. Others had blogged, but creating an academic, historical work online felt entirely new to them. The constraints students faced in creating a digital history project were typical of those faced by historians doing analog history. Like professional historians, students reported that they spent much of their time trying to figure out how to cull their research and hone in on the emerging story. How do you know what is important? How do you analyze the sources in relation to one another in a systematic and valid way? How do you know your interpretation is reasonable? How do you tell a story—how do you craft a history—that is interesting and significant?

These questions were not resolved in writing for *Wikipedia;* they were magnified. The digital aspect of the project likewise brought forth an existential predicament: what if people do not want to read long-form history online? As one student said, "Websites aren't supposed to be wordy." If this is the case, what does it mean for the stories and narrative analyses that historians create? How are they to be organized and told? What does it mean for the profession, let alone individual projects? The project's digital aspect also brought forth an epistemological conundrum—the realization that people do not necessarily read in a linear fashion online as they presumably do with an article or book. Students grappled with these issues head-on in developing their digital histories, and their experimentation and final project products are instructive in highlighting the ways in which digital histories are different from analog articles and monographs.

Creating a traditional five-thousand-word essay was not terribly appealing to students, particularly when the online environment allowed them to provide a range of primary, multimedia sources to readers, instead of just citations. So students created websites and interactive time lines that attended to their curiosity in playing with different ways of doing and presenting history while meeting customary scholarly expectations. As is common with analog histories, students organized their digital history content thematically or chronologically. Though each website features a welcome or home page that explains the central questions and scope of the given study, students generally chose two different methods of organizing their projects: a series of stand-alone essays or a disassembled linear essay.

Two students developed websites using the WordPress[13] platform, creating a series of interlinked, distinct essays. Both of these sites have discrete pages for each essay, which students wrote with a general audience in mind. Each site also has derivative pages, or "child pages," stemming from several of the primary pages and featuring particular essays oriented around a theme. The pages on each site can be read in any order, and both sites use customary methods of documentation, through footnotes or parenthetical notes. The author of one site gives the reader permission to "click around, explore, and gain a better understanding of how exactly we did get here."[14]

The second method of organizing the digital history projects was through disassembly, or carving up a linear essay into distinct pages that include the same content: a title, a statement about the argument, and the corresponding section of text to support that argument. The introductions of these websites read as introductions to cohesive essays, each providing a strong argument and grounding research questions. Each site features multiple pages that comprise sections of the overall essay. While two students acutely felt the challenge of not being able to control the order in which the viewer reads the pages, as their sites utilize a horizontal navigational bar across the top linking each discrete page, another student found a possible remedy through the use of the vertical navigation bar. Students' concern with the order in which viewers read pages originates in the epistemology of their projects as disassembled yet potentially cohesive essays interspersed with primary source evidence. They constructed their text and analysis in a particular way and hoped that they would be read as such.

The question of how to present an argument and a cogent narrative in a digital, multimedia format is a daunting one for historians, and seemingly few shared protocols exist such that they might be considered mainstream or stable in a relatively new and dynamic online environment. One student embraced this. Matthew Henry, who created the *Hollywood Made Kids* digital history project, also used the Prezi presentation tool to design a nonlinear, motion-driven companion time line, titled "Censorship, The Payne Fund Studies and Hollywood's Influence on Children."[15] Using the forward and backward buttons, the viewer can zoom in to a predirected portion of the screen. The section shots, so to speak, have the capability to show embedded video and audio files, and the presentation creator visually moves the viewer from section to section. In effect, the one-line headings and still or moving images become figuratively superimposed on one another, telling a story that the presentation creator has constructed.

Related to the presentation of a clear historical narrative was the issue of opening up the historian's constructive processes for public comment. One of the most interesting conversations that emerged during the final presentations revolved around whether or not to leave the comments feature of the websites live. Having experienced open commenting and editing on *Wikipedia*, students seemed to have faith that comments posted on their sites might well be insightful and constructive. One student was hesitant for aesthetic reasons—she did not want to clutter her site. Others were hesitant for fear of vandalism or extremist views or critique. The two students who had left the comments feature open on their sites countered that it might be a good idea, noting that the comments have the potential to provide an opportunity to rewrite, correct errors, and engage in a public discourse about a topic that greatly interested them, as they experienced on *Wikipedia*.[16] Such transparent conversation and attention to writing and its organization were complemented by the visual environment.

Conclusion

The student work examined in this essay affords a fertile view into the nature of the construction of histories from the vantage point of emergent historians. Most fundamentally, students' concern for the integrity of the historical narrative, its structure, its documentation, and its transparency or opaqueness surfaced, to a large extent, through discussions about audience. Students found that their love of the story conflicted with their intellectual desire to be open with possible readers. That students did not know who their possible readers were or how they would proceed through students' digital histories suggests that the students learned the individualistic nature of historical scholarship early in their training. Students' concern with the changing epistemological nature of historical construction intensified as they moved from a familiar analog environment to the ever-changing digital one. It is necessary to develop protocols for identifying readers of digital histories and to consult the emerging scholarship of cognitive psychologists and specialists in informatics and literacy. Additionally, the question of the long-term accessibility of digital scholarship remains unanswered. Finally, students' experimentation with writing for general audiences and creating a digital history suggests the need for explicit training in both public history and web or graphic design. The orientation of students' scholarship in my Histories of Education course was that of a public good; their experiences underscore the changing forms and norms of doing history.

Notes

1. Peter Novick, *That Noble Dream: The "Objectivity Question" and the American Historical Profession* (Cambridge: Cambridge University Press, 1988).

2. Jack Dougherty and Kristen Nawrotzki, eds., *Writing History: How Historians Research, Write, and Publish in the Digital Age*, October 8, 2010, http://writinghistory.wp.trincoll.edu.

3. Adrea Lawrence, Histories of Education, Fall 2010, American University, Washington, DC, http://www.adrealawrence.org/courses/edhistory/fall2010/.

4. Bruce A. VanSledright and Christine Kelly, "Reading American History: The Influence of Multiple Sources on Six Fifth Graders," *Elementary School Journal* 98, no. 3 (1998): 239–65; Sam Wineburg, *Historical Thinking and Other Unnatural Acts: Charting the Future of Teaching the Past* (Philadelphia: Temple University Press, 2001).

5. Donald Warren, "American Indian Histories as Education Histories" (paper presented to the American Educational Research Association, Denver, CO, 2010).

6. Wayne Urban and Jennings Wagoner, *American Education: A History*, 4th ed. (New York: Routledge, 2009).

7. This assignment is based on Jeremy Boggs, "Assigning Wikipedia in a US History Survey," *ClioWeb*, April 5, 2009, http://clioweb.org/2009/04/05/assigning-wikipedia-in-a-us-history-survey/.

8. Lendol Calder, "Uncoverage: Toward a Signature Pedagogy for the History Survey," *Journal of American History* 92, no. 4 (2006): 1358–70, http://jah.oxfordjournals.org/content/92/4/1358.

9. In this volume, see Shawn Graham, "The Wikiblitz," and Robert Wolff, "The Historian's Craft, Popular Memory, and *Wikipedia*." See also Roy Rosenzweig, "Can History Be Open Source? *Wikipedia* and the Future of the Past," *Journal of American History* 93, no. 1 (2006), 117–46, paras. 1–3, 13, 39–41, 62, 70, http://jah.oxfordjournals.org/content/93/1/117; Lisa Spiro, "Is Wikipedia Becoming a Respectable Academic Source?," *Digital Scholarship in the Humanities: Exploring the Digital Humanities*, September 1, 2008, http://digitalscholarship.wordpress.com/2008/09/01/is-wikipedia-becoming-a-respectable-academic-source/.

10. Boggs, "Assigning Wikipedia in a US History Survey."

11. "Category: Education_stubs," *Wikipedia*, http://en.wikipedia.org/wiki/Category:Education_stubs.

12. Marshall McLuhan, "The Medium Is the Message (1966)," in *Understanding Me: Lectures and Interviews* (Cambridge, MA: MIT Press, 2003), 76–97.

13. WordPress, an open-source web-publishing tool, offers free hosting, at http://www.wordpress.com, and free software from which to run a website on one's own server, at http://www.wordpress.org.

14. Matt, at *Cold War Society and Education*, http://coldwarsocietyanded.wordpress.com/about/.

15. Matthew Henry, "Censorship, The Payne Fund Studies and Hollywood's Influence on Children," December 2010, http://prezi.com/rdkntzm6spjz/censorship-the-payne-fund-studies-and-hollywoods-influence-on-children/.

16. "EDU-596 Digital History Presentations," discussion with Adrea Lawrence, December 9, 2010.

Teaching *Wikipedia* without Apologies

Amanda Seligman

April 20, 2008: If I can get the technology set up before the students in my undergraduate historical methods class arrive, I will play a clip from *The Colbert Report*. Stephen Colbert has discovered *Wikipedia;* he demonstrates to his audience how easy it is for individual actors in the 21st century to create the "truth," or at least "truthiness." He alters the *Wikipedia* entry on elephants so that the population of African elephants has miraculously tripled in the past six months,[1] a position on environmental degradation roughly consistent with his conservative persona. I have moments when I think that the only reason for this lesson is to create a pretext for convincing the students that I am cooler than I really am. In fact, however, my purpose is to teach students to think about authority, authorship, and argument in tertiary sources.

Yes, I teach *Wikipedia*. And I teach *Wikipedia* without apologies.

Historians are notoriously skeptical of the value of encyclopedias. When we discuss this topic in class, my students tell me which colleagues have forbidden them to cite any encyclopedia in their papers. *Wikipedia* has come in for particular criticism due to its common production. It lacks authority because anyone—you, me, or Stephen Colbert—can change any entry. Most famously, perhaps, the Middlebury College Department of History adopted a resolution in 2007 informing students that "*Wikipedia* is not an acceptable citation, even though it may lead one to a citable source."[2] This injunction effectively limits the use of *Wikipedia* to what one librarian commenting on an earlier version of this essay called "presearch."[3] Most observers perceived this policy as an outright ban; what are students to do with information they locate only on *Wikipedia*? Moreover, college instructors have developed bitter feelings about the ease with which students plagiarize assignments by cutting and pasting from *Wikipedia*.

Despite the skepticism surrounding encyclopedic writing, however, some historians continue to edit, write for, and consult specialized scholarly encyclopedias. A portion of my own career is staked on the intellectual value of encyclopedia writing. While in graduate school, I worked on the staff of *The Encyclopedia of Chicago* at the Newberry Library.[4] In addition to writing entries, I developed and ran the fact-checking process for the project, encountering, in the process, an astonishing array of specialty encyclopedias on topics I never imagined anyone would bother to compile: they ranged from an encyclopedia of serial killers to one about American first ladies. My work for *The Encyclopedia of Chicago* deepened my nascent historical skills and understanding of the site of my dissertation research, persuaded me of the value for humanities scholars of scientists' graduate education apprenticeship model, and built into my career an assumption that encyclopedias are legitimate sites of scholarly productivity. Having written some four dozen encyclopedia entries since 1995, I am now planning an *Encyclopedia of Milwaukee*, a National Endowment for the Humanities–funded project that my collaborators and I hope to launch in print and online in 2017.

Thus, when I started teaching the undergraduate history methods course at the University of Wisconsin–Milwaukee (UWM), it seemed to me only natural to include tertiary sources in the curriculum. In contrast to other instructors who forbid the citation of encyclopedias, I believe that it is a mistake to hide my head in the sand and pretend that particular sources of information and ideas do not exist. My job as a professor of history is to teach students how to critically evaluate the sources they encounter—wherever they find them. We all know that our students' first stop for information in the digital age is on the Internet; for many, the first stop is *Wikipedia*. If my students are going to turn consistently to *Wikipedia* for their research, I am going to contextualize *Wikipedia* for them by embedding it in a larger set of lessons about the utility of tertiary sources for historical research.

The Assignment

Much of my history methods class centers on introducing students to the basic resources of our library.[5] My goal is to ameliorate their fear of the library's mysteries by taking them to all of the major departments where they might find themselves conducting historical research: at UWM's

Golda Meir Library, this includes Research and Instructional Support, Archives, Special Collections, the Media and Reserve Library,[6] and the American Geographical Society Library. At each stop, a librarian orients the students to the department's physical and intellectual features.

For their part, students develop short papers imagining how they might use each department's sources to craft a research paper. Later in the semester they pick their favorite topic and do preliminary work identifying relevant historiography and contextualizing information such as is readily found in tertiary sources like encyclopedias. This task used to involve a lengthy tour of the Reference Room. We walked through the historical section and pulled from the shelves a variety of tertiary sources, examining their contents and marveling at the range of information at our fingertips. In 2009, however, UWM's Golda Meir Library underwent what has turned out to be a typical and wildly successful 21st-century renovation. To make way for several hundred computer stations, high-tech classrooms, and a coffee shop, 90 percent of the reference collection was dispersed to the stacks. To keep the reference collection accessible, the library subscribed to Paratext's Reference Universe database, which enables subject and keyword searching within more than 20,000 reference sources. Many of these tertiary sources are available electronically and linked right from the database; for some sources, however, students must still go up to the stacks and pull a book from the shelf. Although I regret the loss of the hands-on, sensory-oriented approach that allowed for serendipitous discoveries of the riches of evidence available, I applaud the capacity to zero in quickly on desired information. In either case, the initial reference assignment has been the same: using Reference Room or database sources, write a list of 12 questions and answers. The assignment reads: "For each of the three research projects, produce a list of four factually based questions. Using the library's tertiary sources, find answers to those questions. Turn in a list of the questions and their answers. Each answer should conclude with a precisely footnoted citation (including page numbers) where those answers can be found."

Simultaneous with the visit to the Reference Room, I introduce my students to *Wikipedia*. I assign the late Roy Rosenzweig's pioneering 2006 essay "Can History Be Open Source?," which concluded that historians should contribute to *Wikipedia*. Rosenzweig acknowledged some of the most important reasons for historians' reluctance to write for *Wikipedia*, including challenges to their information from other contributors, the site's prohibition on using original research, and the role of expertise in determining historical significance. The most important problem, he saw, was that historians earn no professional credit for contributing to *Wikipedia*, precisely because of its basic, collectivist premise: anyone can contribute to it, so there are no authors. A historian might work very hard to include information he or she knows, from his or her own painstaking research, to be correct, only to find that someone else deletes it.[7]

The purpose of the classroom discussion of *Wikipedia* is to make sure that all my students are "on the same page"—to use a metaphor originating in the days of print culture—in their understanding of how *Wikipedia* works. It is a tertiary source; anyone can contribute to it, subject to a certain increasing range of restrictions;[8] and what appears in an entry one day might be gone or changed the next. As an authoritative reference source, then, *Wikipedia* has advantages and disadvantages. It is often current,[9] and a crowd of dedicated, volunteer editors constantly defend its contents against controversy and vandalism. But some topics are mysteriously given short shrift, while fans and boosters lavish attention on their favorite topics.[10]

The next step on my pedagogical tour of *Wikipedia* is to ask students to compare its contents to those of a more conventional tertiary source. My syllabus instructs the students:

> Part I: find three articles on historical topics on *Wikipedia.org*. One article should be good, one article should be bad, and one article should be excellent. You should use your own best judgment in deciding what counts as bad, good, and excellent. List these articles, indicating which you think was excellent, good, and bad, including the date and time you accessed them. Print the first page of each article and turn it in.

> Part II: for each of the three articles, find a corresponding (as close as you can get) article in a specialty print encyclopedia (such as those found in the reference room). Try to avoid general reference encyclopedias; part of the point of this assignment is to familiarize you with the breadth of tertiary sources available to you. Make photocopies of these articles and on the photocopies write citations indicating where they came from.

> Part III: write a short paper (2–3 pages) comparing the *Wikipedia* articles to those from the specialty encyclopedias, in answer to the question: "What qualities make a tertiary source good and useful for historical research?" Use specific examples from the articles you have selected. The focus of the paper should be about what works and does not work in all six articles; the paper should not try to answer a question about whether *Wikipedia* articles are better or worse than those that appear in

specialty encyclopedias. In writing this paper, you should think about such issues as the interpretive power of the article; the accessibility of the prose; the level of factual detail; the visual layout of the information; and any other issues that strike you as relevant. Turn in copies of the print articles (with citations noted on the copy) with your paper.

In class, we discuss the merits of the various tertiary sources at their disposal. My students tend to notice things like the convenience of the Internet over the library, how long entries are, how much detail they offer, whether they answer the particular questions that they had in mind, and whether they are comprehensive in scope.

Yet no student has hit what I consider to be the crux of the matter: how well the tertiary sources convey their arguments.

"Whoa!" someone might reply here, "Encyclopedias are not supposed to have arguments. They are supposed to convey factual information without bias." *Wikipedia* enshrines this claim with its philosophy that all articles must be written from a neutral point of view (NPOV).[11] When we seek out an encyclopedia article on a topic, we are (theoretically) looking for a basic introduction to the topic, an introduction that is balanced. We are not looking for the cutting edge of a scholarly debate. If we wanted argument, we would go to the monographic literature on the topic. Among the virtues of *Wikipedia* (and other tertiary sources) is the ease of locating just that quick hit of information that we need to write a lecture.

I suggest, however, that even in a brief encyclopedia entry, argument—whether coherent or not—is unavoidable. In his article "A Place for Stories," environmental historian William Cronon explains the impossibility of NPOV. Cronon conducts a thought experiment: describe the history of the Great Plains. Cronon argues that the only "pure chronicle would have included every event that ever occurred on the Great Plains, no matter how large or small, so that a colorful sunset in September 1623 or a morning milking of cows on a farm near Leavenworth in 1897 would occupy just as prominent a place as the destruction of the bison herds or the 1930s dust storms." Choosing which details to include and exclude is implicitly an act of argument, prioritizing one facet of an experience over another.[12] Similarly, in his essay "The Wikiblitz" in this volume, Shawn Graham suggests that NPOV is itself a point of view that enables certain kinds of rhetoric but not others.

Editors of scholarly encyclopedias recognize that their authors are making arguments. I learned this multiple times as my own encyclopedic career unfolded. My first professional publication was an encyclopedia entry about Canada's Montagnais-Naskapi people.[13] Native American study is far afield for me intellectually, so when I got to the point in my reading where I understood the essence of the anthropological debate about the Montagnais-Naskapi, I concluded that I had done enough research and should start writing. Although I did not know enough to intervene in the debate about whether the Montagnais-Naskapi were precapitalist or extra-capitalist, my narrative structures an argument into the article by threading throughout it observations about how the European colonial encounter changed the name by which these small bands of nomadic people were known, culminating in the rise of their preference for the name *Innu* at the turn of the 21st century.

My work for *The Encyclopedia of Chicago* reinforced the lesson about the centrality of argument. Editor James Grossman explained to me that the reason authors' names appear on their entries is that they are making arguments, sometimes controversial ones. For example, the editors anticipated that Joseph Bigott's article on balloon frame houses would argue that this form evolved over the course of two centuries of white settlement in the continental interior rather than springing up de novo in Chicago—contrary to general belief in popular Chicago architectural history.[14] The majority of my entries were about city neighborhoods. My goal was to make legible the history of each area as revealed in its modern landscape. The argument of each entry rested in its explanation for the neighborhood's development over time. For some neighborhoods, this meant that the class origins of their initial subdivisions dictated their present condition; for others, periods of economic deterioration and overcrowding determined their future; for still others, deliberate interventions in the area, such as those wrought by urban renewal or community organizations, shaped a dramatic change in the neighborhoods' statuses. Sometimes, editors treat length as dictating the capacity of an article to offer an argument. In addition to the 1,000-word entry on the Montagnais-Naskapi in *The Encyclopedia of North American Indians*, I wrote several unsigned, short, "factual" entries on US-Indian treaties. Because these pieces were supposed to convey only introductory information, the publisher chose to leave these anonymous. But at *The Encyclopedia of Chicago*, authors received credit even for entries as short as 100 words.

Students, I have found, have enormous difficulty detecting argument in encyclopedia entries. I am not sure why that is the case, but I have some theories. First, they operate on the implicit assumption that all encyclopedias are NPOV. Additionally, in the context of an authoritatively written encyclopedia entry, it is usually very difficult to discern the broader scholarly context that might allow a student to envision an alternative argument. Unless the author explicates the alternatives, the novice reader has no way of knowing what other lines of argument might be possible. That very novelty is probably what impelled the student to a tertiary source in the first place. Additionally, the emphasis on narrative writing in history makes it hard for students to grasp what arguments are present even in longer secondary sources. Historians do write dissertations that engage explicitly with the relevant historiography. But to compete with popular history for bookstore shelf space, we often drop our overt lines of debate while embedding the argument in the narrative structure of our prose. It takes concentrated training to get advanced graduate students to learn to unpack the arguments and debates of scholarship; asking the majority of undergraduates to see argument as an intellectual puzzle implicit in every act of writing, especially in the context of encyclopedia entries, is probably one of our greatest pedagogical challenges.

Maintaining the argument in a *Wikipedia* entry presents a special problem because of the collective character of authorship. Both the NPOV policy and the ability of "just anyone" to contribute to an entry make it enormously difficult to build and protect a coherent argument in this context. Indeed, the place of argument in the commons—not the issue of credit, as Roy Rosenzweig argued—is the fundamental problem for historians contributing to *Wikipedia*. We are trained and train our students to make careful and sustained historical arguments, considering both the interpretive sweep of our ideas as well as how small nuggets of evidence contribute to our points. Historians who want to participate in *Wikipedia* with the same seriousness that they bring to their individual scholarship need to commit themselves to a long-term relationship with the entries they want to improve. They must prepare themselves to consider whether changes made by others are consistent with the changes they themselves have introduced. As Martha Saxton's essay in this volume makes clear, *Wikipedia* editors with "bots" at their disposal constantly "patrol" entries in their bailiwick, making it necessary for new contributors to prepare not only prose about their topics of interest but also defenses for the inevitable challenge to their planned comments—a state of affairs, incidentally, that neatly underscores Cronon's point that the addition of even an apparently innocuous fact is a form of interpretation. Relatedly, contributing historians should consider whether evidence introduced by another Wikipedian challenges, enhances, or undermines their own arguments. *Wikipedia's* collective character, I suggest here, complicates the labor involved in sharing one of our two greatest scholarly contributions (the other being close scrutiny and interpretation of primary sources). We should keep in mind that writing for *Wikipedia* is making a contribution, not being an author, that is, someone with the primary responsibility for the interpretive power *and* factual accuracy of the writing in question.

I do not mean to dismiss the value of either *Wikipedia* or other 21st-century experiments in commons authorship. I applaud the pedagogical creativity of the other authors in this volume who make *Wikipedia* contributions part of their classes. The model offered for the production of *Writing History in the Digital Age* assumed the capacity of an author (or coauthors) to offer a consistent, untrammeled interpretation, even while the comment feature allowed real-time peer review of the central argument—crowdsourcing to improve the overall quality of the content. The editors' postings of the two versions of their book proposal to the University of Michigan Press and their response to the peer reviewers suggest that they did not entertain the possibility of including an unauthored essay made up of "contributions" from volunteer peer reviewers. They did, however, plan to "invite up to three of the most thoughtfully engaged online commentators to submit reflective essays for the conclusion."[15] This points to the salutary, I think, and unchanged assumption that historians in the digital age should aspire to clean and consistent lines of argumentation in our scholarship, even as we grapple with how real-time commenting pushes us toward having to continuously patrol our "published" work.

Herein lies the challenge of *Wikipedia* for teaching and writing history for the digital natives that make up our 21st-century student body. Our students now enter the classroom with a widely used model of unauthored writing as a standard resource. For their first (and often last) pass at obtaining information, they turn to an asynchronous, nonprofessional community that does not incorporate argument as a central goal. As historians, however, we continue to value sustained argument. The challenge that *Wikipedia* presents to 21st-century history pedagogy is persuading students of the value of embedding argument in historical writing. We must not only teach our students how to make a coherent argument; we must also persuade them of the value of the underlying assumptions about the character of our inquiry.

Notes

1. "The Word-Wikiality," *The Colbert Report*, July 31, 2006, http://www.colbertnation.com/the-colbert-report-videos/72347/july-31-2006/the-word---wikiality.

2. Correspondence with Louisa A. Burnham, Associate Professor of History, Middlebury College.

3. Barbara Rockenbach, comment on Amanda Seligman, "Teaching *Wikipedia* without Apologies," *Writing History in the Digital Age*, web-book ed., Fall 2011 version.

4. Janice L. Reiff, Ann Durkin Keating, and James R. Grossman, *The Electronic Encyclopedia of Chicago* (Chicago: Chicago Historical Society, 2005), http://www. encyclopedia.chicagohistory.org, and its print counterpart.

5. For a recent syllabus, see https://pantherfile.uwm.edu/xythoswfs/webview/ _xy-30013072_1.

6. I take students to the Media and Reserve Library, which has recently absorbed the Microtext Library, for an introduction to microfilm and microfiche formats, because I want the students to experience the evolution of information storage.

7. Roy Rosenzweig, "Can History Be Open Source? *Wikipedia* and the Future of the Past," *Journal of American History* 93, no. 1 (2006): 141–46.

8. One restriction is the locking of a page following "vandalism," like Colbert's enjoining his audience to change the information on African elephants.

9. During the fall 2011 open-review period for this essay, for example, *Wikipedia* incorporated the death of Libyan dictator Muammar Qaddafi into his biographical entry before the *New York Times* had confirmed the news.

10. My students check *Wikipedia* for plot summaries of TV episodes they miss.

11. "Neutral Point of View," *Wikipedia*, http://en.wikipedia.org/wiki/Wikipedia: Neutral_point_of_view.

12. William Cronon, "A Place for Stories: Nature, History, and Narrative," *Journal of American History* 78, no. 4 (1992): 1347–76 (quotation from 1351).

13. Frederick Hoxie, ed., *The Encyclopedia of North American Indians* (Boston: Houghton-Mifflin, 1996).

14. Joseph C. Bigott, "Balloon Frame Construction," in *The Electronic Encyclopedia of Chicago*, http://www.encyclopedia.chicagohistory.org/pages/105.html.

15. "How this book evolved," *Writing History in the Digital Age*, web-book ed., http://writinghistory.trincoll.edu/evolution/initial-proposal/ and http://writing-history.trincoll.edu/evolution/revised-proposal/.

PART 4

Writing with the Needles from Your Data Haystack

How are electronic databases and text-analysis tools changing how historians research and write about the past? Are we finding more "needles in the haystack" that we otherwise might not have noticed? Ansley Erickson launches this section with "Historical Research and the Problem of Categories: Reflections on 10,000 Digital Note Cards," which richly illustrates how using a relational database package reshaped her dissertation source-work and writing process and led her to reflect on broader questions of historical categorization. Reflecting on their long-term collaboration, Kathryn Kish Sklar and Thomas Dublin describe the transformation of their intellectual goals, technology, funding, and global audience, in "Creating Meaning in a Sea of Information: The *Women and Social Movements* Web Sites." Finally, in "The Hermeneutics of Data and Historical Writing," Fred Gibbs and Trevor Owens argue that historians should emphasize our research methods more than traditional narratives, with a case study using such tools as Google Book's Ngram Viewer.

Historical Research and the Problem of Categories

Reflections on 10,000 Digital Note Cards

Ansley T. Erickson

Once while taking a break at an archive, I stood at the snack machine alongside a senior historian. She let out a tired sigh and then explained that she was at the beginning of a project, at the point "where you don't know anything yet." For historians, research often takes a nonlinear or even meandering form, through many phases of uncertainty and redefinition. As global historian William McNeill described it, we begin with a sense of a historical problem and explore it through reading, which cyclically "reshapes the problem, which further directs the reading." This back-and-forth can continue right up to publication. We might be more bold, like Stephen Ramsay, and celebrate the "serendipitous engagement" that happens when "screwing around" with sources, enjoying intellectually productive browsing and exploration. Whether we look forward to or struggle through these phases, much of our work happens while our research questions are still in formation.[1]

Uncertainty is, therefore, a core attribute of our research process, one that we might take as evidence that we are guided by our sources. Yet it can produce challenges as well. How do we proceed to do research—the real nuts and bolts of it—if we acknowledge such uncertainty? How can we organize information and keep it accessible in ways that will facilitate our ongoing thinking and writing, if we acknowledge changing focal points or areas of interest?

To research my dissertation, "Schooling the Metropolis: Educational

Inequality Made and Remade, Nashville, Tennessee, 1945–85," I started with various questions about desegregation in Nashville, Tennessee: Why did black students ride buses more and longer than white students? Was this due to power imbalances, ideologies, or explicit policies? Was the nature of Nashville's economy relevant? I gradually worked my way toward the question I came to address—how the pursuit of economic growth fed educational inequality.[2]

This essay considers a central challenge of historical research, one present in any long-term research endeavor but made more acute by shifting research questions: the challenge of information management. In the summer of 2006, I had a viable dissertation prospectus and was about to embark on the first of my trips to the archives. I was excited and I was scared that I would forget things. I knew what it took to manage the information involved in a seminar-length paper. Earlier, I had filled pages with handwritten notes or word-processed text, filtering through them as I built an argument. But how would I manage a project that would extend over years of research and writing? Where, in the most literal sense, would I put all of the information, so that I could find it when drafting chapters or, much later, revising for publication? I needed something that would backstop my own memory yet allow for shifts in my thinking. I also had to ensure that information stayed in the context of its originating source, while distinguishing between material from the sources and my interpretation of them.

Following the example of some more senior graduate students and one young faculty member in my department, I decided to use a relational database to keep my notes.[3] I was far from the cutting edge of digital history or information sciences. As I designed my database, I leaned on the very analogue metaphor of the note card. Rather than reconceptualizing my historical work in deep interaction with new tools, as many scholars in digital history (including several in this volume) have done, I used a new tool to do familiar aspects of research in a more accessible and efficient way.[4]

In the process, I came to see information management as a consequential aspect of historical research. How we organize and interact with information from our sources can affect what we discover in them. Scholars of the archive and of the social history of knowledge have long observed the consequences of how people keep information, and historians have considered the impact of archival practices on their own findings.[5] Their work raises useful questions about historians' own research processes—questions highlighted during work with databases. Particularly, where, when, and how do we categorize information; how do we interact with these categories as we think and write; and what can we do so that we do not become bound up in the categories we create at the most uncertain stages of our research?

Although the quantity and functionality of digital tools for data management, as well as attention to these tools, has increased in the last few years, they are not yet fully woven into the fabric of the profession. Some of this may be generational; but it also results from our discipline's relative lack of formal conversation about methodology at the granular level. Graduate training programs paradoxically structure their training as internships in the consumption and production of history yet offer little explicit guidance on the mechanics involved.[6] When new tools emerge, their potential utility may not be appreciated fully. Database programs can have broad impact on how we interact with information, but much discussion of them emphasizes their use in the narrower work of bibliographic and citation management.[7]

While neither an early nor an innovating database user, I offer this account to illustrate some potential benefits and learnings from my modest use of this tool. I first lay out how I organized my research and how it related to my thinking and writing. (See images that document my process in the web version of this essay at http://WritingHistory.trincoll.edu.) Then I venture some connections between that process and questions in the social history of knowledge and the scholarship of the archive—questions about the making and impact of categories in thought.

Database Note Keeping

Having decided to keep notes in a database, I selected a program: FileMaker Pro. There are many alternatives: some designed for qualitative research (NVivo, Atlas.ti), some free and web-compatible (such as Zotero), and others emerge periodically.[8] Historians who write code can create their own. I began by creating two FileMaker layouts, one for sources and another for the "note cards" from those sources.[9] Guessing at how I might later sort and analyze my notes, I made a keyword field for themes I expected to recur. Zotero, which I use in current projects, provides a similar structure for sources, notes, and keyword "tags."

In trips to several archives over a year, I collected tens of thousands of pages of documents by taking digital photographs of these.[10] I read and took notes on a portion on site, in those collections that prohibited digital copying or charged exorbitantly for physical copies. Because I had very limited time to work on-site at archives, most of my note taking happened once I returned home. I read digital copies on one screen. On the other, I entered notes in the database, putting direct quotes in one field, my observations and tentative analysis in another (see fig. 5). (Zotero uses a single note-taking field.) The vast majority of my note cards were descriptive, but when I had a thought that tied various sources together or hinted at an argument, I made a new note card, titled "memo to self," and then these entered the digital stack as well, tagged with keywords.

Once I had worked through most of my documents, I had nearly 10,000 note cards. I used the database as I began my analysis and sense making. I first ran large searches based on my keywords: searching hundreds of note cards on "vocational education," for example. I organized these cards chronologically—an action that takes only a few keystrokes—and spent a day or more reading them through. As themes or patterns began to emerge or as there were connections to other sections of my research that were not under the "vocational" heading, I ran separate searches on these, incorporating that material into the bin of quotes and comments I was building by cutting and pasting into a new text document. (Databases often have "report" functions that could help this process, but I did not explore that route.) Of course, sorting information can be done without a database. But I found it to happen quickly and more easily with one.

Having reviewed my research material, I began to draft a section of a chapter. I started to write before I was sure of the precise structure of the chapter or my detailed argument. I used writing as a way to find and refine my argument. Crafting a basic narrative often helped me identify what I was missing, what I needed to find out more about. Writing in this exploratory fashion was made easier by quick access to bits of information from the database as needed.[11]

Using a database did accomplish the most basic of my goals. It proved a reliable and convenient way to keep notes and contextual information in the same place, and it addressed my most basic fear of forgetting, by allowing searches for information in myriad ways—by title, content of notes, direct quotations, keywords, dates. As my writing advanced, I came to appreciate how the database's full-text searchability allowed me not only to follow my original questions but to explore ones that I had not anticipated at the start of my research. This mode of note keeping allowed me, as I thought and wrote, to access information that I would have missed otherwise—likely because of the difficulty of tracking down and reordering notes without such a database. Two examples illustrate this accessibility.

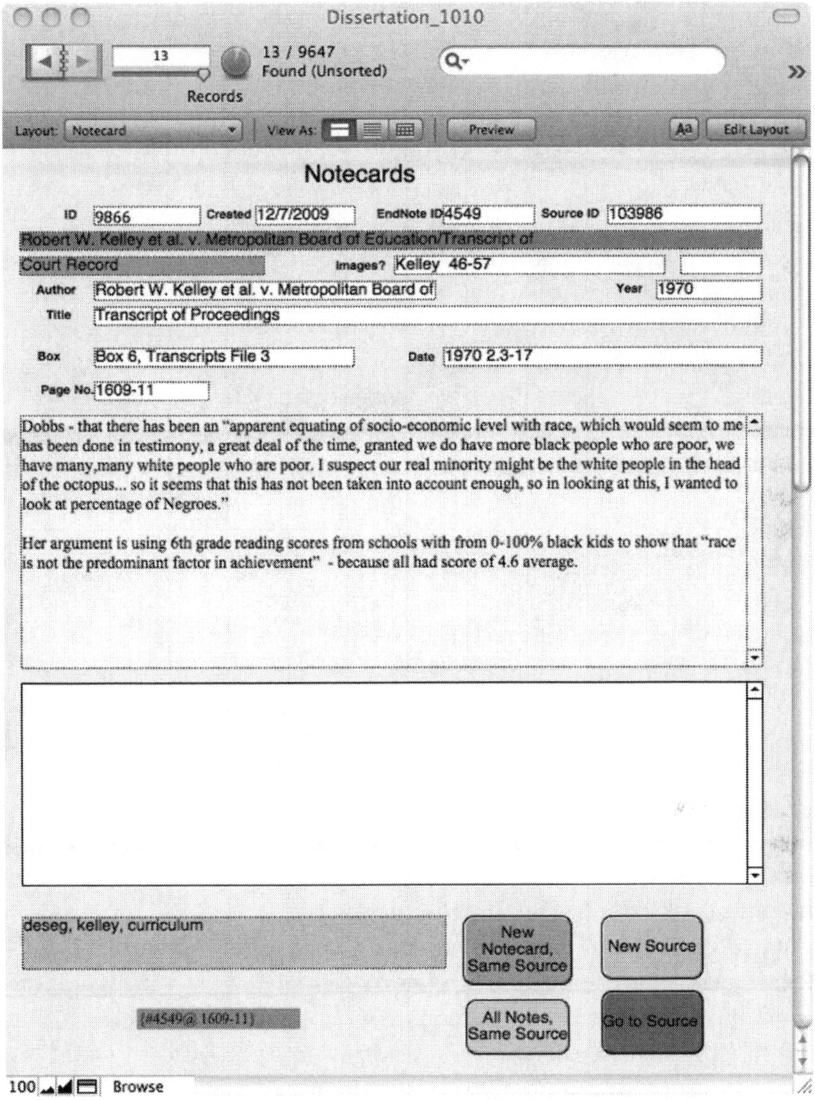
Dissertation_1010
13
13 / 9647
Found (Unsorted)
Records
Layout: Notecard
View As:
Preview
Edit Layout
Notecards
ID 9866
Created 12/7/2009
EndNote ID 4549
Source ID 103986
Robert W. Kelley et al. v. Metropolitan Board of Education/Transcript of Court Record
Images? Kelley 46-57
Author Robert W. Kelley et al. v. Metropolitan Board of
Year 1970
Title Transcript of Proceedings
Box Box 6, Transcripts File 3
Date 1970 2.3-17
Page No. 1609-11
Dobbs - that there has been an "apparent equating of socio-economic level with race, which would seem to me has been done in testimony, a great deal of the time, granted we do have more black people who are poor, we have many,many white people who are poor. I suspect our real minority might be the white people in the head of the octopus... so it seems that this has not been taken into account enough, so in looking at this, I wanted to look at percentage of Negroes."
Her argument is using 6th grade reading scores from schools with from 0-100% black kids to show that "race is not the predominant factor in achievement" - because all had score of 4.6 average.
deseg, kelley, curriculum
New Notecard, Same Source
New Source
{#4549@ 1609-11}
All Notes, Same Source
Go to Source
100
Browse

Fig. 5. FileMaker Pro screenshot of sample notes on a court transcript

One central problem in my work has been understanding the multiple layers of inequality at work in Nashville's desegregation story. There are, of course, salient and central differences by race and by class, but these divisions were often expressed in the language of geography. By the mid-1960s, residents, planners, and educators used the phrase *inner city* to indicate predominantly black neighborhoods or neighborhoods where planners predicted black population growth. I had noticed this pattern in my own reading and had captured examples of such language and other descriptions of geographic space with a keyword: *cognitive map*. To read about this phenomenon, I worked through all of my "cognitive map" notes, in chronological order. Through several conference papers and draft chapters, I developed an argument about how pro-suburban bias informed Nashville's busing plan. In early versions, I seemed to imply that in Nashville residents' cognitive maps, the correlations between suburban space and white residents and between urban space and black residents were absolute. But were there exceptions? What could I do to test this? I searched for instances where my sources used the phrase *inner city*. Of course, I may not have not written down each instance, as I did not plan for this textual analysis. Nonetheless, I had enough to begin.

When I read my sources in this way—some of which I had labeled "cognitive map," some not—I saw something new. Among the critics of schooling in the "inner city" and the smaller group of its defenders, there was a case that proved that the identification of urban space with black residents was not complete, at least for some city residents. I had earlier made notes and then forgotten about the story of a central-city school that was historically segregated white, remained largely working class, and had a local council representative fighting to retain the school in conjunction with what he labeled its surrounding inner-city neighborhood. William Higgins, the council representative, asked, "You're taking children from the inner city and busing them to suburbia. Why place the hardship on them? Why not bring children from suburbia to the inner city?" He later proposed, "All new schools . . . should be unified with the inner-city, otherwise the city finds itself a lonely remnant, disunited and eventually abandoned."[12] When I read these passages in the first years of my research, I had not thought to tag them with the keyword *cognitive map*. Thus they did not show up in that keyword search over two years later. I was able to discover them again because I could search for a phrase laden with meaning and insinuation. Doing so yielded access to notes that influenced my understanding of how categories of race, geography, and class overlapped in my story and where they diverged.

In another case, I found that the database allowed me to reframe an initial research question into a broader one. From the start, my dissertation was concerned with why schools were built where they were, how locations got chosen, to suit whose interests. I thought of schools as a good being struggled over in political and economic terms. After analyzing the local politics of school construction, I understood that my story was not about schools alone but about how the distribution of public goods reflected the political and economic structures that supported metropolitan inequality.

I had been tracing how urban renewal funds subsidized school construction and how, in the context of a metropolitan government, such subsidies could allow a municipality to shift more of its own tax revenues to its suburban precincts. I suspected that this use of urban renewal dollars to reduce the local commitment to supporting city areas in favor of suburban ones was visible in other areas of city services as well. How could I illustrate that broadened claim? I could see what my sources—planning reports, maps, records of community meetings—said about another kind of public good, to see if the dynamics were similar. I knew that I had made some notes about the building and repair of sewer lines for the city and surrounding suburbs, but I had not expected to write about them, so I had no related keyword. Text searchability of the database meant that I could very easily track down everything I had about sewers, organize it chronologically, and test if the pattern I saw for schools fit for sewers as well. Without fully searchable notes, I would have been looking through stacks of note cards, organized to fit another set of categories entirely. I may not have felt I had the time to expand my original question to a broader one.

In each of the examples just presented, the database helped relevant information jump out of the noise of years of research and thinking. It helped make that information available relationally, easily connected to other information.

Categories and the Making of Historical Knowledge

Reflecting on my use of this digital tool for note keeping has led me to questions about how we think about our research practice, how we understand the relationship between how we research and what we learn. Recent work in the social history of knowledge and the history of the archive share a core interest in categories—where they come from, what assumptions or values they represent, how they can be reified on paper or in practice.[13] These interests are relevant to our research methods. In researching and writing my dissertation, I was able to set out initial categories of analysis (via keywords), but it was possible, at no great expense of time, to throw these out. Sometimes I used my initial keywords, and sometimes I skipped over these to evaluate new connections, questions, or lines of analysis. If I had used pens and notebooks or a set of word processing documents, regrouping information would have required a great expenditure of time. I would have been less likely, then, to consider these new avenues, and my earlier categories of analysis would have been more determinative of my final work. Those categories would have been highly influential even though I created them when, in the words of the historian at the snack machine, I really did not know anything yet. Since there was virtually no time expended in trying out new questions utilizing the database, I could explore them easily. Thinking about how my database facilitated my analysis got me thinking about how historians construct, use, and rely on categories in our work.

It makes sense that historians would think about categories, as we encounter them frequently in our work. As graduate students, we learn to identify ourselves by subfield: "I do history of gender" or "I'm an Americanist." We are trained implicitly and explicitly to organize information and causal explanations into categories of analysis—race, class, gender, sexuality, politics, space, and so forth—when, in fact, these categories are never so neat and separate, whether in an individual's life or in a historical moment. Then we research in archives that establish and justify their own categories—legal records divided by plaintiff or defendant, institutions that keep their records with an eye to confirming their power or reinforcing their independence. To make sense of a sometimes overwhelming volume of fact, all of which needs to be analyzed relationally, we rely on categories that we create as we work—like my database keywords.

This matter of categories connects to at least two fields of scholarship. Scholars of the history of knowledge, such as Peter Burke, have examined the organizational schemes embodied in curricula, in libraries, and in encyclopedias and have shown how these structures and taxonomies represent particular ways of seeing the world. For Burke, such schemes reify or naturalize certain ways of seeing, helping to reproduce the view of the world from which they came. They also make some kinds of information more accessible, and some less.[14]

Think, for example, of the encyclopedia. We are accustomed to its alphabetical organization of topics, but this structure, in fact, represented a break from previous reference formats that grouped subjects under the structure of classical disciplines. The alphabetized encyclopedia came about at a point when the previous disciplinary categories no longer could contain growing knowledge. A new, more horizontal model took their place, a model that allowed readers access to information by topic, outside of the hierarchies of a discipline. Burke points us to the importance of how we categorize information, where these categories come from, and how categorizations affect our access to and experience of information.[15]

Anthropologist Ann Stoler comes to the problem of categories from a different perspective. She thinks of the archive as an active site for ethnography and seeks to understand how archives are live spaces in which the Dutch colonial state in Indonesia built, among other things, social categories. She traces how colonial administrators' use of archiving categorized and assigned particular rights and privileges to people with different national heritages. As they categorized, they made some peoples' experiences of the colonial state visible and obscured others. Stoler writes that categories are both the explicit subject of archives and their implicit project: "The career of categories is also lodged in archival habits and how those change; in the telling titles of commissions, in the requisite subject headings of administrative reports, in what sorts of stories get relegated to the miscellaneous and 'misplaced.'" She then frames the archive as a place to understand "how people think and why they seem obliged to think, or *suddenly find themselves having difficulty thinking*," in certain ways.[16]

The work of scholars like Burke and Stoler implies questions for historians' research processes. Burke's work suggests that we investigate how categories of thought, either between disciplines or within them, affect us. Think of academic subfields, for example, the boundaries of which still shape the literatures we read (even as many try to transcend them) and still guide which archives we pursue or whether we think of particular questions as part of our domain. Stoler raises a different kind of question. At what points in our research, out of pragmatic necessity, out of a desire for intellectual order, or for yet other reasons, do we set out categories of evidence or thought that influence what we see and what we do not see? What kinds of tools could help us be more aware of these categories or could give us the flexibility to move beyond them when necessary or desirable?

I hypothesize here that databases offer a kind of flexibility that can allow us to create and re-create categories as we work with notes, to adjust as we know more about our sources, about how they relate to one another and how they relate to the silences we are finding. That flexibility means that we can evaluate particular ways of categorizing what we know and then adapt if we realize that these categories are not satisfactory. In doing so, we are made more aware of the work of categorization and are reminded to take stock of how our ways of organizing help and what they leave out.

The matter of flexible categorization touches on another strand of scholarship: archivists debating what postmodernism means for their work. How does the growing understanding of archives as spaces in which certain kinds of power are codified and justified and where information has to be understood relationally matter for the practice of archiving? Archival theorist Terry Cook argues that finding aids and item descriptions should be constantly evolving, adapting to new relevant knowledge about the item's sources and its relationship to other archived and unarchived materials.[17] Working with databases provokes historians to think about how our note-keeping practices could seek such flexibility and relationality.

Yet there are at least two cautions as well. One comes from the flatness of databases like the one I used. In Burke's terms, my database was not a reference text organized along disciplinary lines. It was more like an alphabetized encyclopedia. Without hierarchies that keep each fact locked in relationship to others—through the structure of earlier historiography, for example, or through the categories of an archive's collections—the historian has to be more intentional about seeing information in its context. If we can look across all of our notes at a very granular level and make connections across categories that we or others created, it becomes too easy to look at these bits of information devoid of context—a danger visible even in my own way of cutting and pasting out of my database. I linked bits of notes only to a source code, meaning that they could be read in less-than-direct connection to their origins. Digital bits seem very easily severed from their context. Zotero's structure links sources and notes visually, which may help safeguard against this.

More important, despite its usefulness in helping us see things we might otherwise have forgotten or missed, no database does the work of analysis. The two are, of course, interdependent—as they are in any digital or non-digital form of note keeping. The analytical work, the crucial sense making that pushes history writing from chronology to critical interpretation, still happens in our own heads. There other implicit categories or habits of thought might shape our analysis. There we decide whose stories to tell first, or we prioritize one set of historical drivers over another. Some of these habits reflect our deepest-held assumptions and beliefs. It is less easy to talk of these, and certainly less easy for an author to identify his or her own, than it is to speak of note keeping. Maybe bringing critical consciousness to the mechanical can prompt more reflection about the conceptual as well.

It is also worth considering what kinds of concerns may arise for historians who have not yet made use of digital tools like databases in their own research. Historians surely value, maybe even romanticize, the encounter with sources in the archives. Does converting that textual, even textural, experience into digital note cards somehow deaden it? Does it render our research uncomfortably close to a social scientist's coding and writing up of findings? Charlotte Rochez, responding to an earlier version of this essay, explained that she worried about sacrificing "some of deeper insights, interpretations and understanding induced from being more involved in sorting and interpreting the sources."[18] Digital note taking may add to but does not of necessity replace varied encounters between researcher and sources— even "serendipitous engagement." It remains possible to meander through your notes from a given collection or source, to look back at the original page (even in PDF or photocopied form). But it becomes newly feasible to look broadly across those collections and sources.

One prompt for this volume came from the *Journal of American History*'s 1997 special issue that made public the process of academic peer review. David Thelen's introduction to that issue raised questions about the work of history writing that seem important to revisit in light of digital innovations. The centerpiece of the issue was a submission by Joel Williamson, in which Williamson recounted his failure to perceive lynching's centrality to and origins in American and Southern history. Two reviewers received Williamson's piece with shock and dismay that he could have missed what they had appreciated as central for years. Despite this disagreement, or perhaps because of it, Thelen saw Williamson's piece as issuing a challenge to historians to "think about what we see and do not see, to reflect on what in our experience we avoid, erase, or deny, as well as what we focus on."[19] I see my attention to categories, to the possibilities and implications of how we choose to organize the information on which our interpretations rest, as a kindred effort.

Acknowledgments: The author thanks Jack Dougherty and Kristen Nawrotzki for the invitation to reflect on research practice and for good feedback on this essay, Courtney Fullilove for reading suggestions, Seth Erickson for ongoing conversations about archives and information architecture, and all those who commented on earlier versions for their helpful remarks. The dissertation research described here was supported by a Spencer Dissertation Fellowship, a Clifford Roberts/Eisenhower Institute Fellowship, and a Mellon Interdisciplinary Graduate Fellowship at the Paul Lazersfeld Center, Institute for Social and Economic Research and Policy, Columbia University.

Notes

1. McNeill quoted in Tracy L. Steffes, "Lessons From the Past: A Challenge and a Caution for Policy-Relevant History," in *Clio at the Table: Using History to Inform and Improve Education Policy*, ed. Kenneth Wong and Robert Rothman (New York: Peter Lang, 2008), 267–68; Stephen Ramsay, "The Hermeneutics of Screwing Around; or What Do You Do with a Million Books" (paper delivered at the conference "Playing with Technology in History," History Education Network/Histoire et Éducation en Réseau, Niagara-on-the-Lake, Canada, April 2010), http://www.playingwithhistory.com/wp-content/uploads/2010/04/hermeneutics.pdf.

2. Ansley T. Erickson, "Schooling the Metropolis: Educational Inequality Made and Remade, Nashville, Tennessee, 1945–1985" (PhD diss., Columbia University, 2010), http://faculty.tc.columbia.edu/upload/ate11/Erickson_TitlePage&Abs_DEP.pdf.

3. A relational database keeps bits of information in relationship to one another without establishing hierarchies. In my database, as discussed in this essay, each source was related to multiple notes, yet I could also search across notes from multiple sources. More elaborate uses of relational databases can include specifying types of relationships between sources or analyzing the density of relationships between attributes of the database so as to discern patterns that may not be otherwise apparent.

4. Consider other examples of database technology in historical writing, such as the archival collection *as* database (full-text searchable to facilitate text mining) or the database as scholarly product. See Jean Bauer, The Early American Foreign Service Database, 2010, http://www.eafsd.org/.

5. See, for example, Peter Burke, *A Social History of Knowledge: From Gutenberg to Diderot* (Cambridge: Polity, 2000); Ann Laura Stoler, *Along the Archival Grain: Epistemic Anxieties and Colonial Common Sense* (Princeton: Princeton University Press, 2010); Antoinette Burton, ed., *Archive Stories: Facts, Fictions, and the Writing of History* (Durham: Duke University Press, 2005); Joan M. Schwartz and Terry Cook. "Archives, Records, and Power: The Making of Modern Memory," *Archival Science* 2 (2002): 1–29.

6. For views of this problem, see Steffes, "Lessons," 267–68; Amanda Seligman, comment on "Historical Research and the Problem of Categories," in *Writing History in the Digital Age*, web-book ed., Fall 2011 version.

7. For one recent example, see Amanda Morton, "Review of Digital Tools: Zotero and Omeka," *Journal of American History* 98, 3 (2011): 952, http://jah.oxfordjournals.org/content/98/3/952.

8. FileMaker Pro, http://www.filemaker.com; NVivo, http://www.qsrinternational.com/products_nvivo.aspx; ATLAS.ti, http://www.atlasti.com/; Zotero, http://www.zotero.org. New options include DevonThink and Adobe Lightroom, discussed in the "History and the Digital Image Forum," *Perspectives* (October 2012), http://www.historians.org/perspectives/issues/2012/1210/index.cfm.

9. You can download my FileMaker template at http://faculty.tc.columbia.edu/upload/ate11/Erickson_FMTemplate.fp7.

10. Kirklin Bateman et al., "Taking a Byte out of the Archives: Making Technology Work for You," *Perspectives*, January 2005, http://www.historians.org/perspec-

tives/issues/2005/0501/0501arc1.cfm; Konrad Lawson, "The Articulated Arm of an Archive Raider," *Chronicle of Higher Education, ProfHacker,* December 7, 2010, http://chronicle.com/blogs/profhacker/the-articulated-arm-of-an-archive-raider/29243.

11. Lynn Hunt argues for a similar approach, encouraging scholars not to delay writing by organizing notes or other getting-ready activities, as well as to use writing to further thinking, in "How Writing Leads to Thinking (and Not the Other Way Around)," *Perspectives,* February 2010, http://www.historians.org/perspectives/issues/2010/1002/1002art1.cfm. Digital note keeping helps earlier and more fluid writing, as the accessibility of information reduces barriers between getting ready and actually writing. James B. McSwain shared a similar story about his experience with Nota Bene in *Writing History: How Historians Research, Write, and Publish in the Digital Age,* ed. Jack Dougherty and Kristen Nawrotzki, October 6, 2010, http://writinghistory.wp.trincoll.edu/2010/10/06/organize/#comment-148. I wrote more about my approach on the same site, in "Keeping the Writing (and Thinking) Going," http://writinghistory.wp.trincoll.edu/2010/10/06/erickson-thinking/.

12. William Higgins, "Suggestions for Development of Guidelines for an Unitary Plan for the Metropolitan Board of Education," 1979, box 69, file 8, Kelly Miller Smith Papers, Vanderbilt University Special Collections and University Archives; Saundra Ivey, "School Closing Plan Draws Fire," *Tennessean,* November 23, 1977.

13. See the works cited in note 5, and see Geoffrey C. Bowker and Susan Leigh Star, *Sorting Things Out: Classification and Its Consequences* (Cambridge, MA: MIT Press, 1999).

14. Burke, *Social History.*

15. Burke, *Social History,* especially 184–87.

16. Stoler, *Along the Archival Grain,* 36.

17. Terry Cook, "Fashionable Nonsense or Professional Rebirth: Postmodernism and the Practice of Archives," *Archivaria* 51 (Spring 2001), http://journals.sfu.ca/archivar/index.php/archivaria/issue/view/428/showToc.

18. Charlotte Rochez, comment in *Writing History: How Historians Research, Write, and Publish,* http://writinghistory.wp.trincoll.edu/2010/10/06/organize/#comment-803.

19. David Thelen, "What We See and Can't See in the Past: An Introduction," *Journal of American History* 83, no. 4 (1997), http://www.jstor.org/stable/295898. This idea also supports Fred Gibbs and Trevor Owen's call for "a new kind of methodological transparency," in "The Hermeneutics of Data and Historical Writing" in the present volume, pp. 159–70.

Creating Meaning in a Sea of Information

The Women and Social Movements *Web Sites*

Kathryn Kish Sklar and Thomas Dublin

In 1997, funded by a small grant from the National Endowment for the Humanities (NEH), we set out to give U.S. women's history a more substantial presence on the World Wide Web, then a rather modest and marginal new domain for history publishing. For six years, we focused on work with undergraduates at Binghamton University, State University of New York, and then with faculty and students at a dozen colleges and universities around the United States.[1] In this first stage, we published more than 40 document projects that constituted original research about the history of women and social movements in the United States.

These document projects consisted of 20 to 30 primary documents complemented by an interpretive essay and other scholarly components, organized to answer a central historiographical question. Document projects have questions for titles, because our goal is to generate more focused scholarship than a topical framework might create. We sought, in this way, to combine new historical interpretations with the publication of valuable and often inaccessible primary sources. In launching this effort, we were struck by the way primary documents and interpretation supported one another and provided a distinctly richer combination for students and scholars than typically emerges from the scholarly article format.

It was not simply a matter of the conjunction of the two kinds of resources; the electronic medium itself dramatically shaped and enriched our undertaking in important ways. The document project format was a felicitous combination of what historians do (analyze documents) with the Internet's spaciousness and hypertext capacity. By publishing documents in their entirety and arranging them in document projects that are much more monographic than is economically feasible in print media, as well as by providing a robust database and search engine, our format and research tools permit readers to evaluate the evidence and arguments much more fully than is possible with a traditional journal. For example, our first document project, published in 1997, "How Did African-American Women Define Their Citizenship at the Chicago World's Fair in 1893?," is by far the most extensive monographic treatment of that topic. Bringing together 27 documents, including all the speeches of African American women at the World's Congress of Representative Women, accompanied by an interpretive essay that analyzes the documents, it makes a substantial historiographic contribution to U.S. women's history, African American history, and U.S. history.[2]

We immediately recognized the power of this innovative but labor-intensive format, and with the support of NEH grants, we taught courses and employed graduate students that together produced dozens more. But since we wanted to produce authoritative, rather than student, work, we also began to involve a small group of colleagues in U.S. women's history. In 2003, we came to a crossroads when we anticipated running out of grant funding and the modest support of Binghamton University. That year, we solved our financial crisis and entered a new stage of growth by partnering with Alexander Street Press (ASP) and becoming a peer-reviewed, online journal, *Women and Social Movements in the United States, 1600–2000*. ASP distributed our journal/database through subscriptions and purchases by academic libraries. Along with financial stability that permitted us to pay our staff, we thus acquired access to much more powerful database and search technology.[3]

Innovative in its format and medium, the journal has grown remarkably in nine years. Because our partnership with ASP made it possible for us to use database functionalities and a powerful search engine, we decided that we would publish full-text scholarly collections of primary sources, often with accompanying interpretive introductions, as well as our signature document projects. Before long, we added book and website reviews, teaching tools, and news about U.S. women's history from the archives. We also created another new format, the "document archive." Bringing together a distinctly larger collection of primary documents—typically 60 to 80 in number—the document archive combines a brief interpretive introduction with a more extensive collection of documents. Document projects seek to "prove" a scholarly interpretation. Document archives provide a minimal interpretive framework for a larger group of documents.

These gains came at a price—our site was no longer freely accessible. Our initial concern on that score was alleviated as the number of subscribing libraries grew, and we were soon accessed by more users than had visited our smaller Binghamton University site. By early 2013, almost 400 libraries provided access to the site for their students and faculty, about the same number of institutional subscribers as many print media journals. While subscription access imposes limits on our site's use, we work with an online publisher that is highly respected by librarians for maintaining high standards in their online publications. So we consider ourselves part of a process by which libraries gain access to high-quality online scholarship, even though it is not funded by foundations or major research universities.

Women and Social Movements in the United States (WASM) has steadily expanded over the years because faculty and librarians have thought well enough of it to fund it with library subscriptions. We hold ourselves directly accountable to those subscribers. In that regard, there is a more democratic aspect to our funding structure than in freely accessible sites that are designed at and funded by well-endowed institutions and foundations but are not accountable to end users.

Our primary goal is to create new knowledge. We do so by integrating documents with the interpretation of documents. Sites that contain only documents predominate in U.S history. Particularly notable among these are the *American Memory* site at the Library of Congress and Ed Ayers's *The Valley of the Shadow* site, which includes documents from two counties in the Civil War period.[4] The documents on these wonderful sites are very valuable for students and scholars of U.S. history, who can use them to create new knowledge off-site. Our goal is to generate new knowledge on our site—with the publication of document projects and with extensive database functionalities that permit users to organize the data in new ways.

To generate new knowledge, we take very seriously our responsibility to be authoritative with the documents and interpretations we publish. Our goal of being authoritative makes our editorial process extremely labor-intensive. Space prohibits us from describing it fully here, but a few examples will show what we have undertaken. First, our interaction with authors is extensive and complex. Scholars are not familiar with the document project format, so we need to help them navigate a steep learning curve. Each project presents unique challenges and new frontiers. We begin by asking authors to pose a historiographically meaningful question and then prepare an annotated list of documents that address the question and a brief essay that shows us how the documents can be read to interpret the question. This stage of the process often takes about a year and a half, with frequent communication between us and an author to address historiographic issues or gaps or redundancies in the documentation. Then our peer review process evaluates the result, almost always suggesting more work, sometimes clarity of interpretation based on the documents, and frequently calling for different or more documents. After authors accommodate peer review suggestions, the next stage of the process involves our Binghamton University work with authors to provide authoritative citations and headnotes about the documents' provenance. We and our authors contact archives to secure permission to publish online and verify that we have accurate metadata. We transcribe the documents because scanning and OCR do not produce sufficiently accurate texts for our database. Our Binghamton University shop carefully compares our transcriptions to the original documents. Our authors provide annotations for the documents and footnotes for their interpretive text, as well as bibliographies. The journal is indexed in *America: History and Life* and the "Research Scholarship Online" section of the *Journal of American History*, the two leading bibliographic resources in U.S. History, so *WASM* publications enter ongoing historiographical debates.

Our search engine and database functionalities are central to our purpose of providing users the opportunity to create new knowledge by organizing the documentary data in new ways that are meaningful to them. We are constantly developing and enhancing the database functionalities. We began our site by key entering documents into HTML so that they could be more effectively indexed and made full-text searchable. With our partnership with Alexander Street Press, we shifted to standards in the Text Encoding Initiative, TEI-SGML and then TEI-XML.

In addition to our goal of creating authoritative new knowledge, we also want to facilitate use of the site by scholars who are not historians of American women. The stream of scholarship published about American women in the past 40 years is underrepresented in the mainstream of U.S. history. Perhaps scholars who are not able to explore the wide range of secondary writings about American women might be able to read and use documents on our site in their research and teaching of primary documents about women, especially if they relate to the scholars' own research interests. Thus, for example, historians of the American Revolution might be interested in the writings of Esther Reed and other elite Philadelphia women who raised funds to support the patriot army during the war. Or they might want to explore Woodrow Wilson's reimposition of segregation in federal offices in 1913.[5] In the document project format, these topics invite the exploration of historical methods associated with cause, effect, periodization, audience, power, and, of course, class, race, and gender. But they can also be used simply to supplement what readers already know.

We have a third goal of drawing scholars in U.S. women's history (and women's history generally) into greater dialogue across specializations. Like other historical fields, women's history has developed subfields that often make it impossible for scholars to learn about work outside their own precincts. Thus scholars of the history of women's health in the antebellum era might not know about recent work on women's labor history in the Progressive Era or on the history of African American women in the civil rights movement. It might be easier for scholars to learn about fields outside their own specialty by having the opportunity to access primary sources. Secondary works sometimes require a considerable commitment of time and familiarity with related historiography to digest. Primary documents offer a more direct route to learning.

One brief example can show how a document project in U.S. women's history might contribute to all three of these rationales: to generate new knowledge, to influence other fields of U.S. History, and to facilitate more communication among historians of American women. Carol Faulkner's document project "How Did White Women Aid Former Slaves during and after the Civil War, 1863–1891?" analyzes the gendered construction of power in the freedmen's aid movement during Reconstruction.[6] She offers documents that demonstrate women reformers' opposition to the policies of such leading men as General Oliver O. Howard, head of the Freedmen's Bureau, or Horace Greeley, noted editor of the *New York Tribune*. These men supported the early closing of the Freedmen's Bureau in 1869 because they feared that assistance to freed people would create economic dependency. Eric Foner, the leading historian of Reconstruction, has described the dominant ethos in the bureau as reflecting "not only attitudes towards blacks, but a more general Northern belief in the dangers of encouraging dependency among the lower classes."[7] Faulkner's exploration of correspondence between General Howard and freedmen's aid advocate Josephine Griffing shows that this group of women reformers sought to provide more generous long-term aid to freedmen and challenged Howard's concern about dependency. Thus Faulkner's document project alters our understanding of the possibilities during this major period of American history. By offering the full text of the sources on which its interpretation rests, it invites scholars and students to use those documents in their own work of interpreting American history.

Our partnership with Alexander Street Press allowed us to expand each issue of our journal to include extensive full-text sources that are not part of document projects. This enhances the site's resources and the meanings that can be derived from the site's database. We now publish about 5,000 pages annually of full-text sources. Our first group in the fall of 2003 included about 30,000 pages of books, pamphlets, and convention proceedings related to the struggle for woman suffrage in the United States from 1830 to 1930. There, we brought together for the first time the published proceedings of the three women's antislavery conventions of the 1830s and the proceedings of 15 women's rights conventions that were held between 1848 and 1870. These resources enable scholars to analyze change over time in the women's rights convention movement, viewing that movement much more fully than ever before. The database permits the retrieval of new knowledge in response to new questions. For example, researchers can identify the number of speeches or letters in convention proceedings that mentioned married women's property rights or education or health. By exploring topics addressed, speakers named, and rhetoric employed at these conventions, historians can explore change over time much more systematically.

Thus *WASM* offers the advantages of a database as well as a journal. Another example is our indexing of the six-volume *History of Woman Suffrage*, totaling some 5,800 pages.[8] These volumes were largely compilations of published and unpublished documents, and the database indexes these works in ways that permit scholars to search for the authors and titles of hundreds of separate documents included in the volumes. The database reveals more than 800 individual documents in those volumes, including 152 speeches, which users can further identify by author, race of author, date, and place (among other variables). We also reprinted, as full-text sources, works by the national and state branches of the League of Women Voters originally published between 1920 and 2000. This collection consists of 660 items totaling 8,000 pages and provides a valuable resource for exploring women in American public life after suffrage was achieved.

We took on a big project of compiling all the publications that we could find by state and local commissions on the status of women between 1961 and 2005. This database, fully integrated into *WASM*, dwarfed our earlier efforts, including almost 1,900 items with some 90,000 pages. In a practice that we began to follow increasingly for the website, we commissioned scholarly essays to explore various dimensions of the state commissions' publications. We have published eight essays in all, exploring such issues as economic security, race, sexuality, labor feminism, and conservatism as they can be found in the publications by commissions in the *WASM* database.

The combination of these two threads—the work of scholars in document projects and the publication of full-text primary sources—means that

WASM is much more than a journal whose articles are accessible online. This is a lot of work, and we fully understand why most websites in U.S. history do not weave together interpretation and documentation and why those that do so usually focus on one historical actor, event, or time period. But now that the World Wide Web offers a sea of information, we wish there were more sites that took the next step and helped scholars construct meaning within that sea.

As with other venues for scholarship in U.S. history, we have witnessed and promoted the expansion of the field to include more international perspectives. Our authors have increasingly brought us projects pertaining to U.S. women and international social movements. Nancy Hewitt and her students at Rutgers University prepared a document project, which we published in 2003, on the relationship between the women's rights movement of the mid-19th century in the United States and contemporary British and European feminism. Colonial themes also added an international dimension to the website: Tracy Leavelle explored the interactions of 17th-century French explorers and Jesuit missionaries with Illinois women, and Patricia Cleary researched women's sexual, familial, and public roles in 18th-century St. Louis, successively an outpost of Spanish and French empires.[9]

As we saw this focus emerging, we actively sought to nurture it with two collaborations. First, we established a "Canadian initiative," aimed at encouraging document projects for a special issue on Canadian women and social movements that we published in September 2009. Second, we organized a collaborative project with Japanese and American historians, encouraging the submission of document projects that explore the interaction of women reformers from Japan and the United States since the Meiji Restoration of 1869. From this collaboration, we have already published three bilingual document projects, beginning in March 2009, and we see this project as a model for how we can contribute to the internationalization of the history of women and social movements in the United States.

In 2007, we began to create a new, complementary online archive, *Women and Social Movements, International—1840 to Present (WASM International)*.[10] For this project, we have drawn heavily on the international community of historians of women, on archivists around the world, on our talented Binghamton University graduate students, and on the technical and editorial skills of Alexander Street Press. The project went "live" in January 2011 and should be complete by September 2013. We hope it will greatly enhance scholarship about women and social movements internationally by providing a wide range of systematic sources, including the proceedings of more than 500 women's international conferences.

If *WASM* was "born digital," *WASM International* was "born digital database." Both were constructed by scholars with a view to creating new knowledge. *WASM International* was much larger at its creation and designed with a view to its systematic analysis. With that analysis in mind and with a self-imposed limit of 150,000 pages of documents, we knew we needed to be thoughtful. We assembled an international advisory board of scholars who assisted in the selection of the archive's resources, meeting with 40 of them at the Berkshire Conference on Women's History at the University of Minnesota in June 2008. They helped us move beyond our U.S.-centric beginnings and construct a truly international resource.

As the work of the project progressed, the international advisory board grew dramatically, reaching more than 130 scholars in 2011. Another women's history conference, at the Aletta Institute in Amsterdam in August 2010, gave us a second opportunity to present the project-in-progress to an international group of women's history scholars. Their comments and assistance have been enormously helpful. Throughout our work, we shared bibliographies with members of our advisory board and received excellent recommendations for additions to the archive. We also expanded the archival dimension of the project over time; by 2011, we had secured extensive materials—scanned or digitally photographed—from the Sophia Smith Collection, the Schlesinger Library, the Swarthmore College Peace Collection, the Library of Congress, Hollins University, the Aletta Institute, the International Institute of Social History, and the National Library of Australia.

All our work on *WASM International* was shaped and facilitated by the electronic revolution that had taken place since we first worked in 1997 with Binghamton students on *Women and Social Movements in the United States.* For example, we relied from the outset on the powerful database program Zotero, which allowed us to download online catalog records from WorldCat to our own database.[11] This ensured the accuracy of our metadata and permitted us to construct intermediate bibliographies to view how the archive was taking shape. We relied on the new media and posted our topical bibliographies on the website of the Center for the Historical Study of Women and Gender at Binghamton University, which our editorial advisors accessed on the Internet.[12] We also downloaded Zotero entries to spreadsheets that permitted us to keep track of our work, particularly the major effort involved in securing permissions to publish copyrighted materials. With these spreadsheets, we could analyze the contents of our archive as it grew—analyzing it by dates, geographical regions, and topical coverage so that we could periodically take stock of our work and identify areas that remained underrepresented in the archive. This work permitted us to contact our international scholarly advisors and ask them for help with our coverage in their areas of expertise.

The electronic revolution assisted our work in still other ways. From the outset, we had decided that a focus on organizations would help us identify a core of publications relevant to the history of women's international activism. Drawing on scholarly writings and using keyword and corporate author searches in WorldCat permitted us to identify the publications of about a hundred organizations that had emerged as key players in promoting women's networks and activism from the mid-19th century to the present.

As we worked, we became aware that library catalogs provide a biased vision of women's international organizing. Established organizations with North American and European memberships and long histories were much more fully represented in library holdings than groups founded recently in the Global South. To complement resources found in major academic libraries, we searched the World Wide Web for online publications of contemporary nongovernmental organizations (NGOs). In this way, we identified 15 to 20 particularly important organizations, found compelling samples of their online publications, and worked with the organizations to improve our coverage of their activism.

In the course of constructing the online archive, our work took on preservation dimensions. For example, when we could not find a good run of the annual proceedings of the World's Woman's Christian Temperance Union (WWCTU) in library catalogs, we contacted (at the suggestion of a colleague in Australia) the national WCTU office in Evanston, Illinois. The WCTU library in Evanston no longer maintains regular hours, but a volunteer addressed our request and soon sent us a duplicate set of the WWCTU proceedings, for scanning and future donation to an appropriate research library. Thus our project unearthed rare copies of proceedings that were not really available to the public, and we were able to publish the proceedings online for scholarly use.

We have had a similar experience with the International Women's Tribune Centre in New York. As our work progressed, a professor at Hollins University who had heard about our work told us that an important international activist, Mildred Persinger, had donated her papers to Hollins. Focusing on the United Nations world conferences on women, from Mexico City in 1975 to Beijing in 1995, her papers constituted an international gold mine. We visited the archive and arranged to photograph more than 3,000 pages of manuscript and published documents.

A preservation project emerged when, anticipating our archival trip, we met Mildred Persinger at her home in Dobbs Ferry, New York. From her, we learned that the International Women's Tribune Centre (IWTC), which she had founded and directed for many years, was closing its office and moving its files to storage. She mentioned that we should try to get copies of slideshows that the IWTC had produced for each UN conference and find a way to include them in our archive. After months of intense effort, we eventually secured copies of slides for all four of the conferences and scripts and cassette tapes of the audio portions of the original slideshows. The resources dated back to 1975, 1980, 1985, and 1995. The slides were discolored with age, and the cassette tapes were uneven in quality, but we had everything digitized, and student workers at Binghamton University skillfully restored the slides. A skilled off-campus videographer then melded together slides and audio for each slideshow, following the scripts that IWTC staff had originally created. From the aged and deteriorating slides and cassettes of an earlier generation of activists, we now have produced four high-quality videos of the original slideshows, which should be useful to scholars and activists for decades to come. This success was only possible because of the networking that was a part of our project, the cooperation of IWTC activists who wanted the history of the conferences to be widely disseminated, and the skills and resources we were able to mobilize at our university.

Our experiences with the WWCTU and IWTC materials were repeated with other resources. Many of the published works we have included in the online archive are available at only one or two of the libraries whose collections are recorded in the WorldCat online catalog. By borrowing resources through interlibrary loan, scanning them, and securing permission from the original copyright holders to publish the works online, we have made these rare works accessible at what we anticipate will be hundreds of research libraries around the world. Similarly, we are including hundreds of online publications of contemporary NGOs, most of which cannot be found in academic or public libraries. These documents will have brief lifetimes on NGO websites, soon to be displaced by more recent publications that better fit the organizations' changing programmatic and fund-raising priorities. We have created an online archive that presents a slice in time, documenting the priorities of women's international activism between the mid-1990s and 2010 as expressed on these NGO websites.

Finally, the preparation of an online archive dramatically expands the potential audience for the rare and fugitive materials we have chosen for inclusion. We have included about 30,000 pages of manuscript and published materials from archives in the United States and Europe, selected to provide depth of coverage of significant international women's organizations and events. In each case, we secured permission from the archive and from copyright holders and then made arrangements for digital photography or scanning to produce electronic copies of the documents that best seemed to fit the selection criteria we established for the archive. These materials do not circulate, and in many cases, it is difficult to determine that the archive actually owns the items in question. Previously, users would have had to visit the archive and conduct research onsite; now, these resources will be accessible in hundreds of academic libraries around the world. While the number of the site's subscribers at this point is quite small, what is striking about early trends is that about a third of early subscribers or purchasers are libraries outside of the United States. Institutions in Canada, Iceland, Norway, the Netherlands, the United Kingdom, China, New Zealand, and Australia are among the site's early subscribers.

Although the site's resources are not freely available on the Internet, they could never have been created without the subscription plan that funded the four years of work that produced them. Access is limited but is steadily expanding over time as more libraries subscribe. We expect that *WASM International* will eventually reach as broad a base of subscribers as *WASM*. Users who are not students or faculty at subscribing institutions can access the databases by visiting a subscribing library and using the resources there. This is the best we can do right now. We are still at an early stage in the evolution of this subscription model, and we continue to consider how we might better serve the needs of scholars and students at nonsubscribing libraries.

A related issue is the concern about how access might be affected should Alexander Street Press decide to stop supporting the databases. Two provisions in the contracts related to the databases anticipate this possibility. First, we, as editors, hold the copyright on the documentary content of the databases, while ASP holds the copyright on the software that provides the user interface, the search engine, and the associated database. If ASP went out of business, we would be free to try to find another way to keep the sites' content on the Internet—for example, by approaching a large research university or foundation and securing the needed funding to create a new site for our documents and document projects. Second, many academic libraries that provide access to the databases have purchased them from ASP. The press supplies purchasing libraries with a copy of the database, thereby ensuring its availability in the future. For *Women and Social Movements in the United States,* more than 180 libraries have purchased the database, assuring its online availability whatever might happen to ASP.

What conclusions can we draw from this survey of our work on the *Women and Social Movements* websites since 1997? How does our work illuminate the emergence of electronic resources for historians in the past 15 years? First, while our topic might be perceived as narrow—women and social movements—it actually cuts a broad swath through all of women's history, as well as U.S. and world history, and speaks to broad issues of social reform that have shaped the mainstream of other national and international histories. So it models how meaning can be constructed in the oceans of information flowing on the Internet. Second, our document projects on *Women and Social Movements in the United States* point to the crucial connection between historical interpretation and primary source documents, permitting historians to share their methods with others and permitting readers to examine historians' primary sources and reach their own interpretive conclusions. Third, both projects draw on the participation of a broad community of scholars. At the same time, these sites help build and reinforce that community. The electronic revolution—supplemented by face-to-face meetings—has enabled us to involve hundreds of historians of women in the United States and elsewhere in publishing *Women and Social Movements in the United States,* and we have relied on the editorial advice of hundreds of historians, librarians, archivists, and activists internationally to construct *Women and Social Movements, International.* The electronic revolution has made this kind of collaboration easier, and we hope that our example might be useful to others who set out to create collaborative projects.

From our reliance on WorldCat and other online catalogs to our use of the Zotero database program, *WASM* and *WASM International* have been born digital. Only with the electronic circulation of e-mail messages, attachments, bibliographies, and document scans have we been able to mobilize the women's history community in the construction and use of these resources. The digital age is especially meaningful for historians. It is an exciting time to be working in circumstances so different than those we encountered when we first acquired the tools of our craft.

Notes

1. For an early description of this work, see Thomas Dublin and Kathryn Kish Sklar, "Democratizing Student Learning: The *Women and Social Movements in the United States, 1820–1940* Web Project at SUNY Binghamton," *History Teacher* 35

(February 2002): 163–73, http://www.historycooperative.org/journals/ht/35.2/dublin.html. For a discussion of the teaching dimension of the project, see Kathryn Kish Sklar, "Teaching Students to Become Producers of New Historical Knowledge on the Web," *Journal of American History* 88 (March 2002): 1471–76, http://chswg.binghamton.edu/sklararticle.htm. See also Kathryn Kish Sklar and Thomas Dublin, "Keeping Up with the Web, 1997–2008: *Women and Social Movements in the United States*," *Perspectives on History* (May 2009): 44–47, http://www.historians.org/perspectives/issues/2009/0905/0905for9.cfm.

2. Kathryn Kish Sklar and Erin Shaughnessy, "How did African-American Women Define Their Citizenship at the Chicago World's Fair in 1893?," *Women and Social Movements in the United States, 1600–2000*, vol. 1 (1997), http://womhist.alexanderstreet.com/ibw/abstract.htm.

3. Thomas Dublin and Kathryn Kish Sklar, eds., *Women and Social Movements in the United States, 1600–2000*, http://womhist.alexanderstreet.com/ (hereafter cited as *WASM*). About one-fifth of the document projects on this site are freely available; access to the remainder requires an institutional library subscription.

4. Library of Congress, *American Memory*, http://memory.loc.gov; Edward Ayers, *The Valley of the Shadow*, http://valley.vcdh.virginia.edu.

5. Kathryn Kish Sklar and Gregory Duffy, "How Did the Ladies Association of Philadelphia Shape New Forms of Women's Activism during the American Revolution, 1780–1781?," *WASM*, vol. 5 (2001), http://womhist.alexanderstreet.com/amrev/abstract.htm; Nancy Unger, "How Did Belle La Follette Oppose Racial Segregation in Washington, D.C., 1913–1914?," *WASM*, vol. 8 (2004), http://womhist.alexanderstreet.com/lafollette/abstract.htm.

6. Carol Faulkner, "How Did White Women Aid Former Slaves during and after the Civil War, 1863–1891?," *WASM*, vol. 3 (1999), http://womhist.alexanderstreet.com/aid/abstract.htm.

7. Eric Foner, *Reconstruction: America's Unfinished Revolution, 1863–1877* (New York: Harper and Row, 1988), 153.

8. Elizabeth Cady Stanton et al., eds., *History of Woman Suffrage*, 6 vols. (New York: Fowler and Wells, 1881–1922).

9. Nancy Hewitt *et al.*, "From Wollstonecraft to Mill: What British and European Ideas and Social Movements Influenced the Emergence of Feminism in the Atlantic World, 1792–1869?," *WASM*, vol. 7 (2003), http://womhist.alexanderstreet.com/awrm/abstract.htm; Tracy Neal Leavelle, "Why Were Illinois Indian Women Attracted to Catholicism, 1665–1750?," *WASM*, vol. 11 (2007), http://womhist.alexanderstreet.com/leavelle/abstract.htm; Patricia Cleary, "How Did Living in an Outpost of Empire Influence Perceptions of Women's Sexual, Marital, and Public Roles in Eighteenth-Century Colonial St. Louis?," *WASM*, vol. 12 (2008), http://womhist.alexanderstreet.com/Cleary/abstract.html.

10. Kathryn Kish Sklar and Thomas Dublin, eds., *Women and Social Movements, International—1840 to Present*, http://wasi.alexanderstreet.com/.

11. Zotero, Roy Rosenzweig Center for History and New Media, http://www.zotero.org.

12. "WASI Bibliographies," Center for the Historical Study of Women and Gender, http://chswg.binghamton.edu/wasi.

The Hermeneutics of Data
and Historical Writing

Fred Gibbs and Trevor Owens

Ongoing digitization of primary sources and the proliferation of born-digital documents are making it easier for historians to engage with vast amounts of research material. As a result, historical scholarship increasingly depends on our interactions with data, from battling the hidden algorithms of Google Book Search to text mining a hand-curated set of full-text documents. Even though methods for exploring and interacting with data have begun to permeate historical research, historians' writing has largely remained mired in traditional forms and conventions. This essay discusses some new ways in which historians might rethink the nature of historical writing as both a product and a process of understanding.

We argue that the new methods used to explore and interpret historical data demand a new level of methodological transparency in history writing. Examples include discussions of data queries, workflows with particular tools, and the production and interpretation of data visualizations. At a minimum, historians' research publications need to reflect new priorities that explicate the process of interfacing with, exploring, and then making sense of historical sources in a fundamentally digital form—that is, the hermeneutics of data.[1] This may mean de-emphasizing narrative in favor of illustrating the rich complexities between an argument and the data that supports it. It may mean calling attention to productive failure—when a certain methodology or technique proved ineffective or had to be abandoned. These are precisely the kinds of lessons historians need to learn as they grapple with new approaches to making sense of the historical record.

In this essay, we consider data as computer-processable information.

This includes measurements of nearly every kind, such as census records, as well as all types of textual publications that have been rendered as plain text. We must also point out that while data certainly can be employed as evidence for a historical argument, data are not necessarily evidence in themselves. Nor do we consider data necessarily to be a direct representation of the historical record, as they are also produced by tools used to investigate or access large datasets. Given the myriad forms that data can take, making sense of data and using them as evidence has become a rather different skill for historians than it has been. For that reason, we argue that the creation of, interaction with, and interpretation of data must become more integral to historical writing.

We call on historians to publicly experiment with ways of presenting their methodologies, procedures, and experiences with historical data as they engage in a cyclical process of contextualization and interpretation. This essay hopes to encourage more dialog about why historical writing must foreground methodological transparency and free itself from the epistemological jitters that make many historians wary of moving away from close readings or embracing the notion of the historical record as data.

Data in History

Use of data in the humanities has recently attracted considerable attention, no project more so than Culturomics, a quantitative study of culture using Google Books.[2] Of course, the idea of using data for historical research is hardly new, whether in the context of quantitative history, early work from the Annales school, or work done under the rubric of humanities computing. Yet the nature of data and the way it has been used by historians in the past differs in several important respects from contemporary uses of data. This is especially true in terms of the sheer quantity of data now available that can be gathered in a short time and thus guide humanistic inquiry. The process of guiding should be a greater part of our historical writing.

Some scholars who work within the domain of the digital humanities have begun to think and write more explicitly about data and its potential for new kinds of research. For example, some Shakespeare scholars have been using statistical procedures to identify language features that signal classification in dramatic works.[3] The Stanford Literary Lab has been rethinking the nature of genre through semantic analysis. Yet most projects, including these, continue to be largely confirmatory, like reinforcing the periodization of Shakespeare's plays or confirming the codified family of literary genres. To be clear, this is not a criticism of these projects and their outcomes—they are, in fact, a crucial step forward. As humanists continue to prove that data manipulation and machine learning can confirm existing knowledge, such techniques come closer to telling us something we do not already know. Other large-scale research projects, like those funded through the Digging into Data initiative, have begun to explore the transformative potential of data in humanities research as well.[4]

However, even these projects generally focus on research (or research potential) rather than on making their methodology accessible to a broader humanities audience. To some extent, legitimizing digital work requires an appeal to the traditional values (and forms) of the nondigital humanities. But how can digital historians expect others to take their new methodologies seriously when new ways of working with data (even when not with sophisticated mathematics) remain too much like an impenetrable and mysterious black box? The processes for working with the vast amounts of easily accessible and diverse large sets of data suggest a need for historians to formulate, articulate, and propagate ideas about how data should be approached in historical research.

Toward a Hermeneutics of Data

What does it mean to "use" data in historical work? To some extent, historians have always collected, analyzed, and written about data. But having access to vastly greater quantities of data, markedly different kinds of datasets, and a variety of complex tools and methodologies for exploring it means that the term *using* signifies a much broader range of data-related activities than it has previously. The rapid rate of data production and technological change means that we must continue to teach each other how we are using and making sense of data.

We should be clear about what using data does *not* imply. For one, it does not refer only to historical analysis via complex statistical methods to create knowledge. Even as data become more readily available and as historians begin to acquire skills in data manipulation as part of their training, rigorous mathematics is not necessarily essential for using data efficiently and effectively. In particular, work with data can be exploratory and deliberately without the mathematical rigor that social scientists must use to support their epistemological claims. Using data in this way is fundamentally different from using data for quantifying, computing, and creating knowledge as per quantitative history.

Similarly, historians need not treat and interpret data only for rigorous hypothesis testing. This is another crucial difference between our approach and the approaches of the cliometricians of the 1960s and '70s.[5] Perhaps such a potential dependence on numbers became even more unpalatable to nonnumerical historians after an embrace of the cultural turn, the importance of subjectivity, and a general epistemological stance against the kind of positivism that underpins much of the hypothesis testing baked into the design of statistical procedures and analytical software.

But data does not always have to be used as evidence. It can also help with discovering and framing research questions. Especially as increasing amounts of historical data is provided via or can be viewed with tools like Google's Ngram Viewer (to take a simple example), playing with data—in all its formats and forms—is more important than ever. This view of iterative interaction with data as a part of the hermeneutic process—especially when explored in graphical form—resonates with some recent theoretical work that describes knowledge from visualizations as not simply "transferred, revealed, or perceived, but . . . created through a dynamic process."[6] Data in a variety of forms can provoke new questions and explorations, just as visualizations themselves have been recently described as "generative and iterative, capable of producing new knowledge through the aesthetic provocation."[7]

As the investment of time and energy to acquire data decreases, rapidly working with data can now be a part of historians' early development and exploration of a research question. It can quickly illustrate potentially interesting pathways that are ultimately dead ends of scholarly research—"negative results," perhaps, that should not be discarded as they likely would be for a typical scholarly book or journal article. It bears repeating that using large amounts of data for research should not be considered opposed to more traditional use of historical sources. As historical data become more ubiquitous, humanists will find it useful to pivot between distant and close readings. More often than not, distant reading will involve (if not require) creative and reusable techniques to reimagine and re-present the past—at least more so than traditional humanist texts do. For this very reason, it becomes insufficient to simply write about research as if it is independent of its methodology.

Furthermore, rich datasets (like the Access to Archival Databases of the National Archives) and interfaces to data (like Google Fusion Tables) are making it easier than ever for historians to combine different kinds of datasets—and thus provide an exciting new way to triangulate historical knowledge.[8] Steven Ramsay has suggested that there is a new kind of role for searching to play in the hermeneutic process of understanding, especially in the value of "screwing around" and embracing the serendipitous discovery that our recent abundance of data makes possible.[9] This could result, for example, in noticing within the context of London's central criminal court, the Old Bailey, that trials about poisoning tend to refer to coffee more than to other beverages and very rarely refer to food.[10] Thus our methodologies might not be as deliberate or as linear as they have been in the past. This means we need more explicit and careful (if not playful) ways of writing about them.

Methodology in Writing

Despite some recent methodological experimentation with data, historians have not been nearly as innovative in terms of writing about how they use it. Even as scholars (at least in certain fields) have embraced communication with new media, historical writing has been largely confined by linear narratives, usually in the form of journal articles and monographs. The insistence on creating a narrative in static form, even if online, is particularly troubling because it obscures the methods for discovery that underlie the hermeneutic research process.

Historical work has needed to tell a good story, but methodology has not made for a very good story or the kind of historical writing that is likely to be published in traditional venues. Although relatively simple text searches or charts that aid in our historical analysis are perhaps not worth including in a book, our searches and work with data have grown increasingly complex, as has the data available to us. While these can present new perspectives on the past, they can only do so to the extent that other historians feel comfortable with the methodologies that are used. This means using appropriate platforms to explain our methods. Does it make sense to explain new research methods that are wholly dependent on large datasets and their manipulation and visualization in a static book that distances the reader from the tools and techniques being described? Of course, the realities of the profession restrict publishing freedoms (no one has gotten tenure for a really good website version of their dissertation), but our work need not be restrained by a false dichotomy between new media and old media. We suggest that exploratory methodological work can exist online in a perfectly complementary way to more traditional publication venues—and that the symbiotic pairing will make both elements the better for it.

Regardless of form, we need history writing that explicates the research process as much as the research conclusions. We need history writing that interfaces with, explains, and makes accessible the data that historians use.

We need history writing that will foreground the new historical methods to manipulate text/data coming online, including data queries and manipulation, and the production and interpretation of visualizations. As John Unsworth suggested long ago with respect to hypertext projects, history writing should explicate failure wherever possible.[11] As Tim Sherratt and Bethany Nowviskie suggested in their comments on an earlier version of this essay, one inspiring model for a new kind of publication is the artist's sketchbook that maps out ideas, explorations, false starts, and promising leads.[12]

There is no question that humanists can be—and, in fact, are trained to be—skeptical of data manipulation. This is perhaps the preeminent reason why methodology needs to be, at least for now, clearly explained. With new digital tools, we are still groping to understand how to identify the best methods for very messy circumstances of historical data. However, the reasons why many historians remain skeptical about data are not all that different from the reasons they can be skeptical about text. Historians have long reflected on the theoretical advantages and practical limitations of various methodologies and approaches to textual research. Critical theorists and historians alike have commented on the slippery notion of a text; some excellent theoretical work on cybertext and hypertext have muddied the waters further. The last few years have complicated such a notion even more, as many traditional texts have come to be seen as data that can be quickly searched, manipulated, viewed from a variety of perspectives, and combined with other data to create entirely new research corpora. Just as the problematic notion of a text has not undermined the hermeneutic process, nor should the notion of data. It is clear that a new relationship between text and data has begun to unfold.[13] This relationship must inform our approach to writing as well as research.

One way of reducing hostility to data and its manipulation is to lay bare whatever manipulations have led to some historical insight. Methodological tutorials, for example, not only would help legitimate the knowledge claims that employ them but would make the methodology more accessible to anyone who might recognize that the same or slightly modified approach could be of value in their own work. Beyond explicit tutorials, there are several key advantages in foregrounding our work with data: (1) it allows others to verify historical claims, (2) it is instructive as part of teaching and exposing historical research practices, (3) it allows us to keep pace with changing tools and ways of using them. Besides, openness has long been part of the ethos of the humanities, and humanists continually argue that we should embrace more public modes of writing and thinking, as a way to challenge the kind of work that scholars do. For example, Dave Perry's blog post "Be Online or Be Irrelevant" suggests that academic blogging can encourage "a digital humanism which takes down those walls and claims a new space for scholarship and public intellectualism."[14] This cannot happen unless our methodologies with data remain transparent.

Case Study: Becoming Users and Communities of Data

Our theoretical and prescriptive remarks thus far will benefit from a concrete example—in this case, one that explores the history of the user. The notion of the user has become ubiquitous. We live in an era of usernames, user experiences, and user-centered design; we tacitly sign end user license agreements when we install software; we read user guides to figure out how to get our software to do what we want. But our omnipresent conception of ourselves as users obscures the history of the term.

Of course, it now takes only seconds to follow this line of inquiry (the history of a term) and see the relationship between the presence of that term and any other similar terms, as Google's Ngram Viewer allows anyone to chart the frequency of words or phrases across a subset of the digitized Google Books corpus.[15]

Needless to say, the chart in figure 6 is not historical evidence of sufficient (if any) rigor to support historical knowledge claims about what is or is not a user. (See the original image in the web version of this essay at http://WritingHistory.trincoll.edu.) For one thing, Google's data is proprietary, and exactly what comprises it is unclear. Perhaps more important, this graph does not indicate anything interesting about *why* usage of the term *user* spiked as it did—the real question that historians want to answer. But these are not reasons to discard the tool or to avoid writing about it. Historians might well start framing research questions this way, with quick uses of the Ngram Viewer or other tools. Conventionally, this work would remain invisible, and only "real" data would appear in published work, to support an argument of influence or causation. But foregrounding such preliminary work (like Ngram charts) will help readers to understand the genesis of the question, flag possible framework errors, and identify category mistakes, and it will perhaps inspire them to think about how such techniques might benefit their own work.

To investigate the term *user* in more detail, one can use other online corpora to generate a series of radically different interpretive views. For example, searching in the Time Magazine Corpus allows one to see all of the collocates (words that appear within a specified number of words from

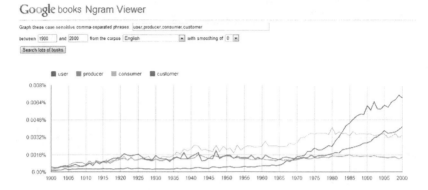

Fig. 6. Google Books Ngram view of the frequency of selected words (*user, producer, consumer, customer*) from 1900 to 2000

the search term) and to display counts by decade.[16] A resulting list of the words that appear most often within a four-word window of the term *user* makes it easy to see that the word *drug* appears within four words of *user* thirty-two times. (See the image in the web version of this essay at http://WritingHistory.trincoll.edu.) To better make sense of these results, the collocates can be coded into two categories: those that have to do with drugs and those that have to do with technology. A spreadsheet created to chart these results drew attention to patterns in the data via cell highlighting to differentiate terms with two hits from those with more than two hits.

On the whole, this charting of collocates of "users" lends itself to some quick observations. For example, as far as the keywords in the Time Magazine Corpus suggest, the growth around the term *user* happened for drugs a bit earlier than for technology, although the latter context came to be the predominant one. We can also see that one of the first technology terms to appear is *telephone*, which perhaps suggests that the rise in usage of the term *user* may have may have to do less with the rise of computing (our typical conception of it now) than with the rise of networks.

Going beyond the data—making sense of it—can be facilitated by additional expertise in ways that our usually much more naturally circumscribed historical data has generally not required. Owens blogged about this research while it was in progress, describing what he was interested in, how he got his data, and how he was working with it, as well as providing a link for others to explore and download the data.[17] Over the next week, the post was viewed over two hundred times; twenty-two researchers and librarians tweeted about the post. Most important, Owens received several substantive comments from scholars and researchers. These ranged from encouragements to explore technical guides, scholarship on the notion of the reader in the context of the history of the book, and suggestions for different prepositions that could further elucidate semantic relationships about "users." This discussion resulted from Owens having foregrounded his initial forays into data online, where it was easy to give different views of his data. Sharing preliminary representations of data, providing some preliminary interpretations of them, and inviting others to consider how best to make sense of the data at hand quickly sparked a substantive scholarly conversation. This is not to say that we should expect everyone to help with our own research. But because we have so much raw data that ranges widely over typical disciplinary boundaries, a collaborative approach is even more essential to making sense of data, and it benefits everyone involved, as the discussants can learn about data and methodologies that might be useful in their own work.

In addition to accelerating research, foregrounding methodology and (access to) data gives rise to a constellation of questions that are becoming increasingly relevant for historians. How far, for example, can expressions of data like Google's Ngram Viewer be used in historical work? Although a chart from historical data should not be automatically admitted as historical evidence in itself, it certainly *can* be used to identify curious phenomena that are unlikely to be artifacts of the data or viewer alone. But how does one cite data without "black-boxy" mathematical reductions and bring the data itself into the realm of scholarly discourse? How does one show, for example, that uses of the term *sinful* in the nineteenth century appear predominantly in sermon and other exegetical literature in the early part of the century but become overshadowed by more secular references later in the century? Typically, this would be illustrated with pithy, anecdotal examples taken to be representative of the phenomenon. But does this adequately represent the research methodology? Does it allow anyone to investigate for themselves or to learn from the methodology?

It would be far better to explain the steps used to collect and reformat the data; ideally, the data would be available for download. The plain text file that was reformatted to show the aforementioned linguistic shift in the usage of *sinful* would be considerably useful for other researchers, who, in turn, would certainly make other observations and draw new and perhaps contradictory conclusions. Exposed data allow us to approach interesting questions from multiple and interdisciplinary points of view, in the way that citations to textual sources do not. Again, we are arguing not for wholly replacing close readings and textual analysis in historical research but, rather, for complementing them with our explorations of data. As it becomes easier and easier for historians to explore and play with data, it becomes essential for us to reflect on how we should incorporate this exploration and play as part of our research and writing practices. Is there a better way than to simply provide the raw data and an explanation of how to witness the same phenomenon? Is this the twenty-first century footnote?

Conclusions

Overall, there has been no aversion to using data in historical research. But historians have started to use data on new scales and to combine different kinds of data that range widely over typical disciplinary boundaries. The ease and increasing presence of data, in terms of both digitized and increasingly born-digital research materials, mean that the historian—irrespective of historical field—faces new methodological challenges. Approaching these materials in a context-sensitive way requires substantial amounts of time and energy devoted to understanding and exploring the particular ways and the degree of precision with which we can interpret data. Consequently, we have argued that historians should deliberately and explicitly share examples of how they are finding and manipulating data in their research, with greater methodological transparency, to promote the spirit of humanistic inquiry and interpretation.

We have also argued that working with and writing about data does not mean that historians need to shoulder the kinds of epistemological burdens that underpin many of the tools that statisticians or quantitative historians have developed. This is not to say that statistics are not a useful tool for inquiry. But the mere act of working with data does not obligate the historian to rely on abstract data analysis. Historical data might require little more than simple frequency counts, simple correlations, or reformatting to make it useful to the historian looking for anomalies, trends, or unusual but meaningful coincidences.

To argue against the necessity of mathematical complexity is also to suggest that it is a mistake to treat data as self-evident or that data implicitly constitute historical argument or proof. Historians must treat data as text, which needs to be approached from multiple points of view and as openly as possible. Working with data can be playful and exploratory, and useful techniques should be shared as readily as research discoveries.

While typical history scholarship has largely kept methodology and data manipulation in the background, new approaches to writing can complement more traditional methods and venues and thus avoid some of their well-documented limitations, especially as those new approaches enable sharing data in a variety of forms.

To best use the new kinds of historical data that have opened up new avenues of inquiry for virtually every historical specialty, gathering data, manipulating it, representing it, and, of course, writing about it should be required of all historians in training—not just those in digital history or new media courses. Of course, not all research projects will require facility with data. But just as historians learn to find, collect, organize, and make sense of the traditional sources, they also need to learn to acquire, manipulate, analyze, and represent data. Access to historical sources makes the historical record look rather different in the twenty-first century than it ever has before. Writing about history needs to evolve as well.

Notes

1. The authors prefer to use the term *data* as a singular mass noun, referring not to multiple datum but to the historical record that can be represented as digital text. Such usage parallels our use of the term *text* as comprising all relevant texts.

2. Jean-Baptiste Michel, Yuan Kui Shen, Aviva Presser Aiden, Adrian Veres, Matthew K. Gray, The Google Books Team, Joseph P. Pickett, et al., "Quantitative Analysis of Culture Using Millions of Digitized Books," *Science* 331, no. 6014 (2011): 176–82.

3. Michael Witmore and Jonathan Hope, "Shakespeare by the Numbers: On the Linguistic Texture of the Late Plays," in *Early Modern Tragicomedy*, ed. Subha Mukherji and Raphael Lyne (Cambridge: D. S. Brewer, 2007).

4. Stanford Literary Lab, http://litlab.stanford.edu/; Digging into Data Challenge, Office of Digital Humanities, National Endowment for the Humanities, http://www.diggingintodata.org/.

5. For a more detailed history of cliometrics and its impact on the digital humanities, see William G. Thomas III, "Computing and the Historical Imagination," in *A Companion to Digital Humanities*, ed. Susan Schreibman, Raymond George Siemens, and John M. Unsworth (Oxford: Blackwell, 2004).

6. Martin Jessop, "Digital Visualization as a Scholarly Activity," *Literary and Linguistic Computing* 23, no. 3 (2008): 281–93 (quotation from 282).

7. Johanna Drucker, "Graphesis: Visual Knowledge Production and Representation," *Poetess Archive Journal* 2, no. 1 (2010), http://paj.muohio.edu/paj/index.php/paj/article/view/4.

8. Access to Archival Databases, National Archives, http://aad.archives.gov/aad/; Google Fusion Tables, http://www.google.com/fusiontables/public/tour/index.html.

9. Stephen Ramsay, "The Hermeneutics of Screwing Around; or What You

Do with a Million Books," (paper presented at the conference "Playing with Technology in History," History Education Network/Histoire et Éducation en Réseau, Niagara-on-the-Lake, Canada, April 2010), http://www.playingwithhistory.com/wp-content/uploads/2010/04/hermeneutics.pdf.

10. *The Proceedings of the Old Bailey, 1674–1913*, http://www.oldbaileyonline.org; Fred Gibbs, "Beware the Coffee," *With Criminal Intent*, March 29, 2011, http://criminalintent.org/2011/03/beware-the-coffee/.

11. John Unsworth, "Documenting the Reinvention of Text: The Importance of Failure," *Journal of Electronic Publishing* 3, no. 2 (1997), http://dx.doi.org/10.3998/3336451.0003.201.

12. Tim Sherratt and Bethany Nowviskie, comments on "The Hermeneutics of Data and Historical Writing," in *Writing History in the Digital Age*, web-book ed., Fall 2011 version.

13. Julia Flanders, "Data and Wisdom: Electronic Editing and the Quantification of Knowledge," *Literary and Linguistic Computing* 24, no. 1 (2009): 53–62.

14. Dave Perry, "Be Online or Be Irrelevant: Thoughts on Emerging Media and Higher Education," *AcademHack*, January 11, 2010, http://academhack.outsidethetext.com/home/2010/be-online-or-be-irrelevant/.

15. Google Books Ngram Viewer, http://books.google.com/ngrams.

16. Time Magazine Corpus, Brigham Young University, http://corpus.byu.edu/time/.

17. Trevor Owens, "When Did We Become Users?," August 5, 2011, http://www.trevorowens.org/2011/08/when-did-we-become-users/.

PART 5

See What I Mean? Visual, Spatial, and Game-Based History

Digital scholarship allows historians to integrate visually rich source materials and interactivity into our writing, and several of the contributors to this volume took the opportunity to demonstrate their work and reflect on how it is changing our field. In "Visualizations and Historical Arguments," John Theibault presents a broad overview of how charts and maps have influenced historical thinking from the birth of nineteenth-century social science to today's processor-intensive digital era. Next, Stephen Robertson's essay "Putting Harlem on the Map" recounts how he and his colleagues used spatial history tools to reconstruct the material lives of residents in this predominantly black New York City neighborhood during the 1920s, with examples of how these maps reshaped his historical analysis and writing. Finally, in "Pox and the City: Challenges in Writing a Digital History Game," Laura Zucconi, Ethan Watrall, Hannah Ueno, and Lisa Rosner offer an insiders' view of the storytelling and design challenges they face in creating a role-playing historical simulation on the invention of the smallpox vaccine in nineteenth-century Scotland.

Visualizations and Historical Arguments

John Theibault

The popular aphorism "A picture is worth a thousand words" is a relatively recent coinage, but the idea that images can be an effective complement to or substitute for written description, narrative, or analysis is probably as old as writing itself. In the European tradition, illuminated manuscripts and incunabula incorporated images, some of which conveyed messages related to the text and some of which were mere adornments. By the late sixteenth century, linkage of image and print reached a kind of apotheosis with the publication of emblem books, in which each page consisted of an image, a motto, and a pithy verse that jointly communicated moral precepts.[1] Western historians have always made use of visualizations in this broad sense. Reproductions of pictures of the main biographical figures referenced in a book or of other objects that figured prominently in the narrative appear in many historical works. Though the connection of these illustrations to the arguments of the book were often implicit rather than explicit, the text sometimes drew direct attention to elements of the pictures, so that the reader's understanding was enhanced by close attention to the images.

When the term *visualization* is used today, it usually refers to an image that is derived from processing information—often, but not always, statistical information—and that presents the information more efficiently than regular text could. Scholars quickly recognized the potential of computers to help process information and display the results in an easily interpreted format. David Staley has argued for a sharp distinction between visualizations as "the organization of meaningful information in two- or three-dimensional spatial form intended to further a systematic inquiry" and images as a "supplement or illustration to a written account."[2] Staley's definition implies two distinct uses for visualizations in the digital age: as a means of quickly identifying patterns in large datasets during the research process, which can open new lines of research and test qualitative assumptions; and as a way to enhance the presentation of arguments, moving beyond what it is possible to display in two dimensions on paper. Visualizations created for the first use may or may not appear in visual form in the final product. This essay is primarily concerned with visualizations as historical arguments in the second sense: how do we deploy the visual capabilities of the computer to *show* what we wish to communicate? It is slightly more ecumenical in defining visualizations than Staley is, in that it sees as forms of visual argument all uses of visual information to communicate an argument or narrative beyond the meaning of the words in text. It argues that visualizations necessarily have a rhetorical dimension and that the principal challenge facing historians who wish to use visualizations in their work is to align the rhetoric with the audience's ability to follow it. (See the images in the web version of this essay at http://WritingHistory. trincoll.edu.)

The key dimensions of a visualization are the density and the transparency of its information. Density is the sheer amount of useful information the visualization conveys, and transparency is the ease with which that information can be understood by the reader. We have become so accustomed to the visual vocabulary of print books that we scarcely register the visual conventions on which almost all historical work relies, such as the footnote indicated by a small number or asterisk. By now, we are also perhaps so familiar with standard web-page layouts that we no longer notice most of the visual cues that indicate the site structure, especially the relation of one page to another achieved by hyperlink. But many historians still have a print mentality when it comes to information-dense graphics. When designing graphics, authors have to consider how much background information the reader brings to the visualization. The development of more complex visualizations has increased the gaps between expert and novice interpreters, which raises challenges for historians who seek the most effective visual approach.

The problem of information density in visualizations is not a new one for historians. Even the most conventional nineteenth-century political histories made use of three important visualizations: maps, time lines, and dynastic charts. It is, after all, much easier and more informative to create a chart of lines of descent to the kings of France than it is to describe the lineage in paragraphs of "begats." Each of these forms of visualization evolved a distinct visual vocabulary, with periods of experimentation and innovation producing visualization schemes that most modern historians now find completely transparent, with earlier visual dead ends now completely forgotten. Daniel Rosenberg and Anthony Grafton have recently shown how experimentation with designs of chronologies helped produce the modern streamlined edition of the time line and information-rich variants by the end of the eighteenth century.[3]

The emergence of the social sciences in the nineteenth century and the ability to work with large datasets created demand for new ways of visualizing information, beyond maps, time lines, and genealogical charts. Processed numerical information was best expressed in tables, charts, and graphs. Mathematics, natural sciences, and social sciences that employed statistics were at the forefront of the development of charts and graphs. History was a consumer, not a designer, of most of these new visualizations— and mostly a sparing consumer at that, since economic and social history lagged behind political history as an area of research. Simple charts and graphs, such as pie charts, line graphs, and histograms, were not difficult to interpret, and their visual conventions became part of what any ordinary reader would be expected to follow. As statistical analysis became more sophisticated, the visualizations that resulted became more and more central to the argument. In some cases, the visualization made interpretation possible. These success stories demonstrated the worth of statistical analysis and visualization. Perhaps the most notable example is John Snow's map of the incidence of cholera in an 1854 London outbreak, which helped plot the source of the outbreak at a single water pump in the neighborhood.[4] Snow's cholera map showed that visualizations could serve as both narrative and analysis. Authors began to experiment with ways of using visual clues to tell complex stories about events, increasing the amount of information that could be conveyed in a small space and thereby overcoming the limitations of two dimensions in print.

A noteworthy example of innovative presentation occurs in Charles Joseph Minard's 1869 *Carte Figurative des pertes successives en hommes de l'Armée Française dans la campagne de Russie 1812–1813*, which portrays the advance and retreat of French troops in Russia on a scale map, showing the changing size of the force due to death and desertion through the thickness of the line representing the force.[5] The conditions confronting the troops during the retreat are also illustrated by a time line of winter temperatures, graphically connected to the map-based chart. Though Minard was a civil engineer, not a historian, he was able to construct a very powerful single-page narrative of the events of Napoleon's march. Minard's chart

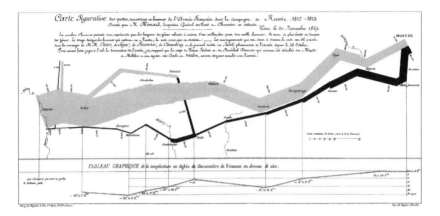

Fig. 7. *Carte Figurative*, by Charles Joseph Minard

is often cited as a model example of information visualization because it is easy to understand, even for people with little background information on the topic or quantitative skills. The challenge for visualization is to be transparent, accurate, and rich in information. Minard's information-rich visualizations set the standard for both transparency and accuracy in the kind of work that could be done before computerization.

As noted already, historians were mostly consumers of statistics-based visualizations from the social sciences, rather than innovators in constructing new kinds of visualizations. The advent of cliometrics and Annaliste total history in the 1960s forced more historians to become conversant with quantitative methods. Though the Annaliste approach to total history predated widespread use of the computer, much of the first wave of social scientific history relied on statistical packages like SPSS and SAS to process large amounts of data. The most determinedly quantitative works often had several pages of tables, most of which would be referenced in the text, though not always at the precise page that made the link between text and table most obvious. Instead of working as a driver of narrative, many of the tables and graphs produced in quantitative works of the 1960s, 1970s, and 1980s sat inert on the page, functioning more like the biographical pictures included in early historical works than as an integral part of the argument. Toggling between explication and evidence slowed reading considerably, so much so that readers of quantitative histories of the era sometimes broke into two broad groups: those who read the text and assumed the charts and graphs confirmed what was said there and those who read the charts and graphs while paying scant regard to the text. To be sure, many more historians developed the ability to rapidly interpret a greater variety of statistical representations. A researcher using a scatter plot with a line of best fit or a Lorenz curve comparing inequalities might reasonably expect that most readers would be persuaded by the results visible in the charts, without requiring significant textual explication. But most social histories continued to rely primarily on bar and line graphs as their most prominent visualizations. The fact that the statistical tools deployed often embedded assumptions that were inapplicable to the messiness of actual historical processes lent a false aura of scientific precision to very tentative conclusions. Many explanations have been offered for the relative decline of social history since its heyday in the 1970s. A failure of imagination in the integration of visualizations with text-based arguments may have contributed to the decline.[6]

While historians debated how to incorporate statistical methods into scholarship, statisticians were becoming more self-conscious about how the results of analysis were being used. This concern with how quantitative information was presented first came to the attention of most humanities scholars with the publications of Edward Tufte in the 1980s. His three key works—*The Visual Display of Quantitative Information* (1983), *Envisioning Information* (1990), and *Visual Explanations* (1997)—placed the aesthetics and explanatory power of graphs and charts under closer scrutiny.[7] Tufte was most responsible for renewing attention to Minard's *Carte Figurative*. Tufte's main target in his books was what he called "chartjunk," unnecessary clutter and contrived images that made visualizations confusing and sometimes deliberately misleading. Chartjunk was mostly associated with news and business publications in what today are called "infographics." Historians, like social scientists writing for scholarly publications, tended to avoid visual embellishments of charts and graphs, but they did have to be attentive to ensuring that legends were clear enough that readers were not deceived by how information was displayed. Even accurate information can mislead if it is presented in a way that creates false visual cues. For example, inexperienced readers might need some guidance with a logarithmic chart so that they do not mistake an exponential change for a linear one. Sometimes, visualizations can be shaped to seem more conclusive than the underlying data actually warrant. For example, if a line graph showing differences ranging from 65 percent to 85 percent has its baseline set at 50 percent rather than zero, it leads people to see the differences in values as starker than they actually are. These issues of what one might call rhetorical honesty in the formulation of visualizations were compounded for historians and other humanists by the hard choices that were required to generate the data to be processed in the first place. As Gibbs and Owens note in their contribution to this volume, historians have traditionally been told to mask the twists and turns of the research process in their finished work, to make their argument as strong as possible.[8] This traditional approach can make any visualization seem like the product of a black box. Their proposal to share both data and methods in as transparent a manner as possible can have the additional benefit of making those visualizations easier to understand, because the logic of how and why they were generated is visible.

Information-rich maps are a particularly good example of the challenge of balancing honesty in visual rhetoric and clarity and persuasiveness. One often has to come to a map visualization with sufficient background information to "read through" peculiarities of delivery. For example, maps of presidential elections that appear in almost any textbook of American history typically color in each state according to which candidate received the electoral votes. It is understood that the visual impact of the color contrast might over- or understate how close the vote actually was. Some states are large in area but small in population; others are the other way around. There are ways to make maps that account for those differences. For example, a cartogram adjusts the size of geographical areas to make them proportional to their populations, while a choropleth map uses shadings of color to indicate the strength of the victory in a given area.[9] The two adjustments, cartogram and choropleth, can be combined to further the information density. Unfortunately, the distortions of the cartogram when combined with the choropleth can also make the information harder, rather than easier, to interpret, without a very high level of prior knowledge. This raises the question whether it is hard to interpret such a visualization because the format of combining cartogram and choropleth is unfamiliar or because it makes unreasonable demands on the background information of the reader. Most historians have probably encountered a choropleth map and a cartogram in a print history book or contemporary source in the course of their research but probably have not encountered the two combined.

The question whether a visualization is hard to interpret because it is unfamiliar or because it relies on unrealistic expectations of background information assumes greater importance because digitization allows for even greater information density and novelty of form. Geospatial locating of information has been one of the richest areas of development in digital humanities. Complex visualizations based on maps are emerging as part of a "geospatial turn" in the humanities.[10] One particular way that geospatial information density can increase is by animating it, adding time as another dimension of visualization. Just as a map can make one inch equal one mile, an animated time line can make one second equal one year. A simple combination of an animated map and a time line can create a powerful narrative without any text at all. A brilliant example of this is Isao Hashimoto's animated map of the 2,053 nuclear explosions between 1945 and 1998, which dramatically narrates the contours of the nuclear age.[11] Aside from the title, there is no background information associated with the animation. The only text in the piece is in the legend, which emerges as each new nuclear power first explodes a device. Sound, not words, is used as a second way of highlighting the data points. Yet, despite the absence of background information text, almost anyone watching the animation will come away with a deep understanding of the key features of the nuclear age. Only a modest background knowledge (such as knowing who the main antagonists in the Cold War were) makes the presentation of what might seem dry factoids not only informative but moving.

Hashimoto's animation of nuclear testing cannot be manipulated by the user, aside from pausing and resuming the animation. Edward Ayers has coined the term *cinematic maps* to describe map-based animations that show the process of change over time.[12] The University of Richmond's Digital Scholarship Lab has taken the traditional maps of presidential elections from 1840 to 2008 and turned them into an animated sequence.[13] These maps try to overcome the information distortions caused by population differences and the electoral college, by providing not only county-level votes but a dot density map that shows the aggregated votes of five hundred voters. Instead of adjusting the size of the geographical area to make it fit the voting pattern, the dot pattern reflects the density of votes in each region. Still, it is easy to imagine how this information could be converted to cartograms and choropleth maps of presidential elections to tell yet another story about changing voting patterns over the decades.

As part of Stanford University's Spatial History Project, online visualizations have been created to accompany Richard White's recent book on the development of the transcontinental railroad.[14] This project is particularly interesting for understanding the impact of digital humanities on current historical practice, because it is directly associated with a print work and seems likely to serve as a template for future hybrid productions of print and digital. It is also closely aligned with a still more expansive set of visualizations from the Stanford Spatial History Project that relate to the themes of the book, collected under the heading *Shaping the West*.[15]

There are twenty-six different visualizations included at the site, sixteen of which are animated. Not unexpectedly, several of the animations simply plot space and time, like the animations previously described. But others complicate the visualization by layering information in innovative ways. For example, one visualization reframes shipping distances in California in terms of not just track length but also time to delivery and cost. Even though the animations have been created as an accompaniment to an academic work, they offer an interactive opportunity to the reader that those other animations do not. Readers can customize the presentation of data to isolate issues of particular interest to them, rather than depending on the author to frame the question being answered. Interactive engagement with a visualization is yet another innovation made possible by digitization.

As historians ask more complex questions about the data they have assembled, the problem of how best to present the information requires more thought. On the *Shaping the West* site, each visualization has an "About" or "Help" tab that functions as a legend and guide to the information contained in the site. The visualizations are not self-explanatory. A particularly complex visualization links the geography of the railroads with a network diagram of the boards of directors and sources of capital for each. The "About" tab for that visualization includes a "How to Read" statement for the graphic. Such "How to Read" statements recognize that the visual vocabulary of innovative sites may not be familiar enough to make an argument without further explication of methods.

Undoubtedly the biggest advocate for the rhetorical power of statistical animations that incorporate interactive features is the Swedish statistician Hans Rosling. Using a tool called Gapminder, he has created an animation of life expectancy at birth and per capita GDP since 1800 for all countries, to demonstrate the evolution of world health.[16] One can "play" Rosling's animation in a noninteractive mode to see the story he tells. Color coding differentiates countries in different parts of the world. If one scrolls over the circles on the chart, one can see which country each represents. Circles vary in size depending on the population of the country and on change in size over time in response to population growth, so the reasonably well-informed viewer can quickly locate major countries like China, India, and the United States even without scrolling over the circles. The animation contains deep layering of information that is easy to interpret, even without an extensive background. In videos where he talks about the data, Rosling shows that the information illustrates a dramatic narrative of the convergence of the world on higher levels of health and wealth, but the point comes across perfectly clearly even without verbal accompaniment.[17]

Rosling draws on an extremely rich database, and readers are able to customize the display of information according to their own interests. One tab allows readers to orient the circles on a map of the world rather than on two axes of a chart. Another allows readers to choose which country's data to include or not include in the animation. If one wants to isolate countries from a single continent or countries that start out a similar size, one can do so. One can also adjust the time line to focus on narrower periods where crucial changes might be taking place, instead of having to go through the entire time span for "big picture" changes. Because of this option for customization, Rosling's project both makes an argument that is explicit in the first animation one sees and provides the basis for a reader's further exploration of his or her own interests. While the kind of graphs used by Rosling were developed prior to the web, they posed real challenges of presentation and interpretation in the two-dimensional format of print. Animation increases their interpretive force dramatically.

Animation and reader control of the data stream are not the only ways in which digitization affects interpretation. Websites are new enough that there are still opportunities to subvert standard expectations and make readers more attentive to how visual cues structure an argument (in ways that are much less costly than trying to subvert visual cues in print media). A good example is Whitney Trettien's "Computers, Cut-Ups, and Combinatory Volvelles: An Archaeology of Text-Generating Mechanisms,"[18] which encourages a nonlinear reading of her argument about nonlinear texts. The front page of the site does not offer a table of contents or an obvious sequential path through the material. It has a grid of fourteen by twenty-one white squares that light up and change color either when scrolled over or when specific pages of text are clicked. Color coding allows readers to see which sections of the website deal with specific themes, creating a second way of envisioning the argument. Physical proximity of squares and color groupings work together to create a structure to the argument that is as easy to see as it is to read. Interestingly, the idea of color coding in a grid format was presaged in Elizabeth Peabody's nineteenth-century *Universal History: Arranged to Illustrate Bem's Charts of Chronology.*[19] Trettien's experiment with a visual "breadcrumb trail" makes it possible to reimagine how arguments can be presented in an environment where the reader controls what page to turn to next.

As Peabody's work shows, it is possible to use color as a visual cue in print texts, but it is generally prohibitively expensive. Online, color is both efficient and cost-free. A superb example of using color to highlight relationships in text is Ben Fry's concordance of the six editions of Charles Darwin's *Origin of Species* completed in his lifetime.[20] The original text is represented by each sentence being compressed into a single line. The reader can scroll over each line to get a text box of the sentence. The additions in subsequent editions are represented by different colored lines. The colors allow one to quickly grasp, for example, that chapter 4 was most extensively revised in the third and fifth editions, while chapter 6 was most extensively revised in the fourth edition. Dramatic changes are visible because of tiny lines of color. This same principle is taken up in the WordSeer project at the University of California, Berkeley. The WordSeer researchers have digitized a corpus of printed slave narratives and compressed each narrative to a single bar of a heat map. One can search for words across all of the narratives and see how frequently they turn up in each of the paragraphs, represented by lines within each bar.[21] Color, brightness, and lines and bars thus become powerful ways of making interpretive leaps about texts, as long as one has the background knowledge to understand the implications of the visualization.

Much historical writing is implicitly or explicitly about network connections, but historians are less familiar with how social scientists have been visualizing networks than they are with standard statistical visualizations. The *Mapping the Republic of Letters* project at Stanford University shows how network visualizations can be used in historical work.[22] It overlays a networked map of correspondents on the actual map of Europe, with each link in the visualization representing a letter sent between an author at one location and a reader at another. The network described at *Mapping the Republic of Letters* is personal rather than conceptual, as was the network of railroad boards of directors previously mentioned. The railroad visualization was more complicated, because the nodes of the network were not linked to a map but were a pure visualization of relationships. The online prototype of visualizations of network relationships is Thinkmap's *Visual Thesaurus*, which allows readers to move from node to node in pursuit of related concepts.[23] Visualizing networks poses several dangers for historians. First of all, a network theory of graphs adheres to mathematical principles that have little relation to lived human experiences. In an effective network visualization, the location of nodes is not predetermined but is specified by the nature of the links between them. If you remove one source of links from the analysis, the location of nodes may become different. As one undertakes a more complicated kind of network analysis in the mode of *Visual Thesaurus*, it is more likely that following any single link trail can quickly get one lost in the thicket of concepts. Unless one understands the algorithms being used to create the nodes, it is extraordinarily difficult to understand why nodes are in a specific relationship to one another. Thus network analysis demands the kind of "hermeneutics of data" advocated by Gibbs and Owens in this volume. But even when the concepts and relationships being illustrated are relatively straightforward, the task of visualizing them can prove complicated by the volume of connections being analyzed. The sheer density of nodes can make it hard to single out factors that might interest the reader. For example, in the network visualization of those scholars who make up the "vizosphere" (the leading edge of discussion about the future of visualizations), there is a barely differentiated blob of circles instead of a clear pattern of lines between sites.[24]

Innovative visualizations have entered the mainstream of online user experience in the professions and social sciences. Just as SPSS, SAS, and, later, R were created to enable basic statistical analysis, programs like Gephi have been created to undertake network analysis. In the wake of Tufte's work, numerous authors now write about information design, though again mostly targeting a business and journalism audience. Every day, sites like FlowingData highlight innovative uses of visualization to make new arguments, such as PeopleMovin, which illustrates migration flows between countries.[25] It is clear from these sites that people are still expanding the realm of the possible in visualizing information. Looking over these visualizations, even when they are not explicitly historical, will give historians strategies for making more powerful arguments to complement and sometimes even substitute for text. But the task of building those arguments will have to include educating fellow historians about how to interpret visualizations. As we have already noted, it can be very difficult for the uninitiated historian to intuit relationships between entities in a network analysis when they are put into a visualization scheme. Yet networks are often at the center of questions of greatest interest to historians. To the extent that the difficulties in interpreting innovative visualizations like interactive network diagrams are caused by a simple lack of familiarity with them, they can be overcome by building more such sites. To the extent that they are caused by a lack of background knowledge to understand the cues, creators of such sites will have to learn to build new ways of incorporating that background information as economically, in the use of text, as possible. In either case, at some point, historians will have to accustom themselves to "reading" network diagrams as adeptly as they read maps or scatter plots.

Notes

1. The English Emblem Book Project, Pennsylvania State University, http://emblem.libraries.psu.edu/.

2. David J. Staley, *Computers, Visualization, and History* (Armonk, NY: M. E. Sharpe, 2003), 9.

3. Daniel Rosenberg and Anthony Grafton, *Cartographies of Time: A History of the Timeline* (Princeton: Princeton Architectural Press, 2010).

4. Steven Johnson, *The Ghost Map* (New York: Riverhead, 2006).

5. Arthur H. Robinson, "The Thematic Maps of Charles Joseph Minard," *Imago Mundi* 21 (1967): 95–108.

6. One can overstate the degree of that decline. *Social history* was always something of a grab-bag term that included nonquantitative approaches. Nevertheless, the relative decline of social history in comparison to cultural history is unmistakable. See Robert B. Townsend, "Decline of the West or Rise of the Rest?," *Perspectives on History*, September 2011, http://www.historians.org/perspectives/issues/2011/1109/1109pro1.cfm.

7. Edward Tufte, *The Visual Display of Quantitative Information* (Cheshire, CT: Graphics Press, 1983), Edward Tufte, *Envisioning Information* (Cheshire, CT: Graphics Press, 1990), Edward Tufte, *Visual Explanations* (Cheshire, CT: Graphics Press, 1997).

8. Fred Gibbs and Trevor Owens, "The Hermeneutics of Data and Historical Writing," in this volume.

9. Mark Newman, a physicist at the University of Michigan, gives a good overview of the uses of cartograms and choropleth maps for analyzing the 2008 election returns at the level of state and county voting, at http://www-personal.umich.edu/~mejn/election/2008/. Examples include a simple cartogram of county-level results and a choropleth cartogram of the same results.

10. Joanna Guldi, "What Is the Spatial Turn?" *Spatial Humanities*, Institute for Enabling Geospatial Scholarship, Scholars' Lab, University of Virginia, http://spatial.scholarslab.org/spatial-turn/.

11. Isao Hashimoto, "1945–1998," Preparatory Commission for the Comprehensive Nuclear-Test-Ban Treaty Organization (CTBCO), 2003, http://www.ctbto.org/specials/1945–1998-by-isao-hashimoto/.

12. Edward Ayers, "Turning towards Place, Space, and Time," in *The Spatial Humanities: GIS and the Future of Humanities Scholarship*, ed. David J. Bodenhamer, John Corrigan, and Trevor M. Harris (Bloomington: Indiana University Press, 2010), 1–13.

13. "Elections, 1840–2008," *Voting America: United States Politics, 1840–2008*, Digital Scholarship Lab, University of Richmond, 2010, http://dsl.richmond.edu/voting/elections.html.

14. Richard White, *Railroaded* (New York: W. W. Norton, 2011); Toral Patel et al., "Visualization: Transcontinental Railroad Development, 1879–1893," Spatial History Project, Stanford University, http://www.stanford.edu/group/spatialhistory/cgi-bin/site/viz.php?id=341&project_id=0.

15. *Shaping the West*, Spatial History Project, Stanford University, http://www.stanford.edu/group/spatialhistory/cgi-bin/site/project.php?id=997.

16. Hans Rosling, "Wealth and Health of Nations," Gapminder, http://www.gapminder.org/world/.

17. "Hans Rosling Shows the Best Stats You've Ever Seen," TED Talk, 2006,

http://www.ted.com/talks/hans_rosling_shows_the_best_stats_you_ve_ever_seen.html.

18. Whitney Trettien, "Computers, Cut-Ups, and Combinatory Volvelles: An Archaeology of Text-Generating Mechanisms," http://whitneyannetrettien.com/thesis/.

19. Elizabeth Peabody, *Universal History: Arranged to Illustrate Bem's Charts of Chronology* (New York, 1859), referred from http://beineckeroom26.library.yale.edu/2011/09/02/visualizing-history/.

20. Ben Fry, "On the Origin of Species: The Preservation of Favoured Traces," http://benfry.com/traces/.

21. WordSeer, "Search Slave Narratives," University of California, Berkeley, http://wordseer.berkeley.edu/slave_narratives/heatmap.php.

22. *Mapping the Republic of Letters*, Stanford University, https://republicofletters.stanford.edu/#maps.

23. Thinkmap, *Visual Thesaurus*, http://www.visualthesaurus.com/.

24. Moritz Stefaner, "Vizosphere," http://www.visualizing.org/full-screen/29391.

25. Nathan Yau, FlowingData, http://flowingdata.com; PeopleMovin: Migration Flows Across the World, http://peoplemov.in/.

Putting Harlem on the Map

Stephen Robertson

Beginning in 1904, black New Yorkers relocated their residences, churches, and businesses to the streets around the new subway station at 135th Street and Lenox Avenue in Harlem. Waves of African American migrants from the South and immigrants from the Caribbean joined them, creating a community in which blacks resided segregated from whites. By 1920, the area occupied almost exclusively by blacks stretched south to 130th Street, north to 144th Street, and from Fifth Avenue across to Eighth Avenue, encompassing a population of some seventy-three thousand people. In the next decade, Harlem became the "Negro Mecca" (a more cosmopolitan place than America's other "black metropolis," Chicago), deserving of the title "the world's black capital." By 1930, the black population, now numbering around two hundred thousand, had spilled over 8th Avenue to Amsterdam Avenue, and blacks were living as far north as 160th Street and approaching 110th Street to the south. Of course, Harlem's status was about more than simply size or numbers. Harlem was home to the political and cultural leaders of black America: the New York Urban League and Garvey's Universal Negro Improvement Association (UNIA) had their headquarters there; writers Langston Hughes, Wallace Thurman, and Zora Neale Hurston all lodged in the same building; and Duke Ellington and Ethel Waters performed in the neighborhood's clubs and theaters.[1]

The picture of Harlem that I have presented so far is in line with those you would find setting the scene for most studies of the neighborhood or offering a snapshot in some broader account. After six years of using digital geospatial tools to study Harlem, I am struck by how much that picture omits and how little sense of the place it conveys. If urban history is defined by a concern with particular places and spaces, it has long been satisfied with a large-scale or very selective treatment of physical locations. Certainly, when three colleagues and I conceived a collaborative study of everyday life in Harlem in the 1920s, we largely took the place as a given. Our central concern was to identify ordinary blacks, residents other than those familiar from the ever-expanding literature on the Harlem Renaissance and the beginnings of the civil rights movement. In fact, only when we headed to the archives did we even confront having to precisely define the neighborhood's boundaries.[2] (See additional images in the web version of this essay at http://WritingHistory.trincoll.edu.)

The digital tools we used to manage what we found in the archives changed how I thought about Harlem. Our core sources consisted of almost three thousand case files containing accounts of crimes by or involving blacks, as well as hundreds of pages from black newspapers. I had used a simple FileMaker database to organize similar material in a previous project and proposed that we develop a more sophisticated online database for this material, so that all the collaborators could share and use it. In addition, since our research concerned a neighborhood and since legal records almost invariably include information on locations, I envisioned our database as linked to maps. A geographic information system (GIS) offered that combination of a database and a mapping system, and with only a general idea of how such software worked and what it could do, I imagined using it to re-create several key blocks in Harlem. I was imagining this in 2002, when the existing historical GIS projects employed desktop ArcGIS software developed for social scientists, relied on quantitative data, and could not easily be shared online.[3] The designers and programmers who we employed, from the University of Sydney's Archaeological Computing Laboratory (ACL, now Arts eResearch), offered us a different approach. When they constructed our database, in 2006, they linked it to Google Maps, made available online only a year earlier, as a temporary fix to allow me to create preliminary maps of our evidence. As we grappled with a raft of design and technical challenges, it became clear that this simplified, web-based form of GIS would serve the purposes of the project, and *Digital Harlem* became one of the first scholarly sites to employ what has become known as the geospatial web.[4]

GIS organizes and integrates sources on the basis of their shared geographic location—in the case of an urban setting, their street address. Working with addresses involved thinking about Harlem on a much smaller scale than had other scholars.[5] Maps in existing historical studies focused on showing the boundaries of the area dominated by black residents and the location of a handful of landmarks, at a scale that located Harlem in Upper Manhattan, the area above Central Park. With a street map as the background, the area around the boundaries and landmarks appeared only as undifferentiated space.[6] To fill the spaces in these maps, to re-create Harlem at the scale of individual addresses, I turned to a real estate atlas from 1930, from which the ACL eventually created a map to overlay on Google Maps. Real estate maps include the footprints of buildings, with information on how many floors high they stood, on the materials from which they were constructed, and on the presence of elevators and stores.[7] In other words, these maps literally fill in the blocks of the street map, helping, as Ian Gregory and Paul Ell put it, to "subdivide the place under study into multiple smaller places and give some indication of how these places interact."[8] Thinking about Harlem at this scale, you are immediately confronted with how imprecisely most historical scholarship treats location: events and buildings are not given an address or are given only a partial or incorrect address, and little attention is paid to how that location is related to other places, to what is proximate or distant. It is enough to say that the places mentioned are somewhere in Harlem.

Examining Harlem at a smaller scale involved me in what Karen Halttunen identified as the second wave of the spatial turn in humanities scholarship, the move from constructing a spatial analysis that "tended to the metaphorical" and employed the "idiom of borders and boundaries, frontiers and crossroads, centers and margins," to a concern with "spatial issues more materially."[9] While you could argue that my work is spatial history and not digital history, this would ignore the extent to which such mapping is not just enabled by digital tools but, really, only possible when you use such tools. Real estate maps are so small in scale that they cannot be reproduced in print publications, with those covering Harlem amounting to almost an entire atlas volume. However, digitized and overlaid on Google Maps, real estate maps become scalable, making it possible to zoom out from individual buildings to the neighborhood view favored in historical maps of Harlem and to an even larger scale that situates Upper Manhattan in the larger city.

Geospatial tools involve not only maps but also databases. The power of such tools is that they use geographic location to integrate material from a wide range of disparate sources. "What is important about assigning a geographic reference to data," Karen Kemp points out, "is that it then becomes possible to compare that characteristic, event, phenomenon, etc. with others that exist or have existed in the same geographic space. What were previously unrelated facts become integrated and correlated."[10] The sources that feature in *Digital Harlem* are qualitative records, rather than the quantitative data traditionally used in GIS. Few other attempts have been made to use the technology to analyze such sources. The most prominent example is *The Valley of the Shadow*, which maps railroads and roads, agricultural production and farm values, households owning slaves, and voting and the location of churches, in order to compare two communities in the era of the Civil War.[11]

What distinguishes *Digital Harlem* from *The Valley of the Shadow* is not only its sources—legal records and newspapers—but also that the database contains everything in the sources that is associated with an address. The geospatial database allowed us to incorporate and organize a range of material that historians typically treat as ephemera or pass over as too sparse or fragmentary to support an analysis. From the newspapers, we took not just the news stories on which scholars typically focus but also the society columns, sports reports, news from churches and fraternal organizations, and advertisements. From the legal records, we took every offense (not just a particular crime or group of crimes) and information on the victim and witnesses as well as the offender, on the nature of the crime's location, and on the circumstances in which it occurred, which ranged from card games to shopping trips. The range of activity captured by *Digital Harlem* can be seen in the list of event types in the database. (Crimes constitute a minority of the events in the database but are prominent in that list because the variety of different offenses in the law effectively disaggregates crime more than the categories we have used for other events.) Such recurrent events as plays, movies, church services, and street speakers are not included as event types but, instead, can be located by searching for their venues by location type. At the same time, the need for a location excluded some material; every newspaper issue included some stories that did not include an address and therefore could not be included in the database. So, as much as the database offered a way to bring together a wide range of material, it was not a means of creating a "total history," an all-encompassing picture of everyday life.

In making it possible to place the contents of a database on an online map, GIS takes advantage of one of the core properties of the digital medium, that it is visual—an aspect that historians have been slow to develop, exploit, and make integral to historical analysis.[12] As Trevor Harris, Jesse Rouse, and Susan Bergeron argue, "The visual display of information creates a visceral connection to the content that goes beyond what is possible through traditional text documents."[13] (That contrast is evident in a comparison of how traffic accidents appear in the database and displayed on a map.) Not only is mapped data seen in its geographical context, but layers of different data and, hence, large quantities of data can be combined on a single map, providing an image of the complexity of the past. You can examine maps of sources at different scales and "discover relationships . . . by visually detecting spatial patterns that remain hidden in texts and tables."[14] Those spatial relationships prompted questions I might otherwise have ignored, and they facilitated comparisons that I would not have considered. There are definite limits to the visualizations created by *Digital Harlem* and by GIS in general. As Ian Gregory notes, "They provide a simple summary of the distribution of a variable in ways that attempt to stress the spatial by simplifying attribute [the characteristics recorded about entities in the database] and fixing time."[15] The patterns evident on these maps reveal the "where" involved in an inquiry. In the process, they ask, though they do not explain, "Why there?" Pursuing answers to such questions changed the way I thought about Harlem's past and gave me a different perspective on the neighborhood.

One example of the new perspective that *Digital Harlem* offers is the map of Harlem's nightlife (fig. 8), which includes layers showing the neighborhood's nightclubs, the speakeasies that became ubiquitous during Prohibition, and the buffet flats that black residents set up as an alternative to those venues. The nightclubs are the most familiar of Harlem's attractions, described in a range of sources. The presence of speakeasies is also well known, but they and their locations are discussed only in general terms. This map uses lists of locations regularly published in the *New York Age* as part of the editor's efforts to get Prohibition authorities to take action. The third venue, buffet flats operated in residences, attract only a passing mention by scholars, but they became a concern for reformers at the end of the 1920s and the target of a 1928 undercover investigation by the Committee of Fourteen, a white antiprostitution organization. Combining these sources shows that these nightlife venues had very different geographies. Nightclubs, many of which predated Prohibition, clustered around 135th Street and on and east of Seventh Avenue, locations that stretched from the core of black settlement toward the areas of white population. Speakeasies could be found far more widely in storefronts throughout Harlem, mostly on the avenues (including on Eighth Avenue, which had no other nightlife), with clusters in the vicinity of nightclubs. Buffet flats likewise operated at more widely scattered locations than nightclubs, but most were on cross streets, not avenues, with many above 140th Street, a largely residential district distant from whites. Whereas whites owned most nightclubs and speakeasies and catered to white or racially mixed crowds, blacks oper-

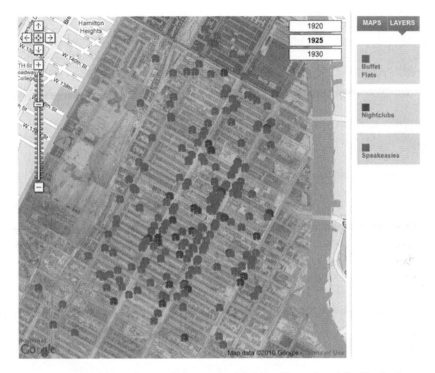

Fig. 8. Screenshot of a search for "nightclub," "speakeasy," and "buffet flat" under "Places" in *Digital Harlem* (http://acl.arts.usyd.edu.au/harlem/)

ated the buffet flats for black patrons, without publicizing their locations, thereby extending some of the privacy of a residence to their customers. Mapping nightlife thus helps identify an unrecognized black response to Prohibition's impact on Harlem: the creation of places where blacks could be apart from the whites who appeared in increasing numbers in the neighborhood's nightlife.[16]

Data on traffic accidents offer another example of how *Digital Harlem* changed my thinking. I would not have paid attention to these incidents if I had not been entering every event that had a location into the database. Reports of accidents appeared regularly in black newspapers but usually amounted to no more than a few sentences. A map of that information showed accidents throughout the neighborhood, concentrated on Seventh and Lenox Avenues, which ran north-south the length of Harlem. These avenues have long been recognized as occupying a central place in Harlem life. Christened the "Black Broadway" by writer Wallace Thurman,

Seventh Avenue featured the nightlife visited by thousands each evening in the late 1920s, as well as many of Harlem's major churches, which drew large crowds each Sunday. On the sidewalks of both avenues, individuals went "strolling," donning their best clothes to display their style, to socialize with friends and to meet strangers. Men and women collecting bets on the numbers occupied the corners each weekday morning, replaced in the evenings by prostitutes. On weekends, residents paraded in the avenues themselves, with their fraternal lodges, as members of the UNIA, or in funeral processions.[17] In addition to these well-known activities, the two avenues saw more traffic than any other roadway north of 59th Street, most of it traveling through the neighborhood en route into and out of the city, joined in the evening by fleets of taxis bringing visitors to Harlem's nightlife. Public transport also ran on both avenues: street cars traveled on Lenox from 116th to 148th Street, and double-decker buses ran on Seventh from 110th to 155th Street.

Accidents revealed an overlooked facet of life in the neighborhood and recast the context and meaning of what happened on the avenues. Whites made up most of those driving on Harlem's streets, behind the wheel of private cars, buses, and streetcars. As a result, traffic accidents often produced interracial encounters, conflict, and occasionally violence. In some cases, efforts to better control the traffic exacerbated that conflict. The traffic police eventually stationed at the most dangerous intersections included black officers, whose direction of white drivers often attracted crowds of blacks and enough controversy that the police department refused to appoint them to posts on 125th Street, where many pedestrians as well as drivers would have been white.[18] In the context of the white presence in the street and the white ownership of the businesses lining the avenues, when blacks paraded, strolled the sidewalks, and spoke on the street corners, they effectively contested white dominance of the avenues and claimed those places for themselves. That such racial contests for space took place within Harlem made me pay more attention to the white places in what I had thought of as simply a black neighborhood. Not only did there prove to be a more extensive white presence than the passing mentions in the historiography implied, but as I argue in a forthcoming article, it was more contentious, introducing the racial negotiation, resistance, and accommodation that characterized the rest of the city into some places in Harlem itself, taking away from the respite that the neighborhood offered blacks.[19]

While mapping traffic accidents made me aware of the white presence in Harlem, visualizing the lives of individuals gave me a new sense of how blacks moved around the neighborhood and the wider city. *Digital Harlem* uses lines to mark two kinds of temporal relations, to link sequences of locations at which events like parades took place and to link an individual's residence with locations where she or he spent time while living at that address.[20] The richest pictures of individual lives are contained in probation files, whose subjects reported their activities on a weekly basis for up to five years. Maps of their lives highlight the distance they had to travel to work and how often many changed their residence. Morgan Thompson, a West Indian on probation after he lost his temper and stabbed a man who had confronted his seventeen-year-old son, worked as a laborer for construction contractors. Between 1928 and 1933, that work took him to fifteen different construction sites, in downtown Manhattan, on the Upper East Side, and in the outer boroughs of Brooklyn, Queens, and the Bronx. Only once did he work in Harlem, on the construction of the YMCA on 135th Street.[21] Maps also identify other largely unexplored occasions when blacks had to move through the city, including to attend sporting events. While basketball games took place in Harlem's dance halls and church community houses, cricket and baseball games involving black teams took place in Washington Heights, the Bronx, and Brooklyn.[22]

Within Harlem, while Morgan Thompson and his family lived at the same address on West 144th Street for over a decade, many black families regularly relocated. Perry Brown, a forty-five-year-old on probation for stealing coats to pay for his wife's medical care, relocated five times in three years, not simply to get better housing, but sometimes to get rooms to lease to boarders, to obtain premises easier for his wife to maintain, or when he could not pay the rent.[23] The variety of apartments that Brown and his wife occupied highlights the range of housing that existed in Harlem beyond the overcrowded tenements and middle-class dwellings that typically draw attention. Moreover, for all the upheaval attending relocation, mapping the Browns' homes highlights that moving generally only involved shifting a few blocks for Harlemites, with little likely disruption of their relationships and involvement in the community.

Working with *Digital Harlem* also led me to write in a different form, a blog.[24] This online writing is typically seen primarily in terms of length, as a short form, but what shaped my blogging was its relationship to other forms of digital history and historical writing. In the first instance, blogging provided a way to supplement *Digital Harlem*. By their very nature, the maps created on the site raise questions rather than answering them, and they could not simply stand on their own online. *Digital Harlem* required additional context, and a blog linked to the site provided a medium in which to tell stories about the maps on the site. In addition,

Digital Harlem's maps are difficult to incorporate into print publications, where dynamic maps have to become static, without scalability or links to the database of sources, and where colored visualizations have to be reproduced in black and white, limiting the layers and quantity of data that can be included. When presented in a blog, screenshots of the maps retain their color and can be linked to the site. They also can be supplemented with images, which are not currently in the database and for which space is limited in print publications. Thus the blog posts can also provide a form of footnote to traditional published writing, where I can elaborate in more detail on a topic that there is only space to touch on in a print article. Relative to a published footnote, the blog is a longer form. Obviously, the blog can serve both as a context for *Digital Harlem* and as a reference for a print publication.

The blog post "Traffic Accidents in 1920s Harlem," for example, provides both context for a map and an extension of an argument in a forthcoming article. The 784-word post describes the broad pattern of accidents, the character of the traffic on Lenox and Seventh Avenues, traffic police posts and the reactions to black officers, and an example of the racial conflict that some accidents produced. It includes screenshots of a map of accidents, that map with traffic police posts added (with instructions on how to create the maps in *Digital Harlem*), and photographs of children crossing the street and of Officer Reuben Carter directing traffic. The article that will link to the post includes two paragraphs focused on the racial conflicts that occurred as a result of accidents, but it has no maps or photographs (only brief mentions of the broader patterns of accidents) and no discussion of the origins of the traffic police posts.[25] The posts on individual lives take a slightly different approach to elaborating on what can be gleaned from the map. In writing about Perry Brown, I drew on his probation file to craft a narrative of this slice of his life and used his membership of a fraternal lodge as a way into a broader discussion of lodges in Harlem, with a map of their locations, a photograph of members of one Elks lodge, and an image of the Temple of Imperial Elks. In this case, the post does not serve as an elaborated footnote; our published analysis of Brown's life is considerably more detailed, but it lacks the maps and images incorporated into the post. Approached from the published article (or via a search engine), posts thus serve a mediating function, offering static screenshots that link to *Digital Harlem*, where dynamic maps can be re-created and explored.[26]

Recently, as I realized I had considered the blog in relationship to my project only and not to the larger Internet, *Digital Harlem* has led me to another form of online writing. When I began this project, I implicitly subscribed to the "build it and they will come" assumption that underlies much digital history, the idea that going online immediately delivers an audience. It does not. Search engines bring some users, but attracting more requires connecting your work to the rest of the web. Following the lead of other digital projects, I have turned to *Wikipedia*. I had hoped to merely add links to existing articles, but the originality of *Digital Harlem* means that few of the topics it deals with were previously mentioned. As a result, I have had to write contributions to articles, grappling with *Wikipedia*'s wariness about primary sources, blogs, and citing yourself and with the existing organization of the articles related to 1920s Harlem.[27] The challenges of writing for *Wikipedia* are well documented elsewhere in this collection; to that discussion, my experience adds an example of why such engagement is more meaningful to digital historians than to other scholars and is hence something not to be left to students.

However I write about it, approaching 1920s Harlem through the maps created by *Digital Harlem*, using the tools offered by the geospatial web, has literally caused the way I think about the neighborhood to go through a spatial turn. Maps of the variety of sources my colleagues and I have gathered confront me with the multiple places that made up Harlem and the wide variety of events that took place there. Trying to understand those maps draws me down to the level of individual places and to the relations between them, into the web of locations in which individuals lived their lives—where they resided, worked, and spent their leisure time. Used in this way, the geospatial web can capture "the confluence of multiple rhythms" that Henri Lefebvre argued make up everyday life, offering a new perspective on what it was like to live *in* Harlem.[28]

Acknowledgments: *Digital Harlem* exists thanks to an Australian Research Council Discovery Grant (DP0343148), on which I collaborated with Shane White, Stephen Garton, and Graham White, all of whom are due thanks for gathering the sources used in the project and for supporting the development of the site.

Notes

1. Gilbert Osofsky, *Harlem: The Making of a Ghetto*, 2nd ed. (New York: HarperCollins, 1971), xvi; James Weldon Johnson, *Black Manhattan* (1930; repr., New York: Da Capo, 1991), 147; David Levering Lewis, *When Harlem Was in Vogue* (New York: Penguin, 1981), 193–94; Jervis Anderson, *This Was Harlem: A Cultural Portrait, 1900–1950* (New York: Farrar, Straus and Giroux, 1981), 128, 174, 236.
2. Shane White, Stephen Robertson, Stephen Garton, and Graham White,

"Black Metropolis: Harlem 1915–1930," Department of History, University of Sydney, http://sydney.edu.au/arts/history/research/projects/harlem.shtml.

3. Ian Gregory and Paul Ell, *Historical GIS: Technologies, Methodologies, and Scholarship* (Cambridge: Cambridge University Press, 2007), 1–19, 89–90; Anne Kelly Knowles, "GIS and History," in *Placing History: How Maps, Spatial Data, and GIS Are Changing Historical Scholarship*, ed. Amy Hillier and Anne Kelly Knowles (Redlands, CA: Esri, 2008), 2–7; David Bodenhamer, "History and GIS: Implications for the Discipline," in Hillier and Knowles, *Placing History*, 222–30.

4. *Digital Harlem: Everyday Life, 1915–1930*, http://www.acl.arts.usyd.edu.au/harlem/; "Arts eResearch," http://sydney.edu.au/arts/eresearch/; Muki Haklay, Alex Singleton, and Chris Parker, "Web Mapping 2.0: The Neogeography of the GeoWeb," *Geography Compass* 2, no. 6 (2008): 2011–39; Trevor Harris, Jesse Rouse, and Susan Bergeron, "The Geospatial Semantic Web, Pareto GIS, and the Humanities," in *The Spatial Humanities: GIS and the Future of Humanities Scholarship*, ed. David Bodenhamer, John Corrigan, and Trevor Harris (Bloomington: Indiana University Press, 2010), 124–42. Damien Evans took the lead in designing our database and site, and Andrew Wilson later created the overlay map.

5. Irma Watkins-Owens does include an analysis of the residents of a single block in her study of West Indians in Harlem, *Blood Relations: Caribbean Immigrants and the Harlem Community, 1900–1930* (Bloomington: Indiana University Press, 1996).

6. Johnson, *Black Manhattan*, 147; Osofsky, *Harlem*, xv–xvii; Cheryl Lynn Greenberg, *"Or Does It Explode?" Black Harlem in the Great Depression* (New York: Oxford University Press, 1991), i; Stephen Watson, *The Harlem Renaissance: Hub of African-American Culture, 1920–1930* (New York: Pantheon, 1995).

7. "The Map," *Digital Harlem Blog*, http://digitalharlemblog.wordpress.com/digital-harlem-the-site/the-map/.

8. Gregory and Ell, *Historical GIS*, 185.

9. Karen Halttunen, "Groundwork: American Studies in Place—Presidential Address to the American Studies Association, November 4, 2005," *American Quarterly* 58, no. 1 (March 2006): 2.

10. Karen Kemp, "Geographic Information Science and Spatial Analysis for the Humanities," in Bodenhamer, *Spatial Humanities*, 32.

11. Edward Ayers et al., "Augusta County Maps" and "Franklin County Maps," *The Valley of the Shadow*, http://valley.lib.virginia.edu/VoS/maps/augustamaps.html and http://valley.lib.virginia.edu/VoS/maps/franklinmaps.html. For discussions of this site, see Gregory and Ell, *Historical GIS*, 195–98; and Knowles, "GIS and History," 5–6.

12. See "Interchange: The Promise of Digital History," *Journal of American History* 95, no. 2 (2008): 484.

13. Harris, Rouse, and Bergeron, "Geospatial Semantic Web," 130.

14. David Bodenhamer, John Corrigan, and Trevor Harris, introduction to Bodenhamer, *Spatial Humanities*, vii.

15. Gregory and Ell, *Historical GIS*, 94.

16. Stephen Robertson, "Harlem Undercover: Vice Investigators, Race, and Prostitution in the 1920s," *Journal of Urban History* 35, no. 4 (May 2009): 486–504; Stephen Robertson, "Harlem Undercover—the Maps," *Digital Harlem Blog*, http://digitalharlemblog.wordpress.com/2009/04/17/harlem-undercover-the-maps/.

17. Wallace Thurman, "Negro Life in New York's Harlem: A Lively Picture of a Popular and Interesting Section" (1927), in *The Collected Writings of Wallace Thurman*, ed. Amritjit and Daniel M. Scott III (New Brunswick, NJ: Rutgers University Press, 2003), 40–41; Anderson, *This Was Harlem*, 319–23.

18. Stephen Robertson, "Traffic Accidents in 1920s Harlem," *Digital Harlem Blog*, http://digitalharlemblog.wordpress.com/2010/04/01/traffic-accidents-in-1920s-harlem/.

19. Stephen Robertson, Shane White, and Stephen Garton, "Harlem in Black and White: Mapping Race and Place in the 1920s," *Journal of Urban History* 39, no. 5 (September 2013).

20. Lines are only one of the ways that *Digital Harlem* can visualize time. Layers can also represent different time periods, providing an image of change over time. A fairly straightforward example, a map with layers for prostitution arrests in 1925 and 1930, can be found in Stephen Robertson, "Prostitution Arrests," *Digital Harlem Blog*, http://digitalharlemblog.wordpress.com/2009/10/05/prostitution-arrests/

21. Court of General Sessions Probation Department Case File 11076 (1928), Municipal Archives, New York City Department of Records. We have employed pseudonyms for individuals on probation, as required by the Municipal Archives. See also Stephen Robertson, "Morgan Thompson—a West Indian Laborer's Life in Harlem," *Digital Harlem Blog*, http://digitalharlemblog.wordpress.com/2009/12/01/morganthompson/; Stephen Robertson, Shane White, Stephen Garton, and Graham White, "This Harlem Life: Black Families and Everyday Life in the 1920s and 1930s," *Journal of Social History* 44, no. 1 (2010): 97–98, 100–104.

22. Stephen Robertson, "Harlem and Baseball in the 1920s," *Digital Harlem Blog*, http://digitalharlemblog.wordpress.com/2011/07/27/baseball-1920s-harlem/

23. Court of General Sessions Probation Department Case File 15872 (1930), Municipal Archives, New York City Department of Records; Stephen Robertson, "Perry Brown: A Lodge Member's Life in Harlem," *Digital Harlem Blog*, http://digitalharlemblog.wordpress.com/2010/07/15/perry-brown-lodge-member/; Robertson et al., "This Harlem Life," 104–8.

24. Stephen Robertson, *Digital Harlem Blog*, http://digitalharlemblog.wordpress.com.

25. Robertson, "Traffic Accidents"; Robertson, White, and Garton, "Harlem in Black and White."

26. Robertson, "Perry Brown"; Robertson et al., "This Harlem Life," 104–8.

27. Stephen Robertson, "Digital Harlem and Wikipedia," *Digital Harlem Blog*, http://digitalharlemblog.wordpress.com/2012/01/11/digital-harlem-and-wikipedia/.

28. The description of Lefebvre's argument is from Stefan Kipfer, Kaniska Goonwardena, Christian Schimd, and Richard Milgrom, "On the Production of Henri Lefebvre," in *Space, Difference, Everyday Life: Reading Henri Lefebvre*, ed. Kaniska Goonwardena, Stefan Kipfer, Richard Milgrom, and Christian Schimd (New York: Routledge, 2008), 15.

Pox and the City

Challenges in Writing a Digital History Game

Laura Zucconi, Ethan Watrall, Hannah Ueno, and Lisa Rosner

Real event or plausible scenario? First-person shooter or third-person isometric perspective? These are some of the questions we confronted as we began the collaborative digital history project *Pox and the City*,[1] a role-playing game funded by a start-up grant from the Office of Digital Humanities.[2] How do we adapt the content into a playable scenario that retains educational and research value? What restrictions do pedagogical concerns place on the actual programming? How are these concepts visually represented in a digital world?

When completed, *Pox and the City* will allow students to explore the interplay of disease, patients, healers, and social institutions in medical history. Set in early nineteenth-century Edinburgh, Scotland, the game is designed to allow players to adopt one of three roles: a newly graduated physician, intent on setting up a paying medical practice by using the recent discovery of vaccination for smallpox; an Irish immigrant, just arrived in Edinburgh's immigrant district and hoping to establish himself in a market stall in the city's central district; and a smallpox virus, "intent" on replicating and spreading throughout the city. Each role has a home base in the city and a distinct set of tasks he/it must perform in order to move to the next level.

The game is a collaboration among scholars with different specialties and different approaches to writing history. Lisa Rosner, a historian of medicine with a long-standing interest in web design as a digital humanities tool, is the content specialist for Edinburgh medicine and for visual representations of the city. Laura Zucconi is both a historian of medicine and an avid gamer, with a previous incarnation as a programmer. Both are based at Stockton College, New Jersey. Ethan Watrall, an anthropologist and a designer of serious games, from Michigan State University, oversees the design team, Adventure Club, also based in East Lansing. Hannah Ueno, a visual artist and 3D graphic designer from Stockton, is creating a virtual world of 1800s Edinburgh as a complement to the game. The project is also a collaboration between the project designers and the staff of the Historical Collections of the College of Physicians of Philadelphia, who provide many of the primary sources on which the game is based. Each of the many partners brings a specific area of expertise to the project, but what may appear as a simple decision in one area suddenly becomes problematic when it intersects with another area. For the authors of this essay, working on *Pox and the City* has transformed the writing of history from a process designed and carried out by a single individual, firmly in control, to an exhilarating, surprising, and, above all, collaborative effort, akin to completing a giant jigsaw puzzle when we are not sure who has all the pieces.

The best way to illustrate the "jigsaw" analogy is to follow the way our collaboration evolved. This project began with Rosner, as the content specialist, firmly in control of the narrative and debating the issue of where to situate the game in time and space. One option was to re-create an actual historical event, Edward Jenner's 1798 research establishing that vaccinating a patient with cowpox matter resulted in his or her immunity to the deadly disease smallpox.[3] Another option was to create a plausible historical scenario, situated in early nineteenth-century Edinburgh, based on Rosner's expertise on the medical history of the city. Since the former is based on historical fact, while the latter would be a kind of historical fiction, Rosner's choice initially seemed clear: we should develop a role-playing game based on Jenner's actual medical research. Such a game would appear to offer the best support for a key facet of history pedagogy, teaching students to make inferences about the past based on historical evidence.

Once Rosner and Zucconi began to collaborate on gamifying the content, though, this choice appeared less clear-cut. We investigated the precise pedagogical purpose served by a role-playing activity, digital or otherwise, and what kinds of assumptions might be embedded within the choice of specific topics to enact. One common purpose is to convey a "you are there" sense of a specific historical moment, to allow students to re-create an event or series of events. Common scenarios used for this are the 1787 debates over the Constitution or the set of alliances leading to the outbreak of World War I. This type of scenario can be easily paired with another pedagogical imperative, getting students to read primary sources. The underlying assumption is that the more students read the sources, the more they will re-create the actual historical events, and the better they will understand how those events took place.[4]

This assumption is deeply ingrained in the pedagogy of the history of science. Many high school and college science courses re-create classic experiments, such as Robert Millikan's oil-drop experiment, in student labs.[5] The goal is not just to teach the scientific facts but also to provide examples of analytical reasoning and scientific creativity. James Conant's seminal work *Harvard Case Histories in Experimental Science*[6] explicitly incorporated this goal into the teaching of the history of science. Like the Harvard Business School case histories, specific episodes in the history of science were to serve as exemplars, negative and positive, of rational inquiry, innovation, and problem solving. This view of the history of science privileged major scientists and has made a very successful transition to new media, such as the Public Broadcasting Service's *Nova*.[7]

But the best-laid plans go awry in role-playing activities as often as elsewhere. The group dynamics of role playing in the classroom are complicated: particularly charismatic or present-minded students may skew the results, so that the Founding Fathers end up abolishing slavery in 1787 or so that Italy succeeds in negotiating a peace settlement that heads off World War I. Within the history of science, the complexities of re-creating even a single individual's process of discovery in the classroom is time-consuming and requires a level of engagement with primary source materials—including lab apparatuses—that is difficult to achieve in a standard semester-length course. The laboratory program at St. John's College,[8] which does use texts based directly on classic works in the sciences, like Isaac Newton's *Principia*, requires a full three years of intensive immersion.[9] In the history of medicine, any kind of hands-on re-creation of historical events—for example, Jenner's inoculation practice—is out of the question.

As our research into serious games told us, adding the game component to role-playing activities creates even more problems. A historical simulation, or case study, is not the same as a game. How can students play at being Edward Jenner? Would they be rewarded—for example, earn points or collect digital tokens—for reading about his life and work and choosing correctly among a set of online scenarios? What would make this a game, rather than an online test, perhaps (but only perhaps) more appealing than a traditional written test? Unlike *Nova* episodes, games do not lend themselves to re-creation of the lives and ideas of specific, well-known individuals, because then players are constrained, not empowered, by their knowledge of real historical events. Instead, games work best when they are open-ended, allowing players a set of choices without predetermined outcomes.

Games also work best when they are visually interesting. One of the appeals of historical games, like the *Caesar* series,[10] is the opportunity to move through a world that no longer exists. This is also an important pedagogical point: not only can students learn about the history of, for example, architecture or urban conditions, but they can also learn to "read" visual as well as text-based historical sources. Yet this was a complicating factor if we made Edward Jenner the focus of the game. We know very little about Jenner's physical environment—what his house looked like, where he performed his vaccinations, how his village was situated in the landscape. It might be possible to re-create the environment by using contemporary images, but such images would only be approximations. They would be, in effect, a kind of historical fiction rather than historical fact.

So we returned again to historical pedagogy to look for alternatives to the traditional role-playing reenactment of a specific historical event. An obvious model is the use of films to teach history. Few historians would argue that films, even those based on real events, are entirely accurate. But they can be ideal media for conveying an understanding of the past, and their use is supported by a growing body of scholarly literature.[11] Games, like films, can be based on serious scholarly research and are as well suited to visual as textual sources. Moreover, the scholarly literature continues to expand through both print and born-digital publications.[12]

We redesigned our jigsaw puzzle: instead of starting with the content and then somehow forcing it into a game, we started with the structure of the game and asked ourselves what kind of content would best serve its purposes. We wanted to create a dynamic and engaging game in a role-playing multiuser format that allowed an exploration of the social history of medicine, rather than just a recapitulation of accepted theories. In this environment, students could more freely explore the medical culture of the nineteenth century by asking themselves questions when presented with problems, such as how a doctor might convince a wealthy patron to be vaccinated and whether the doctor would act the same way toward a patient from the laboring class. The student must figure out on his or her own which documents to access in the archive and how to synthesize that data with the game mechanics. This process of question and discovery makes for a greater impact in terms of active learning.[13]

For the high school or undergraduate student, the plausible scenario helps them learn how to do research. For graduate students and other researchers, the plausible scenario approach can aid them in what to look for when working in the archives. A re-creation of nineteenth-century Edinburgh that permits free-form movement of the players allows them to interact in ways that our current models of historical narrative may not address.[14] As players try to solve game problems, such as where to get money to set up a medical practice, they may devise a novel solution. Their task would then become combing the archives to see if pertinent economic data relevant to their theory had been overlooked by previous histories. Even if such data cannot be found, the researcher would, at the very least, develop a better understanding of nineteenth-century economic values, avoiding the pitfall of accidentally imparting anachronistic perceptions.

A plausible scenario format comes with the difficulties of character creation and developing quests that highlight historically important data. There is also the danger of losing the historical narrative as players create a new environment through their actions. We resolved the issue of what types of characters to create as player characters (PCs) and nonplayer characters (NPCs) by returning to the content, in this case, a central concept for the history of medicine: the interaction of disease, patient, and healer. Thus the PCs would be the doctor, an immigrant laborer, and the smallpox virus itself. This choice of PCs would work well with either a research or pedagogical approach to the game. NPCs would account for any other people that would normally interact with our three standard PCs, such as a wealthy patron for the doctor.

After settling on the basic ideas of both research and pedagogy played in a plausible scenario format, we turned to the look of the game, in consultation with designer Ethan Watrall. He added a new set of pieces for our jigsaw puzzle, and we once again had to shake some out and start rebuilding. Our initial conception was that the game would follow the style made popular by such first-person shooters as *Planet Wolfenstein* and *Doom*.[15] We felt that this would give the player the best feel for nineteenth-century Edinburgh, as they would move through various scenes of closes, markets, and buildings based on contemporary maps, etchings, and watercolors. Such immersive environments have proven effective in simulation-based training games for pilots and military personnel.[16]

Watrall pointed out several technical problems, though, with this popular style of game perspective. The first is that we expect students to play the game on a standard computer using a mouse and keyboard, rather than a joystick or gamepad. The first-person perspective simply does not work well with a mouse interface. The second problem had to do with the design decision, prevalent in the genre of serious games, to program in Flash. Knowledge of Flash is common among game designers and allows comparatively rapid game development. Since students can be competent Flash designers, it helps keep design costs within the grant budget. In addition, because Adobe Flash is both ubiquitous and cross-platform, there are very few issues with compatibility or accessibility. Although Flash-based applications do not work on Apple devices like the iPad and iPhone, that is not a drawback for *Pox and the City*, because we expect students to play it through a web browser on a standard computer. However, Flash programming does not lend itself well to games played in a browser in first-person perspective, because of the variation in download rates.

Watrall suggested that the game design use a third-person isometric perspective, with the "camera shot" above and at an angle to the player character. This perspective plays well with a browser deployment. Watrall pointed out that recent research indicates that a third-person perspective allows for greater immersion in a role-playing game, because the player can see his character within the environment.[17] Additionally, this perspective permits a wider view of the environment, thus richer detail can be built into the game and absorbed by the player. The following illustration of an Edinburgh map adapted for game play demonstrates these points. (See the additional image in the web version of this essay at http://WritingHistory. trincoll.edu.)

The issue of immersion is not limited to just resolving a player's perspective. As our fourth collaborator, Hannah Ueno, pointed out, the style of graphics equally affects how well a player feels connected and interacts with the visual features of the game. A photorealistic quality to the graphics is the ideal environment, but if this is not done well, it will actually detract from player interaction and negatively impact the overall learning outcomes.[18] Studies have shown that a more stylized art approach that is illustrative or "cartoony" creates a certain level of suspended disbelief that allows the player to feel more connected to the game. At the time of writing, we have yet to fit in all the jigsaw pieces associated with a particular art style, but we are leaning toward a graphic look that imitates nineteenth-century watercolors and line drawings depicting Edinburgh's Old Town. From the 1860s through the 1920s, Edinburgh undertook a series of urban construction projects that eventually eliminated the unhygienic alleys and courtyards of previous centuries. Local artists, concerned to record their rich architectural heritage, went street by street through the city, creating a wealth of visual imagery.[19] Of course, they were not merely recording what they saw but, rather, interpreting it as a record of a bygone era—a vanished

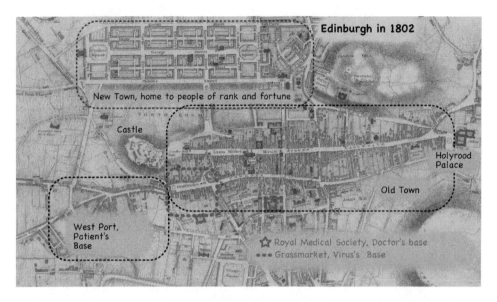

Fig. 9. Map of Edinburgh showing locations of game play in *Pox and the City*, based on John Anderson Junior, 1830; digital reproduction by Carson Clark Gallery; adapted by Lisa Rosner

past, once great, now fallen into decay. We expect these illustrations to work very well in evoking the era and drawing players into the game. That many of the streets can be located on historical and contemporary maps, available online from the National Library of Scotland,[20] adds another layer to the pedagogical goal of the game.

Pox and the City is still in its initial stages, with much work to do even in developing the basic design for the game, let alone working out art assets or detailed scenarios. It is fair to say that our ideas of writing a history game as an isolated process, carried out by an individual in a book-lined study, have been permanently transformed. We hope the game, once completed, will prove to be a similar vehicle for transformation for our students and colleagues.

Update: Since this chapter was written, the game has been publicly released at http://poxandthecity.blogspot.com

Notes

1. "Three Cheers for *Pox and the City*!" School of Arts and Humanities Grants and News, South Jersey Center for Digital Humanities, Stockton College, http://intraweb.stockton.edu/eyos/page.cfm?siteID=69&pageID=246.

2. "NEH Announces 22 New Start-Up Grants," Office of Digital Humanities, National Endowment for the Humanities, April 2011, http://www.neh.gov/ODH/ODHHome/tabid/36/EntryId/161/NEH-Announces-22-New-Digital-Humanities-Start-Up-Grants-April-2011.aspx.

3. Edward Jenner, *An Inquiry into the Causes and Effects of the* Variolae Vaccinae (London, 1798), http://babel.hathitrust.org/cgi/pt?id=ucm.5325107182.

4. A recent example is discussed in Lauren Kientz Anderson, "Exciting New Pedagogy Based in History of Ideas," *U.S. Intellectual History*, January 12, 2010, http://us-intellectual-history.blogspot.com/2010/01/exciting-new-pedagogy-based-in-history.html.

5. For one of many examples, see Ryan McAlister, "The Millikan Oil Drop Experiment," Fall 2003, http://ffden-2.phys.uaf.edu/212_fall2003.web.dir/ryan_mcallister/slide3.htm.

6. James Conant, *Harvard Case Histories in Experimental Science*, 2 vols. (Cambridge, MA: Harvard University Press, 1957).

7. See, for example, "Galileo's Battle for the Heavens," *PBS Nova*, 2002, http://www.pbs.org/wgbh/nova/galileo/

8. "Academic Program: Laboratory," St. John's College, 2008, http://www.stjohnscollege.edu/academic/laboratory.shtml.

9. Dana Densmore and William H. Donahue, *Newton's "Principia": The Central Argument* (Santa Fe: Green Lion, 2003).

10. Jason Ocampo, "*Caesar IV*: Review," *Gamespot*, October 5, 2006, http://www.gamespot.com/pc/strategy/caesar4/review.html?tag=summary%3Bread-review.

11. An excellent teaching resource is Mark C. Carnes, ed., *Past Imperfect: History according to the Movies* (New York: Henry Holt, 1996); see also Robert Brent Toplin, "The Historian and Film: Challenges Ahead," *Perspectives* 34, no. 4 (April 1996), http://www.historians.org/perspectives/issues/1996/9604/9604FIL.CFM. The *Internet Modern History Sourcebook*, maintained by Fordham University, includes a section titled "Modern History in the Movies," http://www.fordham.edu/halsall/mod/modsbookmovies.asp.

12. Much of the current discussion highlights the use of commercial games in teaching, but that can be expected to change as the field of serious games expands. See Russell Francis, "Towards a Theory of a Games-Based Pedagogy" (paper presented at the conference "Innovating E-Learning 2006: Transforming Learning Experiences," JISC online conference, March 2006), http://gu-se.academia.edu/RussellFrancis/Papers/409557/Towards_a_Theory_of_a_Games-Based_Pedagogy; see also Ethan Watrall, "Interactive Entertainment as Public Archaeology," *Archaeological Record* 2, no. 2 (2002): 37–39, http://www.saa.org/Portals/0/SAA/Publications/thesaaarchrec/mar02.pdf; Brian Winn et al., "What Should Higher Education Learn from Games?" (presentation at the National Learning Infrastructure Initiative, San Diego, CA, January 2004, http://www.educause.edu/library/resources/what-should-higher-education-learn-games).

13. David Gijbels et al., "Effects of Problem-Based Learning: A Meta-Analysis from the Angle of Assessment," *Review of Educational Research* 75, no. 1 (Spring 2005): 27–61.

14. In 2008, Edward Castronova of Indiana University designed a version of the *Neverwinter Nights* multiuser game called *Arden: The World of Shakespeare* for exper-

imental economics, as he described in "A Test of the Law of Demand in a Virtual World: Exploring the Petri Dish Approach to Social Science" (CESifo Working Paper 2355, Department of Telecommunications, Indiana University, Bloomington), http://papers.ssrn.com/sol3/papers.cfm?abstract_id=1173642.

15. *Planet Wolfenstein*, http://www.planetwolfenstein.com/; *Doom*, http://www.silvergames.com/doom.

16. J. D. Fletcher, "Education and Training Technology in the Military," *Science* 323, no. 5910 (January 2009): 72–75.

17. S. Bangay and L. Preston, "An Investigation into Factors Influencing Immersion in Interactive Virtual Reality Environments," in *Virtual Environments in Clinical Psychology and Neuroscience*, ed. G. Riva, B. K. Wiederhold, and E. Molinary (Amsterdam: Ios, 1998); Charlene Jennet et al., "Measuring and Defining the Experience of Immersion in Games," *International Journal of Human-Computer Studies* 66, no. 9 (September 2008): 641–61.

18. R. Wages, S. M. Grunvogel, and B. Grutzmacher, "How Realistic Is Realism? Considerations on the Aesthetics of Computer Games," *Lecture Notes in Computer Science* 3166 (2004): 83–92; J. Seyama and R. S. Nagayama, "The Uncanny Valley: The Effect of Realism on the Impression of Artificial Human Faces," *Presence: Teleoperators and Virtual Environments* 16, no. 4 (August 2007): 337–51; Babak Kaveh, "A Fresh Look at the Concept of Immersion," *Game Design Ideas*, March 10, 2010, http://www.gamedesignideas.com/video-games/a-fresh-look-at-the-concept-of-immersion.html.

19. Thomas Shepherd, *Modern Athens, Displayed in a Series of Views* (London: Jones, 1830); James Drummond, *Old Edinburgh* (Edinburgh: G. Waterston Sons and Stewart, 1879); Bruce Home, *Old Houses in Edinburgh* (Edinburgh: Hay and Bagster, 1905).

20. Maps of Scotland, National Library of Scotland, http://maps.nls.uk/.

PART 6

Public History on the Web:
If You Build It, Will They Come?

The potential of public history has been profoundly altered by the democratization of the web. Oscar Rosales Castañeda's essay "Writing Chicana/o History with the Seattle Civil Rights and Labor History Project" describes how students and faculty created a digital public history project to document local activism, indicating the vivid role it played in shaping their lives as well as historical knowledge on the contemporary Pacific Northwest. In "Citizen Scholars: Facebook and the Co-creation of Knowledge," Amanda Grace Sikarskie draws on her experience with the Quilt Index to make a case for lay historians actively contributing to research through social media. Finally, Shawn Graham, Guy Massie, and Nadine Feuerherm offer a behind-the-scenes look and some early conclusions on documenting Canadian memories, in "The *HeritageCrowd* Project: A Case Study in Crowdsourcing Public History."

Writing Chicana/o History with the Seattle Civil Rights and Labor History Project

Oscar Rosales Castañeda

The Seattle Civil Rights and Labor History Project (hereafter referred to as the Seattle Civil Rights Project) has allowed a city to retell its rich, multicultural civil rights narrative. Since its inception in 2004, it has produced a wealth of information that allows Seattle's history to be retold through research reports, digitized documents, and dozens of oral history videos, allowing the fusion of oral history tradition with the newly emergent medium of the digital research project.[1] In 2005, coming off the initial release of the newly minted Seattle Civil Rights Project, a group of undergraduate students, myself included, met with University of Washington (UW) history professor Dr. Jim Gregory and UW PhD candidate Trevor Griffey to dialogue on expanding the civil rights project to include the local ethnic Mexican/Latino community in Seattle. This meeting resulted in what became the largest archive documenting the Chicana/o Movement[2] outside of Southwest United States. Nationwide, this reverberated throughout academic circles as a model for undergraduates to use when producing and writing digital history for K–12, college, and public audiences. (See the images on the web version of this essay at http://WritingHistory.trincoll.edu.)

From the outset, the Chicana/o Movement in Washington State History Project (hereafter referred to as the Chicana/o Movement Project) was intended as a point of departure, an exploration of a local narrative long relegated to obscure, unpublished materials and oral histories passed down from one generation to another. For many Latinos in Seattle and the Pacific Northwest, the thirst for knowledge was tempered by a sense of isolation from the ethnic Mexican/Latino cultural hubs in the Southwest and East Coast, as well as a sense of historical omission in regional narratives. The need for addressing this dual marginalization proved to be the impetus for initiating the Chicana/o Movement Project research.

Latinos in the Pacific Northwest

Interest in Chicana/o activist history at the University of Washington was central to our contingent of freshman students as early as 2002. Most of us arrived from eastern Washington, with some from the Seattle area, as we formed the leadership of the UW chapter of El Movimiento Estudiantil Chicana/o de Aztlan (the Chicana/o Student Movement of Aztlan),[3] or MEChA. For many, this was the first time we came together with other like-minded youth to organize around educational access, economic justice, and civil and human rights. The previous leadership graduated the summer before we arrived. Their departure left an organizational vacuum that prompted us to take over the reins of the leadership to ensure organizational continuity.[4]

Among the initiatives we pressed forth were educational meetings to share skills and knowledge as well as to train ourselves in organizing strategies. We understood that there was a relation between ourselves and the space we inhabited. Far removed from the cultural hubs in the Southwest, yet part of a cultural diaspora that adapted to its new surroundings, we imagined a way of being and collaborating with other communities that represented a smaller portion of the local population, in contrast to other places in the South and East.

Our first encounter with this ethnic Mexican/Latino narrative in the Pacific Northwest came through a class instructed by Dr. Erasmo Gamboa.[5] Though the class introduced material that we had not seen in textbooks on Washington State's history, the material mostly related the rural experience. The urban narrative existed, as we later found out, in various journal articles, master's theses, document collections, and published ephemera that were inaccessible to many readers in our community. As a means of addressing this issue, we undertook the task of consolidating material pertinent to our history in Seattle and the University of Washington.

As this project was underway, we received an e-mail from an alumnus who was a graduate student at California State University, Northridge. While researching on Google, he happened on a web article by former UW activist Jeremy Simer, "La Raza Comes to Campus," published from

Dr. Jim Gregory's independent research seminar at the University of Washington. The discovery of this article impacted how we viewed digital media in collecting this history. We knew that the best way to preserve and build on our work was to make it accessible to anyone curious about the subject. The intent was to make the work available through our organization's website. After serving out my term as the chapter cochair, I looked toward fleshing out this idea and was successful in acquiring a research fellowship for 2005–6. I argued that the project would "aid in incorporating scholarly work from the Pacific Northwest into the study of Latinos on the West Coast, enhancing the already existing historical narrative."[6] I was also fortunate to receive a second fellowship from the UW Center for Labor Studies, which was presented at the center's annual ceremony, where I met Dr. Gregory. As a consequence of having a sizable class from 2002, we had students looking to initiate senior projects. We now had the research contingent and resources to unearth our collective vision.

Urban Activism in Seattle

The project intended to examine the local movement's unique character, in relation to its spatial confines in a city long known for its vibrant history. Unlike the cultural nationalist current prevalent in cities and communities along the Southwest, activity in Seattle mirrored the Third World and internationalist tendencies of the San Francisco Bay Area. Further, unlike the Southwest, activity in Seattle and other communities in Washington State differed, as there was no significant record of social and political mobilization within the ethnic Mexican/Latino community.[7]

Upon reading the primary sources, it was clear that our project would shift focus. A survey of this narrative from early rural farmworker activism to later urban movements had not been written. As we discovered, original writings had been fragmented in four- to five-year increments. Furthermore, much of this story lay in a tapestry of documents buried in archives since at least the 1970s. This forced us to utilize a three-pronged approach, with some researchers conducting oral history interviews, some digging into archival material and newspaper articles, and others writing material and digitizing rare, tattered documents that sat in the file cabinet of the UW chapter of MEChA for decades. We did this to weave these writings on farm labor unionization, student strikes, urban and rural activism, and cultural aesthetic movements into one historical survey that covered the period from 1965 to 1980.

With the project taking form, local interest in the research slowly surfaced. Nationwide, polemic debate around immigration seeped into mainstream parlance. In April 2005, the Minuteman Project began conducting armed patrols of the U.S.-Mexico border under the pretext that borders were porous and susceptible to "terrorist organizations," a reflection of the anti-Muslim and anti-immigrant hysteria of the post-9/11 era. Soon this staunchly nativist group began patrolling the northern border, along Washington State's northern counties. This right-wing anti-immigrant formation influenced policy makers, who, by late December of 2005, passed House Resolution 4437 (commonly referred to as the "Sensenbrenner Bill," after the legislation's primary sponsor, Rep. Jim Sensenbrenner of Wisconsin).[8]

In response to this highly controversial, draconian legislation, immigrants and their allies protested en masse in the spring of 2006 in what was perhaps the largest wave of demonstrations in the United States in a generation. In the Seattle area, immigrants came out in force as never before. In a meeting, Dr. Gregory communicated that queries in search engines for information on the immigrant marches led, during this time, to our rudimentary project site (mostly still under construction). We were months from completing the project, and the need to tie events from the present day to our narrative was a reminder that, regionally, the narrative was still being written. Nevertheless, despite the lack of an accessible established infrastructure for the historical narrative, the demand for this information was visible. These events made our nascent project even more noticeable and further fed interest in regional scholarship.

Teaching and Researching History in the Present Day

Since 2005, scholarship on Latinos in the Pacific Northwest has resurfaced from the last flurry of activity in the early to middle part of the 1990s. Of note, one of the most recent collections of essays, *Memory, Community, and Activism*, edited by Jerry Garcia and Gilberto Garcia,[9] expands this examination of ethnic Mexican communities in the Pacific Northwest by including cross-cultural collaboration in labor, the cultural significance of art in public space, the role of the church in community activism, and, most critical, the role that gender has played in community organizing in the region. In addition, Jerry Garcia also published a book illustrating the formation of the Latino community in Quincy, Washington.[10]

Along with the aforementioned books, there are also recent articles, theses, and PhD dissertations that focus on Chicana and Chicano experiences in the Pacific Northwest. Aside from the Chicana/o Movement Project at the University of Washington, other research projects in existence or transferred to digital format include the Chicano/Latino Archive hosted by the Evergreen State College Library and the Columbia River Basin Ethnic History Archive hosted by Washington State University, Vancouver.[11] The proliferation of these new sources within the last few years complemented and helped strengthen the Chicana/o Movement Project's visibility. Our work confronts collective amnesia within textbooks on Washington State history and challenges textbooks on Chicana/o history to include the stories of northern communities. In effect, the literary definition of "borderlands" takes on different meaning as the experience at the U.S.-Canadian border region becomes a part of the larger historical narrative, augmented by the use of digital media to teach this unique history.

It has been over five years since the Chicana/o Movement Project was officially unveiled in August 2006. Three years later, a sister project, the Farm Workers in Washington State History Project, went live in September 2009.[12] Following a pattern much like its predecessor, the latter project worked to acknowledge the history of union organizing for Washington's socially and economically marginalized population of farm laborers. Besides influencing additional research projects, the Chicana/o Movement Project has also been used as required reading for U.S. history classes at the following institutions, among others: the University of Washington; Whitman College (a liberal arts college in Walla Walla, Washington); Washington State University; Western Washington University; the University of California, Los Angeles; and the University of Minnesota, Twin Cities.

These digital history projects, in addition to the larger Seattle Civil Rights Project, also have been featured in the American Historical Association's *Perspectives* publication, various publications oriented toward oral history and diversity, and newspapers ranging from the *Seattle Times* and *Seattle Post-Intelligencer* to the *New York Times* and *USA Today*, and the local National Public Radio affiliate KBCS.[13] The research has also been listed in the Civil Rights Digital Library and reviewed by the National History Education Clearinghouse.[14] Likewise, the local Public Broadcasting System affiliate KCTS Seattle produced a brief documentary detailing the experiences of the first class of Latino students at the University of Washington, entitled *Students of Change: Los del '68*, which used much of the background material researched by our project.[15]

Perhaps most profoundly meaningful for many of us who produced the project are comments and e-mail messages from community members who have happened upon the project or were referred to the site by a teacher or professor. For many, it was their first introduction to the local history of the Latino community in Washington State. They validated not only the struggle in producing the material but also the reasons why it matters and why it merits further research. This project was one of the first projects nationwide to fuse academic writing and public history on the open web. Even more remarkable, perhaps, is that this project gave undergraduate students the opportunity to produce Chicana/o scholarship and has drastically changed the way that this history is taught in the state of Washington.

Notes

1. For detailed information on the project, see "About the Project," Seattle Civil Rights & Labor History Project, http://depts.washington.edu/civilr/about. htm.

2. The Chicano Movement in the United States was, at its essence, the rejection of assimilation into the larger dominant U.S. culture that simultaneously sought to erase all semblance of cultural distinction (e.g. customs, language, music, ancestral knowledge) and to keep the community in a state of secondhand citizenship, locked in the cyclical poverty, disempowerment, and racism that were commonplace for many communities of color in the United States prior to the formation of the civil rights movement. See George Mariscal, *Brown-Eyed Children of the Sun: Lessons from the Chicano Movement, 1965–1975* (Albuquerque: University of New Mexico Press, 2005), 250.

3. MEChA is a student organization that has over four hundred loosely affiliated chapters throughout the United States. See "About Us," Movimiento Estudiantil Chican@ de Aztlan, http://www.nationalmecha.org/about.html.

4. In Washington State, the emergence of a youth movement first took root in rural central Washington's Yakima Valley with the emergent farmworker movement in 1966 and 1967 and established itself in Seattle with the first significant recruitment class of Chicana/o students to the University of Washington. See Jeremy Simer, "La Raza Comes to Campus: The New Chicano Contingent and the Grape Boycott at the University of Washington, 1968–69," Seattle Civil Rights & Labor History Project, http://depts.washington.edu/civilr/la_raza2.htm.

5. See "Erasmo Gamboa," Seattle Civil Rights & Labor History Project, http://depts.washington.edu/civilr/Erasmo_Gamboa.htm.

6. Oscar Rosales Castañeda, "McNair Project Proposal," document in the author's personal collection, June 6, 2005.

7. Oscar Rosales Castañeda, Maria Quintana, and James Gregory, "A History of Farm Labor Organizing, 1890–2009," Seattle Civil Rights & Labor History Project, http://depts.washington.edu/civilr/farmwk_history.htm.

8. HR 4437: Border Protection, Antiterrorism, and Illegal Immigration Control Act of 2005, Bill Summary, Library of Congress, http://thomas.loc.gov/cgi-bin/bdquery/z?d109:HR04437:@@@D&summ1&.

9. Jerry Garcia and Gilberto Garcia, eds., *Memory, Community, and Activism: Mexican Migration and Labor in the Pacific Northwest* (East Lansing: Michigan State University Press, 2005).

10. Jerry Garcia, *Mexicans in North Central Washington* (San Francisco: Arcadia, 2007).

11. Chicano/Latino Archives, Evergreen State College Library, http://chicano-latino.evergreen.edu/; Columbia River Basin Ethnic History Archive, Washington State University, Vancouver, http://archive.vancouver.wsu.edu/crbeha/home.htm. See also Oscar Rosales Castañeda, "Bibliography: Farm Workers in Washington State History Project," Seattle Civil Rights & Labor History Project, http://depts.washington.edu/civilr/farmwk_bib.htm.

12. "Special Section: Chicano Movement in Washington State History," Seattle Civil Rights & Labor History Project, http://depts.washington.edu/civilr/mecha_intro.htm; "Special Section: Farm Workers in Washington State History Project," Seattle Civil Rights & Labor History Project, http://depts.washington.edu/civilr/farmwk_intro.htm.

13. "News Coverage about the Seattle Civil Rights and Labor History Project," Seattle Civil Rights & Labor History Project, http://depts.washington.edu/civilr/publicity.htm.

14. Civil Rights Digital Library, http://crdl.usg.edu/topics/boycott_direct_action/; National History Education Clearinghouse, http://teachinghistory.org/history-content/website-reviews/24033.

15. *Students of Change: Los del '68*, KCTS 9, Seattle, 2009, http://video.kcts9.org/video/1491354319/.

Citizen Scholars

Facebook and the Co-creation of Knowledge

Amanda Grace Sikarskie

Doing historical research and writing on Facebook or Twitter may still seem like a strange notion to some. Social networks once had a reputation as frivolous spaces in which young people entered into and out of romantic relationships faster than one can click the "like" button and where "older" people (read "over 25") posted incessantly about the rare finds they made at the local organic farmer's market and consumed in their latest meal. While these uses of social media have not gone away (stop telling me about your arugula!), the value of social media sites such as Facebook for historians, both academics and those outside academia, has become increasingly apparent. This essay seeks to present and contextualize the role of the lay historian—what I am calling the "citizen scholar"[1]—in the production of historical research and writing through social media.

In her 2011 blog post "More Crowdsourced Scholarship: Citizen History," Elissa Frankle wrote, "In the history museum of the future, curators' work will be driven by our audiences' curiosity, and their preference for inquiry over certainty."[2] This growing preference for inquiry over certainty, for co-creation of content rather than consumption of content, is the basis of citizen scholarship in social media. Through the lens of a case study of interactions with citizen scholars on Facebook, I seek to illustrate the small yet profound ways in which lay historians are crowdsourcing the production of historical knowledge.

Connecting through "Quilts of the Day"

I am currently a faculty member in public history at Western Michigan University. Previously, from 2008 to 2011, I worked as a doctoral research assistant for the Quilt Index, a digital repository providing preservation and access to images and metadata for over 50,000 quilts.[3] In addition to my regular work, I also managed the project's social media campaign, including a Twitter feed, a blog, a wiki, and our most popular social media channel, a fan page on Facebook.[4]

As of this writing, in January 2012, the Facebook fan page has over 2,250 fans, most of whom seem to be middle-aged to older women who are either hobbyist quiltmakers or self-styled lay quilt historians, though we do, of course, have many fans who do not meet this description. It is a geographically diverse group, with around 20 percent of our fans living outside the United States, in such far-flung places as Ethiopia and Pakistan, and with huge followings in Canada, Italy, the United Kingdom, and South Africa.[5]

The Quilt Index social media strategy on Facebook includes engaging with the audience via trivia questions, which are designed to foster a personal connection to content, and by posting a "Quilt of the Day" daily. Themes for the Quilt of the Day (a particular pattern, period, region, etc.) are often suggested by the fans themselves. I facilitated this collective curatorial choice by posing several similar options the week before and inviting fans to use the comment feature to make their choice. For example, in July 2010, I asked the audience to choose from among five "quilt-specific" fabric colors (each of which are very much rooted in specific historical periods): cheddar orange, chocolate brown, indigo blue, Nile green, and Turkey red.

Negotiating this mass curatorial process and engaging in the co-creation of knowledge with the audience on Facebook has been fascinating. On several occasions, fans have demonstrated strong historical knowledge of a particular historical period or type of quilt or have even suggested ways in which a quilt's metadata record might be more complete. This has then prompted me and other Quilt Index staff to do additional research and post the findings. Comments posted on the Quilt Index Facebook page often provide obscure information about pattern origins and early or out-of-print publications.

Citizen Scholars and Collective Knowledge

One out-of-print publication that we learned more about through our Facebook page is Roderick Kiracofe's *Homage to Amanda.*[6] In June 2011, I posted a Quilt of the Day and noted in my post that according to the quilt's metadata record, the quilt had been published in a book called *Homage to Amanda.* I inquired if anyone had ever heard of it, and several people reported that they had, including the author of the book, who happened to be our fan. The author even offered to send me a free copy of the book, as it is out of print. Skeptics might argue that those with such historical knowledge to share are the exception, rather than the rule, and that the majority of those on the Quilt Index Facebook page are there just to look at quilts or because they simply wanted more pages to "like." Indeed, many of our fans do come to the page to self-identify with a quilt-related community or to gain intellectual or emotional uplift from the quilts (both of which are worthy outcomes as well), rather than to engage in some form of knowledge production.

Referring to the dynamic of a teacher and student (or a Facebook manager and Facebook fan) is perhaps a more apt way of describing the work we are doing on Facebook with this population of "self-identifiers." However, even this top-down model of scholarly communication is still a process of co-creation of knowledge to an extent. As Elissa Frankle noted,

> In the age of the twenty-four hour news cycle and a well-researched, well-policed Wikipedia, museums like to believe that we still have the advantage of being Authorities. We know how to do Research. We know how to pose the Right Questions. We know, most importantly, how to Give Our Visitors The Answers. Citizen History is an experiment in finding out what happens if we trust our visitors enough to allow them to bring their diverse perspectives and boundless enthusiasm into the research work of the museum and share our authority. . . . Citizen History opens up a museum's existing data to participants and, through scaffolded inquiry, invites participants to draw conclusions to answer big questions.[7]

This sort of "scaffolded inquiry,"[8] which allows for a sharing but not a relinquishing of authority, provides a space in which those who might be better defined as simply citizens, rather than citizen scholars, can still work alongside us.

The Quilt Index fan page does have several individuals who are clearly visiting the fan page for the purpose of participation in research. In fact, one of our fans in Pakistan (another indicator of the very international nature of this scholarly exchange) alerted me that a ralli quilt[9] that I had posted during "International Week" had an incorrect provenance. According to its donor-submitted metadata, the quilt was made in India. However, the fan argued that it was actually made in Pakistan. I was later able to do some research to prove the fan's assertion, resulting in the updating of the quilt's record. (See the image in the web version of this essay at http:// WritingHistory.trincoll.edu.)

Taken together, these short anecdotes on co-curating Quilts of the Day, crowdsourcing the ralli quilt record, and connecting with the author of *Homage to Amanda* (culled from numerous examples of such interactions on the Quilt Index Facebook page) may be understood in the context of what cybertheorist Pierre Lévy termed "collective intelligence." In *Cyberculture*, Lévy describes the collective intelligence brought about by online communication.

> My hypothesis is that cyberculture reinstates the copresence of messages and their context, which had been the current of oral societies, but on a different scale and on a different plane. The new universality no longer depends on self-sufficient texts, on the fixity and independence of signification. It is constructed and extended by interconnecting messages with one another, by their continuous ramification through virtual communities, which instills in them varied meanings that are continuously renewed.[10]

One can understand the collective intelligence of lay scholars' crowdsourcing of history in this way: no one historian knows everything, and everyone actively posting content has something slightly different to offer the community. All of the content produced and posted by lay quilt scholars amounts to the collective intelligence of the quilt world, a body of knowledge that no one individual can ever know in its entirety, for it is simply too vast. Collectively, these social citizen scholars have created a massive, fairly cohesive body of knowledge online. I see this collaborative, corporate way of producing and sharing knowledge as a new genre of historical writing and research,[11] a genre that challenges but need not overthrow traditional academic assumptions about single authorship and the roles of lay scholars.

Social media shifts the role of authority from being vested solely in a historical cultural domain, such as the museum or the university history department, to being shared with a community- or user-generated body of information that is critiqued within the community. Academic historians are beginning to recognize that this outpouring of lay scholarship on Facebook and through other social media outlets is neither to be ignored nor to be feared. The ability of citizen scholars to engage in historical inquiry on Facebook pages such as the Quilt Index's fan page is strengthening, rather than eroding, the connection between lay historians and museum professionals and other academics. In fact, I myself (an academic historian) have cited Facebook comments before. Facebook is challenging the traditional channels of scholarly communication, and crowdsourcing is changing the way in which I approach the writing of history.

Acknowledgments: I am grateful to my colleagues at the Quilt Index— Marsha MacDowell, Mary Worrall, Justine Richardson, and Amy Milne— for their help and guidance with this project. I also very much thank those who provided comments and questions during the open peer review, especially Timothy Burke, Bethany Nowviskie, and Barbara Rockenbach. A big thank-you goes to Beth Donaldson, herself a lay quilt historian, who recently took over for me as Quilt Index social media manager after I accepted my current faculty position.

Notes

1. In this essay, the terms *lay scholar*, *lay historian*, and *citizen scholar* are all used more or less interchangeably, to indicate someone who produces (historical) scholarship without having attained a postbaccalaureate academic degree, the MA or PhD in history or a related discipline. These terms are all used to contrast such scholars to the academic historian, who possesses such a credential and often works within a university or museum setting. When used on its own in this essay, the term *scholar* refers simply to a person who participates in historical research and writing.

2. Elissa Frankle, "More Crowdsourced Scholarship: Citizen History," blog of the Center for the Future of Museums, July 28, 2011, http://futureofmuseums. blogspot.com/2011/07/more-crowdsourced-scholarship-citizen.html.

3. The Quilt Index (http://www.quiltindex.org) is a partnership project between Michigan State University's MATRIX: The Center for Humane Arts, Letters, and Social Sciences Online, the Michigan State University Museum, and the Alliance for American Quilts. It has been funded in part by grants from the National Endowment for the Humanities and the Institute for Museum and Library Services.

4. Quilt Index Twitter feed, http://www.twitter.com/quiltindex; blog, http://www.quiltindex.org/news; wiki page, http://www.quiltindex.org/~quilti/wiki/index.php/Main_Page; Facebook fan page, http://www.facebook.com/quiltindex.

5. Statistics and countries given are according to Insights, Facebook's internal analytics application for managers of fan pages.

6. Roderick Kiracofe, *Homage to Amanda: Two Hundred Years of American Quilts* (San Francisco: R K Press, 1984).

7. Frankle, "More Crowdsourced Scholarship."

8. In learning theory, the term *scaffolded inquiry* refers to a social constructivist idea in which learning is facilitated by a framework, or scaffold, constructed by the content expert. Scaffolded inquiry can also facilitate collaboration with peers.

9. Ralli quilts are a traditional form of quilted patchwork produced in Pakistan and northwestern India.

10. Pierre Lévy, *Cyberculture* (Minneapolis: University of Minnesota Press, 2011), xiv.

11. Bethany Nowviskie, comment on Amanda Grace Sikarskie, "Citizen Scholars," in *Writing History in the Digital Age*, web-book ed., Fall 2011 version.

The *HeritageCrowd* Project

A Case Study in Crowdsourcing Public History

Shawn Graham, Guy Massie, and Nadine Feuerherm

Digital history is public history: when we put materials online, we enter into a conversation with individuals from all walks of life, with various voices and degrees of professionalism. In this essay, we discuss our experience in relinquishing control of the historical voice in order to crowdsource cultural heritage and history. What is the role of the historian when we crowdsource history? Whose history is it anyway—the historian's or the crowd's? Which crowd can lay claim to it?

Wikipedia, the exemplar par excellence of what crowdsourcing can accomplish, has perhaps the most succinct and elegant definition of the term: "a distributed problem-solving and production model."[1] This definition dovetails nicely with recent polemics about the nature of the digital humanities more generally, where digital work is not just about solving a problem but also about "building things," as Steven Ramsay has argued.[2] Notice that this definition says nothing about the nature of the crowd, its professionalism, or its training; there is an implicit suggestion that "anyone" can be part of the crowd. Notable projects that crowdsource historical problems range from *Ancient Lives*, a project to transcribe the Oxyrhynchus papyri; to *Transcribe Bentham*, a project to transcribe the papers of Jeremy Bentham; to the National Geographic Society's *Field Expedition: Mongolia*, where contributors study satellite images of Mongolia to help direct the archaeological survey team on the ground.[3]

Roy Rosenzweig has made the case for the need for historians to engage audiences outside the discipline, as well as for the power of historical narratives to bring about social justice.[4] On a similar note, in 1932, Carl Becker, taking part in what was already an old discussion about the professionalization of history, wrote, "If the essence of history is the memory of things said and done, then it is obvious that every normal person, Mr. Everyman, knows some history."[5] In the age of *Wikipedia* as the go-to place for historical knowledge and of increased funding cuts to humanities research, the need to reach out to the public has never been greater. Edward L. Ayers argued that while a "democratization of history" has taken place since the emergence of new historical fields in academia, a "democratization of audience" has yet to come.[6] Digital history has the potential to address these concerns by linking members of a community together to collaborate on historical projects.

Nevertheless, the Internet is not an inherently even playing field; to digitize is not to democratize.[7] Technical literacy, closed algorithms for search engines, unequal access to quality hardware, and poor Internet connections mean that there is a disparity among users in their ability to manipulate the Internet for their own purposes.[8] Colleen Morgan points out that "when even considered," the audience for digital work "is almost always assumed to be male, white, western users of technology, a broadly defined 'public' for whom digitality is an obvious boon."[9] To put historical materials online is not a neutral process; to ask the crowd to solve a problem has the effect of creating self-selected groups, people who participate not just by interest but also by technological proficiency.

Our own project, which we christened *HeritageCrowd*, attempts to take these issues into account as we provide tools for the group expression of local history and heritage in certain rural communities in Eastern Canada, using low-tech "old digital media," such as short message service (SMS) and voice mail, built into a web-based system.[10] We wanted to bring the potential of digital technology to bear on a region with relatively low Internet access but also a relatively high interest in local history. (See the images in the web version of this essay at http://WritingHistory.trincoll.edu.)

Canadians may lead the world in Internet use,[11] but this usage is not distributed equitably—for instance, across the rural and urban divide.[12] Many rural museums and cultural heritage organizations do not have the technical expertise, human resources, or funding to effectively curate and interpret their materials, let alone to present them in a comprehensive manner over the Internet. These organizations constituted our ideal "crowds" for this project. We used two web-based platforms. The first platform is Ushahidi, a system developed in Kenya in the wake of the 2008 election violence, allowing for quick "reports" to be posted to a map via SMS messaging, voice mail (using voice-to-text software), Twitter, e-mail, and web forms.[13] The second platform is Omeka, from the Rosenzweig Center for History and New Media at George Mason University, which we use to archive and tell "stories" built around the contributions submitted on the Ushahidi platform.[14]

Local history associations and other heritage groups form the backbone of a community's collective memory, preserving and performing their sense of historicity. At its more elementary level, the goal of our project was simply to assist local heritage initiatives by creating a web-based system that could store and accept short, text contributions. The submissions that came in were then approved by members of the project team and enabled on the Ushahidi-powered site, where they were placed as reports on a map of the region.[15]

Research Objectives

In the initial proposal for this project, we were particularly interested in trying to address the rural-urban digital divide in Canada, by using the SMS system as the project's backbone. We asked, can public history be crowdsourced? What does that even mean? How could the SMS system be used to collect local knowledge of heritage resources? What can be curated in this way? In what ways would such a system change the nature of local knowledge, once that knowledge becomes available to the wider world on the web?

We targeted a local area with which we were familiar, Pontiac County in Western Quebec, known locally as "the Pontiac."[16] Internet connectivity in the Pontiac has only recently transitioned from dial-up Internet connection.[17] More important, over half the population does not have a high school diploma,[18] an indicator of low Internet use.[19] The Pontiac's sister county in the neighboring province of Ontario, Renfrew, was also a target region, for similar reasons.[20] Both of these counties together are known as the "Upper Ottawa Valley." Could a low-tech approach to crowdsourcing history reach this particular crowd, and what kind of history would emerge?

Strong institutional narratives were already at play, given the provincial boundary between our two target counties. Education is a provincial responsibility in Canada, and the province of Quebec teaches a very different historical narrative than the province of Ontario.[21] The histories of the regions and of minority groups do not have any real role in the "official" history taught at the high school level. Our project, then, has the political and social goal of validating those marginalized histories, to give a sense of legitimacy to the historical narratives of the local community. This made us question the role of the historian in this context; by crowdsourcing local history, we had transcended the traditional role of the historian as being an arbiter of historical truth.[22] Historians who crowdsource the writing of historical narratives may be able to empower members of a given community who may not have the same institutionalized or professional authority conceded to "experts" in the discipline. This mission is distinctly different from that of most academic historians, whose work is centered around the construction of historical narratives based on the analysis of sources, and from that of museum or public historians, who attempt to provide an impartial and objective narrative of the past for public consumption.

Initial Results

To encourage submissions from visitors to the website, we created a number of reports to "seed" it, assuming that visitors would be less likely to submit reports if the site was empty or contained few reports. As of the end of July 2011, we have received 25 reports (5 contributions by voice mail, 7 by SMS, and 13 by e-mail, from unique contributors), and the site has 50 reports listed (this number includes the previous amount listed plus reports submitted via the website). At the time of writing, the site had been open to the public for a total of 54 days. As the Upper Ottawa Valley has a population of approximately 90,000 people, this suggests that about one in four thousand people living in the targeted area made a submission to the project.

It is difficult to judge whether or not this figure represents a low participation rate, since we have no comparable data. The promotion of the project took place by contacting local history associations and genealogical groups, churches, and museums via mail and e-mail. A brief labor disruption with Canada Post, the national postal operator, occurred in the early phases of the project, but we do not believe it to have been responsible for any significant delays in processing our mail. A large spike in submissions took place immediately after the publication of a newsprint article about the *HeritageCrowd* project in the urban newspaper the *Ottawa Citizen* (Renfrew and the Pontiac are in the city of Ottawa's hinterland).[23] As Amanda Sikarskie describes in this volume, her experience with the Quilt Index database, another important historical crowdsourcing project, shows that an effective and well-organized social media campaign has the ability to vastly increase the size of the "crowd" that participates in the project.[24]

Reflections

From a technological point of view, our mission was simply to give people the digital tools to more easily express and share their sense of heritage and local history. During the course of the project, however, it became evident that a second crowdsourcing method could be used for a similar goal. This approach, which could be called "retroactive crowdsourcing" (for lack of a better term), involves gathering representations of local history and heritage from disparate online sources that already exist and then collecting them in an online database.[25] This is different from our original concept of crowdsourcing, where we actively solicited submissions to our project from a wide community.

We trawled through a number of different kinds of sites (such as Flickr. com), other amateur and local historical and genealogical websites (such as Bytown.net), blog posts, and online exhibits. This produced a sizable collection of heritage materials. We created an example report, "St. John's Lutheran Church and Cemetery, Sebastopol Township."[26] A picture of the church taken by a Flickr user was uploaded (with permission) to the report, and a link was provided to a website that had photographed all of the headstones in the cemetery. The use of automated spiders and other software tools, such as DownThemAll or DevonAgent, could speed up this process and broaden its reach considerably.[27] Indeed, this example shows one sense in which our project's focus was misplaced. Crowdsourcing should not be a first step. The resources are already out there; why not trawl, crawl, spider, and collect what has already been uploaded to the Internet? Once the knowledge is collected, one could call on the crowd to fill in the gaps. This would perhaps be a better use of time, money, and resources.

In hindsight, one of the ways in which the project could have attracted more submissions lay in implementing what Jane McGonigal calls "classic game rewards"—in other words, building a series of gamelike mechanics into the project. These include giving the participants "a clear sense of purpose," as well as giving them the impression that they are "making an obvious impact" and contributing to "continuous progress."[28] *Gamification* is a troubled term, in that while it implies using the classical tools of games to foster engagement, it can also be taken to suggest the trivialization of the task at hand or, worse, exploitation of the user/visitor.[29] Be that as it may, McGonigal cites major crowdsourced collaborations, such as Wikipedia, as being successful because of subtle systems of rewards, satisfaction, and, to some extent, social interaction.[30] *HeritageCrowd* could foster engagement through its "comments" feature on the individual reports in the Ushahidi platform, but here we have a clear case of where the technology, the medium, shapes the message: Ushahidi is for quickly reporting crisis incidents, not for fostering a dialogue about them. For our purpose, a great deal of modification needs to be done to the core platform, perhaps by merging the reporting system with the autocreation of wiki pages.

Although the accumulation of reports on the Ushahidi-powered website's map could be seen as an indicator of progress over time, these reports first had to be approved by us before becoming visible (a decision taken to filter out potential spam or otherwise unsuitable material). The instant satisfaction of having made a contribution to the project was therefore lost. Similarly, one would not have been able to track one's own individual progress (that is, with a personal account and information interface that lists the number of contributions). Either further development of the Ushahidi platform or the use of an additional platform to track this data for users could provide this benefit.

The concept behind the project (crowdsourcing local history and heritage using SMS networks and voice mail) proved to be an obstacle in some cases. When we visited community events or corresponded with individuals who expressed interest, some people were unsure what exactly we were asking them to do. This was most likely because the project was centered on a concept with which many people in the region were unfamiliar. We could easily explain it in person whenever we were asked about the project, but it is entirely plausible that some contributors made submissions to the project (by sending a text message or voice mail, for instance) without having fully understood how the submissions were compiled onto our website. (The article in the *Ottawa Citizen* was published digitally for a while with the headline "Text If You Are a Descendant of Philemon Wright."[31] We duly received a number of text messages with the exact message "I am a descendant of Philemon Wright.") The layout of the main website also provides some confusion, as it is not immediately obvious how or what visitors actually *do* on the site. We believe that this confusion was partly responsible for the evolution of the project from a tool where collaboration and community support was envisioned, a process of sharing authority, to one where we the historians seem to be using the crowd more as a reservoir, contrary to our intentions.

Finally, we had a number of potential contributors who were worried that what they had to contribute was not "professional" enough and who were thus reluctant to actually contribute; in these cases, our role seemed to be to reassure them that what they knew, what they valued, did have "offi-cial" historical value. One community activist approached us with a body of materials that she had collected as part of a continuing negotiation with a local city council in Quebec over the development of a neighborhood. This neighborhood is predominantly Anglophone, while the city itself is largely Francophone. The history and memory of this one neighborhood was thus caught up in larger issues of identity, power, and institutionalized inter-pretations of history. The city council wishes to rezone the neighborhood to allow for high-rise condominiums. The activist approached us to see if we could "legitimize" what she had collected, in the hopes of forcing the city to adopt specific heritage recommendations into its planning process. The act of collecting community knowledge, since it was being done via our university-funded project, seems to put an imprimatur of "truth" and legitimacy on anything submitted and displayed. On all submissions, the Ushahidi platform uses the term *verified* in the sense of crisis management, to indicate that what is described in the submission actually happened. Our approach was initially one where we used the term simply as a spam filter. Clearly, this was far too simplistic and carries implications far beyond what we initially imagined.

Early Conclusions

At this early stage in our project, the single most important observation is the role our project seems to have in validating individuals' and groups' historical knowledge. Even if we have not yet collected masses of docu-mentation, we provide a new avenue for nonprofessional knowledge to enter into the academic world of knowledge production. Consequently, by adapting a platform meant for one domain into another, there is procedural rhetoric that needs to be taken into account when designing how the proj-ect works.[32] Our authority was not shared; rather, the platform and our use of it seem to have reinforced the primacy of the historian.

Were we to start this project over, we would spend more time modify-ing the basic platform to combat this result. The terminology and struc-ture of the platform as it currently stands give more authority to the data displayed than might be warranted. We had imagined that if a contribution was made that might not be factually accurate or that carried political bias, a discussion would take place in the comments for that item and would result in the issue resolving itself (much like what happens on *Wikipedia*). This has not yet happened. Perhaps the fact that this project is university funded and carried out by university researchers and students also gives immediate "weight" and authority to anything displayed on the website, thus inhibiting discussion.

When the aim of a crowdsourced project is to transcribe documents, it is self-evident what needs to be done. When the aim is a bit more nebulous, like in the case of *HeritageCrowd*, we could suggest the following guidelines:

- Choose your base platform carefully, thinking through the technological and epistemological implications. (As it happens, Ushahidi as a platform does work in terms of widening access beyond the tech-savvy: we did get voice and SMS contributions and so met at least that aim of our project.)
- Collect what already exists.
- Seed your site with the collected existing material so that you can identify the gaps.
- Narrow your target when communicating with the public: get them to fill the holes.
- Make sure to design for engagement.
- Put initial resources into publicity. Building your crowd is key. Get out, walk the walk, and talk to people. Identify, contact, and cultivate key players.
- Have an "elevator pitch." Make sure that the project can be described completely in 30 seconds or less. Build your outreach and social media strategy around getting that pitch in front of as many eyes in your target crowd as possible.

The funding for *HeritageCrowd* was limited to only a few summer months. However, by using open-source, freely available software, its continuing operating costs run to that of maintaining the web hosting. We will be taking the lessons we learned in the summer of 2011 and using them to improve our approach. With time, we hope to reach more of our target audience. *HeritageCrowd* will also become a platform for the training of students in digital history, outreach, and exhibition. As we collect more materials, we will be developing the Omeka-based "Stories" part of our site, allowing individuals, societies, students, and researchers to tell the stories that emerge from the crowdsourced contributions. It is still our hope that the role of the digital historian might be shifted away from that of the expert, dictating historical narratives from an academic podium, and toward an activist role for grassroots community empowerment. Digitally crowdsourced history has the potential to be like a cracked mirror: it could reflect what looks into it, and while it might not (cannot?) produce a polished, singular view, the aesthetic pleasure will lie in the abundance of perspectives that it provides.

Acknowledgments: The *HeritageCrowd* project was funded by a 2011 Junior Research Fellowship from the Faculty of Arts and Social Sciences at Carleton University, whose support is gratefully acknowledged. We would like to thank James Miller, Jim Opp, John Walsh, Lisa Mibach, and the contributors to *HeritageCrowd* for their interest, support, and feedback. Errors and omissions are our own.

Notes

1. "Crowdsourcing," *Wikipedia*, http://en.wikipedia.org/w/index.php?title=Crowdsourcing&oldid=470989039.

2. Stephen Ramsay, "Who's In and Who's Out" (text of paper delivered at MLA2011, Los Angeles, January 8, 2011, posted to personal blog), http://lenz.unl.edu/papers/2011/01/08/whos-in-and-whos-out.html.

3. *Ancient Lives*, University of Oxford, http://www.ancientlives.org; *Transcribe Bentham*, University College London, http://www.ucl.ac.uk/transcribe-bentham/; *Field Expedition: Mongolia*, National Geographic Society, http://exploration.nationalgeographic.com/mongolia.

4. Roy Rosenzweig, "Afterthoughts: Roy Rosenzweig," *The Presence of the Past*, 1998, http://chnm.gmu.edu/survey/afterroy.html.

5. Carl Becker, "Everyman His Own Historian," *American Historical Review* 37 (1932): 223.

6. Edward L. Ayers, "The Pasts and Futures of Digital History," http://www.vcdh.virginia.edu/PastsFutures.html.

7. Compare Evgeny Morozov, *The Net Delusion: The Dark Side of Internet Freedom* (New York: Public Affairs, 2011).

8. Lorna Richardson, "The Internet Delusion and Public Archaeology Online" (paper presented at the annual conference of the Central Theoretical Archaeology Group, London, May 14, 2011), excerpted online at http://digipubarch.org/2011/12/14/inequalities-in-public-archaeology-online/.

9. Colleen Morgan, "Contextualized Digital Archaeology—Chapter 3," draft of PhD diss., Anthropology Department, University of California, Berkeley, p. 3, http://middlesavagery.wordpress.com/2011/12/19/contextualized-digital-archaeology-dissertation-chapter/.

10. *HeritageCrowd*, Carleton University, http://heritagecrowd.org. In May 2012, the site was maliciously hacked and, as of this writing, is off-line, as described in Shawn Graham, "How I Lost the Crowd: A Tale of Sorrow and Hope," *Electric Archaeology*, May 18, 2012, http://electricarchaeologist.wordpress.com/2012/05/18/how-i-lost-the-crowd-a-tale-of-sorrow-and-hope/.

11. ComScore, "The 2010 Canada Digital Year in Review 2010," March 2011,

http://www.comscore.com/content/download/7717/133765/version/5/file/comSc
ore+2010+Canada+Digital+Year+in+Review.pdf.

12. Compare Ian Marlow and Jacquie McNish, "Canada's Digital Divide," *Globe and Mail*, April 2, 2010, http://www.theglobeandmail.com/report-on-business/canadas-digital-divide/article1521631/.

13. Ushahidi, "About Us," http://ushahidi.com/about-us. See also "Mobile Services in Poor Countries: Not Just Talk," *Economist*, January 27, 2011, http://www.economist.com/node/18008202.

14. Roy Rosenzweig Center for History and New Media, Omeka, http://omeka.org.

15. "Approving" a report was a step built into the platform; no report could be viewed unless it was approved. We did not edit or turn away submissions unless they were manifestly spam.

16. One of us has deep family ties in the area.

17. MRC de Pontiac, "Plan stratégique—Vision Pontiac 2020," April 2009, http://www.mrcpontiac.qc.ca/documents/vision2020/Diagnostic%20-%20MRC%20de%20Pontiac.pdf.

18. MRC Pontiac, "Demographic and Socio-economic Profile, Pontiac Municipal Regional County," 2006, http://web.archive.org/web/20111011002302/http://mrcpontiac.qc.ca/en/regional/regional_demographic.htm.

19. Statistics Canada, "Internet Use by Individuals, by Selected Characteristics," 2005–9, http://www.statcan.gc.ca/tables-tableaux/sum-som/l01/cst01/comm35a-eng.htm.

20. The proportion of individuals in Renfrew County without a high school diploma is about 26 percent. Statistics Canada, "2006 Community Profiles—Renfrew County and District Health Unit," http://www12.statcan.ca/census-recensement/2006/dp-pd/prof/92-591/index.cfm?Lang=E.

21. Problems with the provincial history curriculum, as it pertains to the Anglophone history of Quebec, have long been recognized. See, for instance, Sam Allison and Jon Bradley, "Quebec Exam Is Bad History, Written in Bad English," *Montreal Gazette*, July 5, 2011, http://j.mp/gazette-bad-english.

22. See, for instance, the papers in the special edition edited by Steven High, Lisa Ndejuru, and Kristen O'Hare, "Sharing Authority: Community-University Collaboration in Oral History, Digital Storytelling, and Engaged Scholarship," *Journal of Canadian Studies/Revue d'études canadiennes* 43, no. 1 (2009).

23. Matthew Pearson, "Text If You Are a Descendant of Philemon Wright," *Ottawa Citizen*, June 25, 2011.

24. Amanda Grace Sikarskie, "Citizen Scholars: Facebook and the Co-creation of Knowledge," in this volume.

25. Guy Massie, "Photos, Exhibit Research, and Thoughts about Crowdsourcing," *HeritageCrowd Journal*, June 24, 2011, http://www.heritagecrowd.org/journal/?p=38.

26. "St. John's Lutheran Church and Cemetery, Sebastopol Township," June 23, 2011, http://heritagecrowd.org/reports/view/39.

27. William J. Turkel, "Spider to Collect Sources," March 23, 2011, http://williamjturkel.net/2011/03/22/spider-to-collect-sources/; DownThemAll, http://www.downthemall.net/; DevonAgent, http://www.devontechnologies.com/.

28. Jane McGonigal, *Reality Is Broken: Why Games Make Us Better and How They Can Change the World* (New York: Penguin, 2011), 222–23.

29. Ian Bogost, "Gamification Is Bullshit: My Position Statement at the Wharton Gamification Symposium," August 8, 2011, http://www.bogost.com/blog/gamification_is_bullshit.shtml.

30. McGonigal, *Reality Is Broken*, 219–46.

31. Philemon Wright was the first major colonist and landowner in the region, *Dictionary of Canadian Biography Online*, http://www.biographi.ca/009004-119.01-e.php?id_nbr=3738.

32. See Ian Bogost, *Persuasive Games: The Expressive Power of Videogames* (Cambridge, MA: MIT Press, 2007), on how software processes force a particular rhetoric of expression in the final representation of digital data.

PART 7

Collaborative Writing:
Yours, Mine, and Ours

Networked computers create more opportunities for historians to engage in collaborative work, and this section offers perspectives on such opportunities from different points in the writing process. First, in "The Accountability Partnership: Writing and Surviving in the Digital Age," coauthors Natalia Mehlman Petrzela and Sarah Manekin share their story of online support for dissertation writing, along with broader reflections on what writing guides do not tell us. Next, Alex Sayf Cummings and Jonathan Jarrett write about their past experiences, future predictions, and friendly disagreements regarding history blogs, in "Only Typing? Informal Writing, Blogging, and the Academy."

The Accountability Partnership

Writing and Surviving in the Digital Age

Natalia Mehlman Petrzela and Sarah Manekin

In 2007, we were struggling to write the dissertations that stood between us and our PhDs in history. Studying different centuries and working in distant cities, we were both frustrated with our lack of writing progress and desperate to find strategies that could help. So we decided to experiment with an accountability partnership. For the next two years, we sent each other daily e-mails that contained our goals for the day, a tentative schedule for how we would achieve those goals, and the occasional rambling reflection on the particular analytical question that had us in knots. Over the course of that two-year period, we kept each other on task, modeled for each other perseverance and life balance, and inspired each other to continue forward on the long marathon that constitutes completing a dissertation.

Now that our dissertations have been securely filed and our careers have moved ahead, we can reflect on our partnership, what it meant, and why it worked. What have we concluded? Our accountability partnership is worth analyzing and sharing as a writing strategy of the digital age. In this essay, we present that strategy and offer some reflections on how it advances the possibilities for collaboration in writing history.

We place our self-designed, daily, online accountability partnership at the center of our analysis here, but rather than simply presenting what we did and why it helped, we examine the wider literature of "writing guides," to enable a richer discussion of the strategies that can be deployed to facilitate success. In general, we found that this literature is perfectly maddening and largely banal and incomplete—and mostly dead right. As much as is written on the topic, we found the advice largely insufficient to address the experiences of novice writers in the digital age. Moreover, in our writing strategy, we discovered a rich possibility for shared enterprise, an experience too often assumed to be absent from the pursuit of historical scholarship.

For as long as young scholars have labored over dissertations and first books, they have wrestled with identifying a research question, finding sources, organizing their ideas, and explaining those ideas in smooth, elegant prose. These intellectual and organizational practices form the core of our craft and are commonly accepted as the sources of our struggles. Historians and scholars across the ages have developed a wide range of strategies to move forward with their work. As the essays in this collection reveal, however, the digital age has changed how we research and what we find; it has changed how we access sources and compile bibliographies, and it has changed how we compose our ideas. This volume makes a strong case for the necessity of rethinking some of the intellectual and organizational challenges of our craft and presents strategies for navigating them.

For us, it was the emotional and psychological challenges of dissertation writing that proved most vexing, and it is difficult to know the extent to which the digital age has altered those challenges.[1] Young scholars such as ourselves are increasingly "digital natives" and, therefore, cannot really compare our experience to anything else.[2] Yet almost every one of us—digital native or neophyte—has experienced those moments when the demons of self-doubt arise and the prospect of sitting down to write feels increasingly unfathomable; we have also experienced the utter isolation and anxiety such emotions evoke. So the question animating our essay resonates with those posed in most essays presented in this volume. As we seek to understand how the digital age has changed the process of writing history, our experience with the accountability partnership leads us to ask how we can best harness technology to address the overwhelming feelings of isolation and anxiety often attendant to the task of writing and to question the assumption that historical writing and research is an inherently solitary process.

We developed our accountability partnership based on our innate sense of why we were struggling and what we thought could help. Unbeknownst to us, a wide range of support mechanisms—packaged in forms ranging from self-help books to coaching sessions to boot camps—already existed to support the dissertators who valiantly resist joining the nearly one-quarter to one-third of humanities and social science students in the United States who fail to complete their doctoral degrees.[3] Apparently, we learned as we explored this literature, legions of ABD (All but Dissertation) candidates out there were just like us: they too felt the gravity of the "rules changing" in the transition from diligent students in coursework to young scholars expected to generate original research.[4] Others also felt stymied by the solitude of the dissertation endeavor and by the total freedom to do nothing (or at least to "procrastinate productively," undertaking discrete tasks that bestow the down-pat sense of accomplishment that working on a major piece of writing fails to provide). This curious little niche of America's twelve-billion-dollar self-help industry, which characterizes "the internal world" of most dissertators as filled with "self-doubt, anxiety, fear, procrastination, perfectionism, and other unwanted experiences," affirmed that our sense of guilt about spending any time away from our dissertations or even away from worrying about our dissertations was hardly unique.[5]

Geared to assist any and all dissertators in surviving thesis writing, these wide-ranging supports vary in their emphases. Some coaches and scholars highlight problems of efficiency and execution, while others focus on emotional and psychological obstacles. But all offer similar strategies for achieving success. Ritualized practice is one mainstay of the literature. Joan Bolker's *Writing Your Dissertation in 15 Minutes a Day* underscores the daily, consistent effort necessary to churn out what Anne Lamott has famously called "a shitty first draft."[6] Dissertation boot camps multiplying on august campuses such as the University of Pennsylvania and Princeton University are primarily mechanisms for making students "show up" to write every day, intellectually and physically.[7] All guides emphasize setting goals that are smaller and more attainable than the elusive and daunting "finish the dissertation." Texts that privilege the emotional and psychological dimensions of novice writers' experience counsel abandoning "negative thoughts" and "self-flagellation" in order to "enjoy the journey" and the inherent "pleasures" of dissertation writing.[8] Completing a successful dissertation, the argument goes, is predicated on practicing "self-care" and "nurture" (e.g., exercise, leisure, and proper eating) in order to escape the "quagmire of self-doubt" that plagues so many graduate students.

So, did our accountability partnership reinvent the wheel? Some might say yes: the literature clearly suggests that almost everyone in our situation feels as we did and that many of the very strategies we "invented" had already been mapped out for and marketed to the dissertation-writing crowd. In the main, the books offered sound, if highly commonsensical, advice; and in general terms, our partnership followed those broad contours. But the personal online partnership we cultivated offered crucial elements that books and boot camps lacked.

First of all, the literature feels incomplete and unsatisfying, due to what scholars of American self-help traditions have identified as a hallmark of the genre: they oversimplify complex problems and offer reductive solutions.[9] Titles such as *Writing Your Dissertation in 15 Minutes a Day* employ facile quantification; the author herself admits that she does not actually know anyone who has completed a dissertation by writing so little and that the title simply evokes the daily commitment necessary to the task (and was certain to "get the reader's attention").[10] Similarly, "surefire" tips and universal solutions fill the dissertation advice literature and diminish its power. Peg Boyle Single's *Demystifying Dissertation Writing* is billed as a "streamlined process from choice of topic to final text" and boasts a glossy image of a lightbulb turning into a laptop morphing into a book, suggesting that a finished project is the inevitable outcome of following her steps to success.[11] While the steps are many, vary depending on scholar and topic, and require consistent commitment, following such a regimen is portrayed as a surefire way to achieve results. Boot camps, one of the newest arrivals on the scene, suggest that laziness is all that stands in the way of a completed dissertation. They invoke a drill sergeant's approach, promising to turn "slackers into scholars."[12] As Barbara Ehrenreich has pointed out in her critique of the "bright-siding" of American culture, the ever-growing "business of motivation," which imparts its advice with annoying sunniness, naively presupposes that dutiful work unconditionally leads to success.[13]

Second, the literature all but overlooked much of what made our partnership uniquely successful: our online relationship. This is in part due to the rapid pace of innovation in our digital age. Bolker's 1998 volume contains an appendix titled "How the Computer Revolution Affects You and Your Dissertation" and almost quaintly enumerates the "disadvantages of the computer," seriously contemplating the possibility that a dissertator might write her manuscript in longhand.[14] Authors writing more recently point out the benefits and pitfalls of a computer for organization and procrastination, respectively: the ability to file and reference notes and drafts is unparalleled, although so are the possibilities for spending hours in the universe of online media, music, and messaging. Single's book comes closest to the type of strategy we devised, as she briefly mentions that the "real-time" experience of trading instant messages with a writing partner improves accountability. But as a group, none of these writing guides consider that a one-on-one online relationship could be crucial to motivating a struggling dissertator to sit down each day to write and, ultimately, to complete a dissertation.[15]

Finally, we cannot help but think that the literature suffers from the fundamental disconnect common to all forms of advice: it is often easier said than done. Before we met, we *knew* what we had to do to complete our dissertations. (We knew we should work consistently and tackle small chunks, for example.) But there is a difference between "knowing you should floss every day and actually doing it," as one of our friends likes to say. We each needed another person engaged in a parallel endeavor—with an understanding of the particularities of writing a dissertation in history and with a comparable sensibility about life and work—in order to get mutually inspired to do the proverbial flossing. We were able to motivate each other in a way that was genuine, personal, and sufficiently rigorous to hold each of us accountable.

At its core, our partnership was effective, firstly, because we turned out to be excellent virtual partners in a field not commonly considered collaborative. A dissertation in history is unique from many other disciplines: it is not merely a write-up of research findings; instead, it is a single-author-generated book-length exposition of a narrow topic, requiring primary and secondary evidence, close analysis, and narrative skill. For these reasons, history dissertators can expect to spend three to five years researching and writing in great solitude. Moreover, as history departments today are characterized by increasing specialization as well as shrinking graduate programs, there seem to be fewer people around who share one's specific intellectual interests, increasing the sense of isolation. For these reasons, our largely online relationship was especially beneficial. We were friendly but not really friends; we knew each other from conferences and worked in the same field, but we attended different graduate schools, lived in different cities, and studied different time periods. This distance gave us necessary space: we did not compete for advisor attention or internal departmental kudos, nor did we try to "scoop" each other with archival finds or analytical insights. Still, we found in each other an interlocutor whose work was more intellectually related to our own than that of anyone on our home campuses. We understood each other's process and project in a way we would not if one of us were writing on medieval illuminated manuscripts and the other were composing an ethnography about contemporary inner-city youth. These affinities made the "virtual office" we shared a particularly necessary haven, especially as we wrote far from our home campuses, a common circumstance for young scholars.

We were also good partners because we shared a commitment to academic professionalism yet were willing to look beyond academia for models that would enable us to meet our scholarly goals. The very title we gave to our relationship, "accountability partners," reeks of a corporate model that is anathema to many academics. Evoking measurable outcomes, deadlines, and time clocks, the idea of accountability runs counter to the freedom and limitless inquiry that many academics consider essential to the life of the mind. Even Natalia's mother, a comparative literature professor, dismissed our plan as needlessly binding us to a structure that would limit our creativity. Yet we saw scholarly utility in the corporate world's use of deadlines and schedules and borrowed those strategies in the service of our academic goals.

Our willingness to seek out other models also led us in a different, albeit similarly "unscholarly" path: a concern for wellness. We recognized in each other a desire to live healthy, balanced lives, with time for exercise, community service, good food, and good friends. Although these features may seem more conducive to graduate life than the aspects we borrowed from corporate culture, too many academics jettison them too often in the rush to read more books, write more pages, and drink more coffee. We found in each other someone who validated our desire to live a life that was attentive to wellness, which enabled us to recognize and validate that value in ourselves.

A second core reason why our partnership worked is that we devised a support structure that made sense to us and that served what we perceived to be our needs. We created a sense of accountability through regular, online interactions that structured our day and fueled the setting of manageable goals. We began each day with a morning e-mail "sign-in." As both of us worked mostly from home, the sign-in became our way of creating a structured work environment. Whether at 7:00 a.m. (Natalia) or the "more reasonable" 9:00 a.m. (Sarah), we announced to each other the moment our workday officially began, and we set forward a series of intentions about what we hoped to accomplish that day. Just as signing in to start the day was important, signing off brought necessary closure. It enabled us to say, "I did all I could do today and now it's time to stop." Sometimes we would send each other long e-mails celebrating what we learned that day. At other times, we would share our frustrations with what we had not accomplished and would write at length about what we needed to do the next day to remedy the situation. Usually, we dashed off a quick "I'm done for the day." We found that regardless of how we signed off, the value was in doing it. Part of our goal of feeling less overwhelmed required that we learn how to walk away from the work, even when the work was unfinished. We knew it would be there the next day, and we knew that our accountability partner would be there too.

While signing in and out was important to our overall sense of accountability and structure, the act of e-mailing a daily schedule enabled us to break down our large writing goals into more manageable parts. The morning sign-in e-mail quickly evolved into a space for creating and sharing a daily schedule. Sometimes the schedule would be as loose:

> Morning: Work on ch. 4
> Lunch
> Afternoon: Work on ch. 4

Sometimes the schedules were far more detailed:

> 8–8:30: Reply to e-mail
> 8:30–9:30: Review/edit stuff from yesterday
> 9:30–11:30: Draft new prose for ch. 3 middle
> 11:30–12:00: Walk to library and pick up books
> 12:00–1:00: Lunch
> 1:30–3:30: Draft new prose for ch. 3 middle
> 3:30–5:30: Read books from library/take notes on connections
> 5:30–6:00: E-mail

In either case, the task of creating a schedule required us to think through the most important work that we needed to accomplish and what period of time we wanted to devote to it.

The daily schedule also became a vehicle for goal setting or, more appropriately, goal managing. The practice of breaking down the big goal (finishing) or even a smaller goal (finishing a specific chapter) was a necessary act of realism and sanity. Over time, we began to schedule things like "Read these two new books and figure out how to incorporate them into my analysis" or "Write three paragraphs that can bridge this section to that section." This shift in precision and clarity in our goal setting allowed us to feel more in control of our progress. In *Bird by Bird*, Lamott reveals that she keeps an empty one-inch picture frame on her desk as a reminder to herself to keep her writing ambitions limited. "All I have to do," she explains, "is to write down as much as I can see through a one-inch picture frame. This is all I have to bite off for the time being."[16] So much of what makes writing a dissertation or book manuscript difficult is the sense that it needs to be finished—yesterday. Lamott reminds us that no one sits down and writes a book in one fell swoop; it takes daily efforts to compile one-inch chunks of prose. Sharing our small goals with a partner forced us to articulate that one-inch frame on a daily basis. Moreover, by stating those goals to each other, we knew there was another person aware of our intention. There was no punishment or disciplining for failing to meet the goal—and often goals were not met, as new ideas generated unforeseen writing and as new reading generated a hunt for unforeseen sources. Still, by stating our small goals in the morning, we gave ourselves enough focus to begin the work.

Central to that focus was the act of writing the e-mail. Unlike phone conversations that can spin off topic or personal to-do lists that can be jotted down and easily tossed, e-mailing your partner a schedule requires *typing*. Thus it necessarily invites revision, reflection, and the type of intentionality that is essential for effective thinking. E-mailing each other our plan for the day required us to think about what we needed to accomplish and gave us space to write, revise, and rework a plan until we felt comfortable with it.

At the time we launched our partnership, e-mail and digital communication in general had become so widespread that it already inspired criticism as "supplanting human connection" and fostering a modern-day anomie, as Sherry Turkle would observe.[17] Interestingly, however, the peculiar circumstance of writing a history dissertation—near solitude being normative—actually meant that our e-mail correspondence forged a powerful interpersonal connection, rather than weakly mimicking one. Turkle's often-cited assumption that our increasing tendency to e-mail and text rather than speak in person or by phone "dials down human contact" did not apply to a situation in which little or no human contact, digital or otherwise, is considered the norm.[18]

As important as forging a personal connection, the act of e-mailing our goals also freed us from guilt about engaging in life pursuits beyond the dissertation. Writing out our daily schedule allowed us to carve out discrete periods not only to exercise, eat, and e-mail but also to nurture a pregnancy, engineer a major move, create a private tutoring business, complete a fitness certification, see friends, and date. The transparency of our daily e-mails showed that neither of us was the "only one" who had other commitments and interests beyond our dissertations. By alleviating the guilt that so many graduate students feel about existing as anything other than a dissertator, we engaged more passionately and productively in all aspects of our lives, including as scholars. Alison Miller describes how her "sense of entitlement to . . . experience pleasure quickly dwindled as the demands of academic life mounted" during graduate school.[19] For us, the accountability partnership disrupted that disempowering cycle, enabling us to undertake our dissertations—and the rest of our lives—with greater pleasure than if we had ventured out alone.

Our experience suggests that the virtual component is essential to a writing partnership in the digital age. For one thing, the online relationship does not involve a physical meeting time or place or even the need to be on the same schedules. We could—and did—sign in or out at wildly different times, and our work patterns never interfered with each other. This created necessary boundaries between our workdays; we were not affected by each other's doctor's appointments or trips to the gym. We were also protected from interferences like phone calls. One can (theoretically) work for hours without checking e-mail; so while the other person is "virtually there," they do not interfere in the actual writing process. In other words, the online aspect of our partnership enabled us to be the solitary, independent scholars we are while, at the same time, offering us virtual and ever-present support and accountability.

Writing a dissertation is hard, and while the general advice literature is largely right, it is woefully incomplete, missing the unprecedented context of the digital age and the singularity of individual intellectual and emotional situations. No existing text acknowledges the burst of motivation that comes from sharing a breakthrough with someone who understands your work, the sense of duty created by knowing someone is waiting for you to check in every morning and to check out every evening, or how much more rewarding the process of writing a dissertation can be when this partner is a respected colleague and, eventually, friend. The digital age provides necessary help for young scholars wrestling with the challenges of writing a history dissertation. We have found this help not in the form of fancy new software but in a relatively old technology that can be altered by the intentionality of how we are using it. E-mail has been around for decades and has certainly been eclipsed by other forms of social media in terms of hipness and hotness. However, as a direct, personal tool of virtual communication and writing support, traditional e-mail is still without peer. It enables daily communication that is flexible, personal, immediate, and noninvasive, and it requires a deliberate act of writing that spurs thinking and enables revision. Perhaps most important, e-mail enables intellectual colleagues of similar goals and temperaments to work together across vast distances, reducing the isolation of academic writing while fostering a rich, supportive collaboration.

We are aware that the strategy we present here risks its own kind of reductive, banal generalization or that some might write it off as a unique result of a unique friendship. But we hope to suggest the value and opportunity in creating a virtual writing partnership that suits the needs of the participants themselves. For us, that meant a daily online partnership; others might prefer to work with a small group or to establish weekly, rather than daily, check-ins. There is a wide array of options. The main point, as we see it, is that technology can and should be used to facilitate the writing process in ways that are necessary and important. We hope that essays such as this one will spur conversations among graduate students and their advisors about successful writing strategies and will challenge the assumption that producing a dissertation in history need be a solitary process. Academia's anxiety about talking about individual writing processes can and should be tackled, as a means to bring about greater intellectual freedom, discovery, and, ultimately, success.

Notes

1. Others address these questions, often building on Robert Putnam's *Bowling Alone: The Collapse and Revival of American Community* (New York: Simon and Schuster, 2001), based largely on research conducted before the digital age. See, for example, Barry Wellman et al., "Does the Internet Increase, Decrease, or Supplement Social Capital?" *American Behavioral Scientist* 45, no. 3 (2001): 436–55; Homero Gil de Zuniga, "The Mediating Path to a Stronger Citizenship: Online and Offline Networks, Weak Ties, and Civic Engagement," *Communication Research*, 38, no. 3 (2011): 397–421; Keith Hampton et al., *Social Isolation and New Technology: How the Internet and Mobile Phones Impact Americans' Social Networks* (Washington, D.C.: Pew Internet & American Life Project, 2009), http://pewinternet.org/Reports/2009/18--Social-Isolation-and-New-Technology.aspx.

2. Marc Prensky, "Digital Natives, Digital Immigrants," *On the Horizon* 9, no. 5 (2001): 1–6.

3. Peg Boyle Single, *Demystifying Dissertation Writing: A Streamlined Process from Choice of Topic to Final Text* (New York: Stylus, 2009), 10.

4. Single, *Demystifying Dissertation Writing*, 2.

5. Alison B. Miller, *Finish Your Dissertation Once and for All! How to Overcome Psychological Barriers, Get Results, and Move On with Your Life* (New York: American Psychological Association, 2008), 19, 74.

6. Joan Bolker, *Writing Your Dissertation in Fifteen Minutes a Day: A Guide to Starting, Revising, and Finishing Your Doctoral Thesis* (New York: Henry Holt, 1998); Anne Lamott, *Bird by Bird: Some Instructions on Writing and Life* (New York: Pantheon Books, 1994), 22.

7. See more about dissertation boot camps at http://www.gsc.upenn.edu/navdiss/bootcamp.php (Graduate Student Center, University of Pennsylvania) and http://www.princeton.edu/writing/university/bootcamps/dissertation (Princeton Writing Program, Princeton University).

8. Miller, *Finish Your Dissertation*, 20.

9. Stephen Starker, *Oracle at the Supermarket: The American Preoccupation with Self-Help Books* (Piscataway, NJ: Transaction, 2002).

10. Bolker, *Writing Your Dissertation*, xvi. Other examples include such best sellers as Steven Covey's *The 7 Habits of Highly Effective People* (New York: Simon and Schuster, 1989), Don Miguel Ruiz's *The Four Agreements: A Practical Guide to Per-*

sonal Freedom (San Rafael, CA: Amber-Allen, 1997), and Wendy Stehling Drumm's *Thin Thighs in 30 Days* (New York: Bantam Books, 1982).

11. Single, *Demystifying Dissertation Writing*, 20.

12. "Dissertation Boot Camp," Graduate Student Center, University of Pennsylvania, http://www.gsc.upenn.edu/navdiss/bootcamp.php.

13. Barbara Ehrenreich, *Bright-Sided: How the Relentless Promotion of Positive Thinking Has Undermined America* (New York: Henry Holt, 2009).

14. Bolker, *Writing Your Dissertation*, 155.

15. Single, *Demystifying Dissertation Writing*, 152.

16. Lamott, *Bird by Bird*, 17–18.

17. Sherry Turkle, *Alone Together: Why We Expect More from Technology and Less from Each Other* (New York: Basic Books, 2011), passim.

18. Turkle, *Alone Together*, 15.

19. Miller, *Finish Your Dissertation*, 157.

Only Typing? Informal Writing, Blogging, and the Academy

Alex Sayf Cummings and Jonathan Jarrett

The late twentieth century saw a staggering growth of media that permitted people to express themselves without going through traditional gatekeepers such as editors, publishers, or record labels. Whether as part of the rise of zines and the alternative press in the 1960s or the development of websites, blogs, and wikis in the 1990s, new technologies and new formats have opened the media up to voices that have often been less formal or polished than the classic published author of yore.[1] These innovations promised greater speed and openness. Computer programmer Ward Cunningham chose the word *wiki*, meaning "fast" in Hawaiian slang, to refer to a site that any number of users can quickly edit without going through the technical process of writing code.[2] Japanese teenagers founded a new literary genre in the cell-phone novel, serialized as discrete bits in the form of text messages—no editors wanted or needed.[3]

Such developments have whizzed by many scholars, especially historians. Being concerned with the past and prone to reflect on the tempo of time itself, we have rarely been known to do things quickly. Our dissertations take years to write and sometimes longer to revise and publish. A scholar sending off an essay to an academic journal can expect to wait four months to a year for feedback. Historians thus have reason to be both wary and curious about the prospect of using technology to do what we do differently and, one hopes, faster than in the past.

One of the central insights of media studies, though, is that a medium is not the same as a particular technology. We may call your iPhone a "phone," but when it makes a call, it uses something more similar to radio than the

Bell technology that still drove the pulse-dial telephones of the 1970s.[4] *30 Rock* and *Hill Street Blues* are still "television" whether we watch them on a broadcast network, cable, or an online video site. The genres and tropes and the commercial considerations and labor relations that shape most TV programs remain sufficiently similar for us to situate the medium of television in a number of technically different platforms. In the same way, the fact that we may now encounter many scholarly journals in the form of individual articles, downloaded as PDFs and read onscreen on whatever device we favor, does not necessarily make the content of them different from the print versions. Academic journals and presses can easily transport the conventions of reviewing, editing, and publishing to the online world, and many already have.[5]

Such models, however, occupy a different route to the reader from writing that is generated online in the informal mode of blogs, wikis, and Twitter. What are the differences between this sort of writing and traditional scholarly practice? What are the benefits and the drawbacks, and can this kind of writing actually be scholarship? The authors of this essay are historians who have experimented with various online formats over the past ten years, most especially blogging, and this essay reflects on these questions by situating the academic blogger in this wider context of informal writing.

The Cultural Form(s) of Online Publishing

The web is ever changing, of course; attempts to sum it up date quickly. If we write at length now about Web 2.0, interactivity, and crowdsourcing, we risk looking foolish if this essay is still online in ten years but Facebook and Twitter have evaporated. There are nonetheless things that can be said about what makes writing for the web distinctive.[6] The medium does exercise pressure: the size of screens and attention spans of readers dictate brevity (or are thought to), and technical issues such as browser capability are an unwelcome consideration. On the positive side, the hyperlink offers the online reader instant passage to citations, and for the creative writer, hypertext allows for wry allusions and the deliberate double-edging of basic statements (for example, silently linking a mention of a police agency to a report on deaths in their custody).

Another characteristic shared by all online material is that it exists in a limbo of semipermanence. On the one hand, websites disappear as their host changes Internet access or host institution or as redesign evolves old content out. Few links from ten years ago remain valid now, even if the content is still online.[7] On the other hand, that which is assumed to be transient may not be: deletion at the source may not keep an ill-considered screed from Google's cache, and the Internet Archive's mission to preserve the disappearing web also contains the implication of preserving such mistakes forever. The Internet Archive's web spiders are far from instantaneous, however, and even its funding is not secure, so one cannot rely on it for permanence.[8] Nothing is safely online for the long term, but not much is certainly lost either: the Internet is an awkward halfway house for an academic culture raised on citability.

On the other hand, for many online writers, permanence is not the point. Generating text online has become a means of social interaction. This can be as true in an academic context as in any other: since the earliest days of the Internet, scholars have embraced its potential for the rapid sharing of unpublished material, feedback, and thoughts, whether via e-mail lists, Usenet, and bulletin boards or, now, Facebook or professional equivalents, such as Academia.edu.[9] These resources not only speed up interchange within the scholarly process; they can also operate as support for an institution's lone specialist in a field who needs to check ideas with a colleague, for example, or for someone in need of perspective on an institutional teaching or management practice.

In these particular lights, blogging, a deliberately personal use of web space, looms large. A blog is not, however, simply a personal website. What makes a blog a blog is its newspaper or diary-like rhythm of discrete, chronological posts; the variable length of posts; and, above all, the relative lack of formal filters or selection processes. The format presumes, displays, and favors immediacy and freshness of output, so that such processes would inhibit it. When Blogger set out to popularize its concept in 1999, the company described its service as "push-button publishing," and its competitor LiveJournal promised a "simple-to-use (but extremely powerful and customizable) personal publishing ('blogging') tool" in 2004.[10] Blogs offered a means for posting and updating one's thoughts without needing to know how to design a website by writing HTML code. Before *blog* became a common term, companies like DiaryLand framed their services in a language of personal, unedited writing.[11] This informality and lack of editorial supervision is key to the enterprise. *Wikipedia*, after all, was preceded by *Nupedia*, an attempt at building an online encyclopedia with credentialed authors and a formal process of review; it generated nowhere near the output of *Wikipedia*, which introduced the little-known format of the wiki to the broader public and spawned countless imitators.[12] Some of its successors were more open than others—the *Mason Historiographiki*, for instance, only includes input from approved contributors—but each embraced the basic principles of rapid editing and multiple authorship that defines a wiki.[13]

This informality can be an advantage. Academic publishers may bring traditions of peer review online or may pioneer new patterns of open review and public commentary, yet we should not shy away from presenting our ideas and research in less-regulated forums like wikis and blogs, which are defined partly by their lack of filters. Indeed, historians have recently taken an interest in blogs, which can accommodate both collaboration and individual authorship. *The Edge of the American West* is a notable example in which scholars such as Eric Rauchway and Kathy Olmstead post about academia, politics, and pop culture, along with, as they put it, "yiddishkeit, WASPhood, the 1980s, Canadiana and, most of all, the Muppets."[14] The tone is loose but intellectual, bringing a perspective informed by history and theory to current events. Other blogs pursue a similar course but specialize in intellectual or legal history, with a committed readership among scholars who work in these fields.[15] (As a friend who writes for such a blog admitted, though, it threatens to be a "career-killing timesuck.")

Readers, Wanted and Unwanted

A blog is a pointless exercise without an audience (as one could achieve the same results with a word processor), but readers are easy neither to attract nor to restrict. To attract them, it is obviously desirable to raise one's site in the rankings of search engines, but the fact that "search engine optimization" is something of a dark art, made so by the understandable reluctance of companies such as Google to expose their heuristics, is amply testified to by the numerous offers of such knowledge arriving in most blogs' spam traps. In fact, many of the more legitimate tactics, such as providing keywords in the unseen parts of a website's code that offer indexing terms for search engines, are denied to users of sites managed by large blog providers, as those users are able to edit only the content of their sites, not such meta-information. It seems that there are no quick, honest secrets to such success. The content that the writer provides is the active ingredient, therefore; it gives the search engines (if one grants them access) something to use to present the blog to inquirers, though what is presented may also be very different from what those parties were actually seeking.[16] Even when they have found what they sought, moreover, it is worth considering who the audience may be.

For those not engaged in scholarship but interested in the author's material, a blog may be an intercession with the academy for those who cannot participate themselves. This can be used by writers as advertising for the academic endeavor as a whole or the field of history large or small or as a chance to correct misapprehensions, but it also requires a reciprocal attempt to engage at an accessible level (keeping terms of art and assumptions of knowledge down), as well as generosity and tolerance in responding to comments.[17] In more social terms, this audience also allows us to demonstrate that (some) academics are approachable and useful human beings, and it can provide the writer with a much-needed sense of wider relevance.

Unless a historical blog is fairly simplistic, its persistent readers will likely be found more among those who are familiar with academic writing. For the nonexpert members of this sector, the historical blogger can help decode the field, cherry-picking interesting work from a jungle of things of which nonhistorians cannot always get hold. Here, blogs can help keep an interested audience informed where history would otherwise lose them because of the commitments required by dedicated study and reading. Such writing also helps circumvent economic exclusion, not just of those not enrolled in a course of study, but also of those without subscription access to print or electronic resources.[18]

A historical blogger is unlikely to avoid discovery by one's academic peers for long, especially if that blogger has used personal names that can be found in web searches. Sometimes one's peers will comment, often friendlily, but one cannot assume an absence of readership from an absence of comments; they may still be aware. This kind of readership can be the most useful and may be the desired one, but it can also be the most dangerous. The dangers are partly in the medium and the expectations thereof and partly in the reaction of the academy to nontraditional publication. Is a colleague (or worse, a potential colleague) wasting time by blogging, or are they doing something valuable? Opinions vary.[19] Some may judge that no matter how carefully written and sourced, blogging is never more than opinion or, at best, a kind of journalism, rather than a proper academic endeavor. We discuss this further shortly, but one does not to have to agree with the argument to see how it might be constructed.

A classic and controversial statement of this point of view was provided in 2005 in a pseudonymous article entitled "Bloggers Need Not Apply," in the *Chronicle of Higher Education*. The author, "Ivan Tribble," recorded with scorn the damage that various applicants for a post in Tribble's institution had done to their applications by mentioning their blogs, which exposed them in various ways as unsuitable in the eyes of the selection committee.[20] It must be recognized that there will continue to be readers like Tribble and his colleagues. Blogging favors an informal approach to writing, because dense writing deters an audience and is hard to produce often enough to keep a blog fresh. An informal approach can obviously become excessive, taking such forms as character assassination or professional gossip (there has been plenty of this), any of which may obviously offend or misrepresent peers.[21] Such offense may, in turn, force retractions, meaning the undoing of work and adding to the transience of the blog. Worse, it may prompt professional complaints or even legal action. These are heavy consequences for killing some time online.[22]

Blogging as Scholarship?

Are those who view blogging as nonscholarly (at best) or unscholarly (at worst) correct? Does such writing have any tangible, professional value?[23] We may, after all, be more prone to sloppy writing or easy generalizations when writing online, knowing that an editor is not going to come along and demand a footnote to support the assertion, for example, that NBC's sitcom *Community* is "well-loved but still-struggling." (Is there evidence that it is well loved? Is it really struggling?) More substantively, no one prevented one of the authors of this essay from stating in a blog post that Arab Americans occupy "an indeterminate place in the US spectrum of race," whereas extensive evidence and reference to an established body of literature would be required to support that assertion if it were published in a journal article.[24]

This is probably the most commonly cited critique of blogging as a scholarly enterprise: it escapes traditional peer review. Self-publication enables blogs' great virtues of speed and freshness but adds problems of credibility. While experiments are being conducted to incorporate peer review and editorial oversight to blog contents, as well as to use blogs to crowdsource peer review of off-blog publications, such efforts threaten to undermine the medium's most salient qualities—speed and currency—and to turn it into the equivalent of an online academic journal, a medium that, as we have suggested, is not substantively different from a regular academic journal except by its apparatus of consumption.[25]

To continue to insist on blogging and online writing in general as academic work thus requires a much more radical shift of position. The recent volume *Hacking the Academy* includes one or two statements of such a case. David Parry, especially, urges his readers,

Given the cost of producing knowledge and the fact that academic journals or academic presses could only afford to produce so many pages with each journal, peers are established to vet, and signal that a particular piece is credible and more worthy than the others. This is the filter-then-publish model. But the net actually works in reverse—publish-then-filter—involving a wider range of people in the discursive production. Why do academics argue for small panel anonymous peer review? One thing we know is diversity of perspective enriches discourse.

We have to give up being authorities, controlling our discourse, seeing ourselves as experts who possess bodies of knowledge over which we have mastery. Instead we have to start thinking of what we do as participating in a conversation, and [sic] ongoing process of knowledge formation. What if we thought of academics as curators, people who keep things up to date, clean, host, point, and aggregate knowledge rather than just those who are responsible for producing new knowledge.[26]

This approach sounds energizing, but it profoundly changes the work of the academic. The onus has shifted here almost all the way from "publish" to "filter," and it is not at all clear where formal publishing fits in this model. The role of the professional scholar becomes one of a fisherman, running their trained mental nets through a sea of otherwise undifferentiable output, from both within and beyond the academy. It may be no bad thing to open the gates of the ivory tower to external ideas (though the business models on which many blame the current crisis of the university have certainly lain that way), but this passive role as pundit or critic resembles our current idea of research little and may make new work much harder to produce amid such an undifferentiated flow of high-speed output.

There are many functions to peer review, and some of them are insidious.[27] One, however, remains a simple provision of credibility, establishing a chain of trust that very digital concerns like encryption continue to require: academic work is taken seriously because others have decided it is worth taking seriously, and they have been allowed to decide that because others, in turn, have done the same for them, and so on. Without this chain of responsibility, the worth of our output is not vouched for, and this process is not yet possible for blogging in isolation.[28]

The two authors of this essay differ in our views of what the preceding concerns mean for blogging in scholarship. For Jarrett, blogging will only serve as a means of *generating* scholarship when peer review ceases to *validate* scholarship. For him, blogging may *contain* scholarship and may be *about* scholarship, but so long as the academy persists in its current practice, blogging will not be where scholarship is done. For Cummings, however, this informal zone of writing, sharing, and discussion can complement, rather than supplant, the main streams of scholarly discourse and publication. He suggests a more expansive definition of scholarship that retains peer review as its core but also encompasses other modes of engaging a wider public in historical work, not unlike the challenge that public historians have presented to the academy in recent years. The defining difference between publications such as this one and a blog remains the issue of filtering and editing, the search for a virtual imprimatur of trustworthiness and credibility, but we differ over whether this difference is remaining solid in the new era or becoming fluid. While this guarantees that one of us will indeed look foolish in ten years for guessing wrong, our amiable irreconcilability on this score makes it all the more compelling that we both see benefits to academics in blogging, and it is with these benefits that we bring this essay to a close.

Blogging and the Writing of History

Blogs are a quintessential feature of the so-called social media of the twenty-first century. As such, they facilitate interaction among "friends," "followers," and the fellow travelers recommended in a site's blogroll— a list of related or like-minded blogs. These are networks of sociability that do more than mutually increase page rankings in web searches. Blogging also offers the other, more social benefits previously described. Graduation from a PhD program leaves a scholar without an advisor or fellow students to read his or her work. A blog can serve a purpose similar to a writing group, as it pressures one to write regularly, meet deadlines, and expose a work in progress to the eyes of others. Faculty can turn to each other for feedback, of course, where suitable expertise exists nearby, but colleagues are often too overburdened with classes, committees, and family to provide regular input, and after earning doctoral degrees, many scholars find themselves in a series of transient positions, such as postdoctoral and visiting positions, with little opportunity to join a discursive community with peers.

Media such as wikis, blogs, and Twitter have the potential to generate such communities where they are otherwise not available. These are the audiences that the academic blogger is, to our mind, best advised to seek; it turns out that peers and, indeed, friends can be found simply by writing interesting things on the Internet. A well-maintained blog has the potential to provide a crowd for crowdsourcing, a forum for validation or advice, and a kind of collegiality that is no less real for being expressed in type. In this respect, the so-called blogosphere can be seen as a set of continual, over-lapping conferences or symposia in an unusually large and friendly institution.[29] Quite apart from the publicity value of having one's name easily associable with well-written and immediately available scholarly-looking content, these are good reasons to blog. While the microblogging service Twitter radically limits the length of posts to 140 characters, effectively barring any long or laborious academic prose, it has been embraced by a growing number of scholars as a means to share ideas, advice, papers, and conference announcements and to highlight useful resources, such as websites and archives.[30]

This kind of informality can be seen as a feature, not a bug. The same quality of blogging that problematizes its acceptance as traditional scholarship, its lack of filters, is the source of its vitality. The blog offers an opportunity to engage with and write about one's area of study in a far less constrained way than, say, a postdoctoral application or a journal submission. Having a less formal outlet for writing serves as a reminder that one's knowledge and creativity are not pressed only into the service of professional goals and a quest for approval.

The benefits of this flexibility cycle back into one's professional writing, through a kind of intellectual cross-pollination. To keep an active blog requires writing often, and this is good practice. Writing for nonacademics can also be fruitful. The variety in audience is good for the prose and good for clarity, and it may be good for employment elsewhere, if the impact of third-stream agendas acquires more force. Ultimately, blogging involves some people writing and others commenting. Writing is central to the practice, but it encourages writing on different topics and in different ways.

As professionals, we may be evaluated largely on peer-reviewed, published writing, but much of what we do as scholars falls in between the formal and informal, the textual and the oral. Writing on a blog might not rise to the standard of a university press or scholarly journal, but neither does a lecture. Rarely will what we write to say in a classroom be subject to the same degree of scrutiny as what we write in a monograph, but that fact does not diminish the value or creativity of the texts we create in the process of teaching.[31] Digital publishing offers an opportunity to recognize the multifaceted nature of our work as historians, which is not limited to the printed page.

Indeed, digital publishing helps us recognize that writing and print are not one and the same. Back in the 1960s, media theorist Marshall McLuhan famously predicted a future "global village" where visual and aural media would eclipse the importance of print, yet the written word has more than held its own in the years since.[32] In the age of Harry Potter and blogs, people write all the time.[33] They compose text messages and e-mails; they write newsletters for church and work and post comments in endless "flame wars" on YouTube videos and news articles.[34] Blogs, wikis, and Twitter are part of this general flurry of written activity. This material may not contribute to tenure and promotion; it may reveal one's work in a less polished or persuasive form than an article or book. However, as an outlet for expression that is freer and faster than traditional publishing, it can offer real benefits to the process of writing, and it provides an arena for collaboration and discussion that can serve the same varied purposes as a graduate school cohort, a writing group, or the process of peer review. It also reaches a public for whom our work is otherwise mediated solely by journalists, allowing us to demonstrate the writing of history as a worthwhile, entertaining, and important thing to do with an intellectual life. These are not small gains. Long ago, Truman Capote slammed Jack Kerouac's work by saying it "isn't writing, it's only typing."[35] When it comes to an important journal submission, online or off, we would be well advised to strive for Capote's standards. But the rest of the time, we should feel free to type.

Notes

1. Stephen Duncombe, *Notes from Underground: Zines and the Politics of Alternative Culture* (New York: Verso, 1997); John McMillian, *Smoking Typewriters: The Sixties Underground Press and the Rise of Alternative Media in America* (New York: Oxford University Press, 2011); Amy Spencer, *DIY: The Rise of Lo-Fi Culture* (London: Marion Boyars, 2008); eHow, "How to Become a Published Author," http://www.ehow.com/how_2057347_become-published-author.html.

2. Phoebe Ayers, Charles Matthews, and Ben Yates, *How Wikipedia Works: And How You Can Be a Part of It* (San Francisco: No Starch, 2008), 41–42.

3. Dana Goodyear, "I Heart Novels," *New Yorker,* 22 December 2008, http://www.newyorker.com/reporting/2008/12/22/081222fa_fact_goodyear.

4. Jonathan Sterne, *The Audible Past: Cultural Origins of Sound Reproduction* (Durham, NC: Duke University Press, 2003), 182.

5. Raymond Williams offered a pioneering analysis of a medium as a "cultural form" in his 1974 text *Television: Technology and Cultural Form;* Roger Silverstone provides an updated perspective in his preface to the 2003 Routledge Classics edition of Williams's book (vi–xii).

6. See Daniel J. Cohen and Roy Rosenzweig, *Digital History: A Guide to Gathering, Preserving, and Presenting the Past on the Web* (Philadelphia: University of Pennsylvania Press, 2005), http://chnm.gmu.edu/digitalhistory/. To their list of types of historical websites could be added social networking sites, such as Academia.edu, or project outreach sites, such as that for the Chester Amphitheatre

Environs Research Project, carried out by the University of Chester (http://www.
univchester-parkdig.blogspot.com/), or *Digging to Understand the Past*, sponsored
by the Norton Community Archaeology Group (http://nortoncommarch.word-
press.com/). On the agendas behind this last category, see Matthew M. Palus, Mark
P. Leone, and Matthew D. Cochran, "Critical Archaeology: Politics Past and Present," in *Historical Archaeology*, ed. Martin Hall and Stephen W. Silliman (Oxford:
Blackwell, 2006), 92–100.

7. Jonathan Jarrett, "Medieval Latin and the Internet, Twelve Years On," *A
Corner of Tenth-Century Europe*, May 15, 2009, http://tenthmedieval.wordpress.
com/2009/05/15/medieval-latin-and-the-internet-twelve-years-on/.

8. Internet Archive, "Frequently Asked Questions," http://www.archive.org/
about/faqs.php#31.

9. Compare the following observation by Lisa Gitelman in *Always Already New:
Media, History, and the Data of Culture* (Cambridge: MIT Press, 2006), 22: "Beyond
CERN, the broader physics community made early use of the World Wide Web.
For instance, the library at the Stanford Linear Accelerator Center (SLAC) soon
offered Web-based access to 'pre-prints'—articles that are on their way through the
peer-review process, but that haven't appeared in print or electronically yet with
the final imprimatur of a refereed journal. The new accessibility of preprints made
them not more authoritative but certainly more integral in the work of physicists.
The practice of doing physics (like doing classics, as it happens) changed in keeping with the accessibility and abundance of what had before been inscriptions that
circulated slowly and in narrow contexts."

10. Blogger, http://www.blogger.com/about; LiveJournal, http://www.livejour-
nal.com.

11. Danah Boyd, "A Blogger's Blog: Exploring the Definition of a Medium,"
Reconstruction 6, no. 4 (2006), http://reconstruction.eserver.org/064/boyd.shtml;
DiaryLand, http://members.diaryland.com/edit/welcome.phtml.

12. "Nupedia," *Wikipedia*, http://en.wikipedia.org/wiki/Nupedia.

13. Stacy Schiff, "Know It All," *New Yorker*, 31 July 2006, http://www.newy-
orker.com/archive/2006/07/31/060731fa_fact; *Mason Historiographiki*, George
Mason University, http://chnm.gmu.edu/courses/schrag/wiki/index.php.

14. "About the Edge of the American West," *The Edge of the American West*,
http://edgeofthewest.wordpress.com/about/.

15. *U.S. Intellectual History Blog*, Society for U.S. Intellectual History, http://
us-intellectual-history.blogspot.com/; Mary L. Dudziak et al., *Legal History Blog*,
http://legalhistoryblog.blogspot.com/.

16. For Jonathan Jarrett, pride of place will always be reserved for the searcher
for "historic annal sex" in October 2008 who found his blog's archive for March
2007 and there presumably learned a new word meaning a chronicle with year-by-
year records.

17. Vellum, "The Language That Locks Others Out," *Vaulting and Vellum*, 15
August 2009, http://vaultingvellum.blogspot.com/2009/08/language-that-locks-
others-out.html.

18. We do not imply or endorse by this the breaching of copyrights, which, in
any case, hardly requires blogs.

19. See A. G. Rud, "Ivan Tribble Unmasked!," *Moo2*, October 10, 2005, http://moodeuce.blogspot.com/2005/10/ivan-tribble-unmasked.html.

20. Ivan Tribble, "Bloggers Need Not Apply," *Chronicle of Higher Education*, July 8, 2005, http://chronicle.com/article/Bloggers-Need-Not-Apply/45022/.

21. For examples, see Ambrose Hofstadter Bierce III, *The Broad-Gauge Gossip*, http://historianbroadgauge.blogspot.com/; C. Vann Winchell, *Nothing Recedes Like Success*, http://www.historygossip.blogspot.com/. However, both those sites have been quiet since early 2010.

22. Such episodes do happen but are inevitably difficult to document, because they tend to result in the removal of materials from the web. At the time of this writing, however, we can point to one example in which the tracks of repercussions are still visible: Edgy Historian, "Why Do We Need the Barbarians?" *Historian on the Edge*, 15 July 2011, http://600transformer.blogspot.com/2011/07/why-do-we-need-barbarians.html; a further case, Damn Good Technician, "Interruption in Service," *Damn Good Technician*, 10 May 2009, http://damngoodtechnician.blogspot.com/2009/05/interruption-in-service.html, was removed from the web while copyediting of this volume was ongoing.

23. Jeffrey Jerome Cohen, "Blogging the Middle Ages," in *Geoffrey Chaucer Hath a Blog: Medieval Studies and New Media*, ed. Brantley L. Bryant (New York City: Palgrave MacMillan, 2010), 38.

24. Alex Sayf Cummings, "Arab American Kitsch: From Ahab to Abed and Back Again," *Tropics of Meta*, 26 July 2011, http://tropicsofmeta.wordpress.com/2011/07/26/american-arab-kitsch-from-ahab-to-abed-and-back-again/.

25. The archaeology blog *Then Dig* intended to classify some of its posts as peer reviewed, according to a standard explained on its page in 2011 ("About This Site," *Then Dig*, http://arf.berkeley.edu/then-dig/about-this-site/), but it had not done so as of its last post in October 2012, whereafter the blog disappeared in a redesign of its parent site. The journal *postmedieval* crowdsourced its review for one issue in 2011 via a blog at http://postmedievalcrowdreview.wordpress.com/.

26. David Parry, "Burn the Boats/Books," in *Hacking the Academy: The Edited Volume*, ed. Dan Cohen and Tom Scheinfeldt (Ann Arbor: University of Michigan Press, 2013), http://www.digitalculture.org/hacking-the-academy/. See also Jo Guldi, "Reinventing the Academic Journal," in the same volume.

27. Dan Cohen, Stephen Ramsay, and Kathleen Fitzpatrick, "Open Access and Scholarly Values: A Conversation," in Cohen and Scheinfeldt, *Hacking the Academy*.

28. Something could also be said about blogging anonymously, but space precludes its discussion here; we assume that it is unlikely that scholars would wish to pursue academic work anonymously. On such issues, see Magistra, "Pseudonymity and Its Discontents," *Magistra et Mater*, 14 May 2010, http://magistraetmater.blog.co.uk/2010/05/14/pseudonymity-and-its-discontents-8591664/.

29. For example, see Jonathan Jarrett, "'Social Networking Gets Medieval,' Does It? A Historian's Take on Some Recent Research on Computing in the Humanities," *A Corner of Tenth-Century Europe*, 5 June 2008, http://tenthmedieval.wordpress.com/2008/06/05/social-networking-gets-medieval-does-it-a-historians-take-on-some-recent-research-on-computing-in-the-humanities/. That post has led to a conference session and an article hopefully forthcoming.

30. See the discussion, relevant to all fields of history, at Michelle Ziegler, "Medieval Tweeting," *Heavenfield*, 11 December 2011, http://hefenfelth.wordpress.com/2011/12/11/medieval-tweeting/.

31. See the preface to *Nonacademic Writing: Social Theory and Technology*, ed. Ann Hill Duin and Craig Hansen (Mahwah, NJ: Lawrence Erlbaum Associates, 1996), xvi.

32. Ivan Kalmar, "The Future of 'Tribal Man' in the Electronic Age," in *Marshall McLuhan: Critical Evaluations in Cultural Theory*, ed. Gary Genosko (New York: Routledge, 2005), 227.

33. Shayna Garlick, "Harry Potter and the Magic of Reading," *Christian Science Monitor*, 2 May 2007, http://www.csmonitor.com/2007/0502/p13s01-legn.html.

34. Alex J. Packer, *How Rude! The Teenagers' Guide to Good Manners, Proper Behavior, and Not Grossing People Out* (Minneapolis: Free Spirit, 1997), 387–88.

35. Robert Emmet Long, *Truman Capote, Enfant Terrible* (New York: Continuum, 2008), 82.

Conclusions

What We Learned from Writing
History in the Digital Age

Jack Dougherty, Kristen Nawrotzki,
Charlotte D. Rochez, and Timothy Burke

What have we learned from creating this collective work of scholarship on
the web? To what extent are new technologies transforming the work of
historians and the ways in which we interpret the past and communicate
our ideas with others? Does the so-called digital turn mark anything truly
different about the trajectory of historical writing? What lessons have we
learned about open peer review and open-access publishing? In this conclusion, we reflect on both the essays in this volume and our experiences in
publishing them, to address these and other questions that arose during the
yearlong process of developing the concept, modifying the existing technology, and cultivating a community of writers and readers who made it all
happen. Since an essential step was to make the "invisible" work of writing
and reviewing more public, the book's coeditors (Jack and Kristen) invited
two of the most thoughtfully engaged participants in the fall 2011 open
peer review (Charlotte and Timothy) to collaborate in authoring these
reflections.[1] Here, by responding to these key questions, we share what we
have learned from *Writing History in the Digital Age.*

Has Digital Technology Transformed Historical Writing, and If So, How?

Much of this volume emphasizes change. Two decades of the web have
expanded the range of creators of historical works, the types of products

generated, and the processes of distribution and evaluation, all of which stand out because they diverge from established practices in our profession. Yet we were surprised to discover the degree of continuity in the content of historical writing. The best of digitally inspired scholarship integrates technology into the art of composing works that feature what many consider the finest qualities in our field: a compelling narrative that unravels the past, supported by insightful argument and persuasive evidence.

Several contributors to this volume vividly describe how digital tools enabled them to uncover richer interpretations of source materials than they otherwise would have discovered. Ansley Erickson explains how a simple relational database not only managed her archival notes but allowed her to rethink how she categorized knowledge during her writing process. Stephen Robertson recounts how digitally mapping everyday life in Harlem pinpointed areas of racial conflict and negotiation that had previously gone unnoticed. Robert Wolff explores how the collectively authored *Wikipedia* platform permits us to peel back the layers of "popular memory" and "professional history" behind each entry, revealing more about contested meanings of the past than do traditional forms of scholarship. Kathryn Kish Sklar and Thomas Dublin describe how they learned to combine primary documents and interpretation on the web to create richer scholarship and expand the scope of women's history. Even Fred Gibbs and Trevor Owens, whose essay pointedly calls for historians to write with greater methodological transparency about our use of data, favor "de-emphasizing narrative," though they do not abandon it. Today's digital media revolution reminds us, argues Stefan Tanaka, that our present-day conceptions of historical writing did not arise until the late eighteenth century, when people began chronicling the past in a linear structure. Taken together, these digitally inspired essays embrace historians' long-standing commitment to narrative, argument, and evidence.

But several contributors also wrestle with changes brought on by the "democratization of history" on the web and our current version of the question, who creates the past?[2] In 1931, Carl Becker, president of the American Historical Association, declared "everyman his own historian," and eight decades later, every woman, man, and child (with Internet access) can view source materials and publish their own interpretations, thereby engaging in work that had previously had been the domain of professional historians.[3] Despite her own misgivings about the web-driven black Confederate myth, Leslie Madsen-Brooks argues that crowdsourcing creates key opportunities for historians to engage with a public that clearly cares about the meaning of the past, and Amanda Sikarskie also emphasizes the role of "citizen scholars" in the "co-creation of content rather than consumption of content." Similarly, essays from history educators Thomas Harbison and Luke Waltzer and also Adrea Lawrence demonstrate how technology can deepen critical thinking and writing about the past in their classrooms. Their perspective is shared by Oscar Rosales Castañeda, who, with other student-activists, digitized civil rights source materials and engaged in the very public act of interpreting their significance on the web.

Yet "the Internet is not an inherently even playing field; to digitize is not to democratize," as Shawn Graham, Guy Massie, and Nadine Feuerherm remind us. Martha Saxton describes how her class collided with today's digital embodiment of Becker's "everyman"—*Wikipedia* and its "neutral point of view" policy—as their efforts to integrate perspectives from women's history were occasionally moved elsewhere or erased. Furthermore, in Graham's innovative "Wikiblitz" classroom activity, he reports "push back from an unexpected quarter" of his first-year seminar—declared history majors—who "already had quite clear ideas about authority, authorship, and intellectual property, ideas that fit in quite well with established ways of writing history." Technology did not create these debates over who "owns" the past, but it does make it harder for professional historians to ignore them.

Another theme across the essays demarcates the lines of debate regarding the products of digital history, particularly how we recognize arguments within these newer types of historical writing. Amanda Seligman illustrates how she teaches her students to identify arguments embedded within "factual" encyclopedia entries, both print and online. John Theibault contends that data visualizations "necessarily have a rhetorical dimension" and that historians must "align the rhetoric" to better communicate their interpretation of maps and charts to the viewer. By contrast, Sherman Dorn's survey of the field challenges the profession to use "the best of digital history work to redraw the discipline's boundaries," by breaking away from long-form argument in journal articles and books as the defining standard of historical scholarship. Together, these essays show how seriously historians debate the role of argument, even when we disagree over how much we should value it.

A fourth set of essays speak directly to the process of creating, sharing, and assessing historical writing in the digital age, with collaboration as a recurring theme. Natalia Mehlman Petrzela and Sarah Manekin narrate their personal accountability partnership within a broader analysis of dissertation advice guides and self-help literature. Similarly, the research and design team behind *Pox and the City* richly describe their collective thinking on writing the history of medicine as a computer game, particularly on issues of historical content, player characters, and third-person perspective. As readers, we benefit when authors' thoughtful disagreements emerge more clearly through collaborative writing: together, Jonathan Jarrett and Alex Cummings attempt to predict the future of blogging in historical writing, but one contends that "blogging will only serve as a means of *generating* scholarship when peer review ceases to *validate*" it, while the other anticipates that "this informal zone of writing, sharing, and discussion can complement, rather than supplant, the main streams of scholarly discourse and publication." Nevertheless, both agree that the Internet is interrupting the traditional academic practice of "filter-then-publish," thereby raising the potential for the practice of "publish-then-filter," as we also discussed in our introduction.

Writing about history in our digital age has its share of internal debates, much like the broader field of the digital humanities.[4] But Kathleen Fitzpatrick persuades us that the most challenging barriers to the transformation of scholarly communication are not technological but, instead, "social, intellectual, and institutional."[5] The academy has been ambivalent about the Internet, observes Dan Cohen, and "this resistance has less to do with the *tools* of the web and more to do with the web's *culture*," specifically its degree of openness that makes many scholars suspicious.[6] By nature, historians are a skeptical breed. Yet by pulling the curtain aside and making the process of writing, reviewing, and publishing history more visible, we hope that this volume of essays—and the debates expressed within it—will help make the case that the digital age offers a valuable opportunity for the profession to reexamine our established practices and realign them with our scholarly values. The extent to which this reexamination puts us on virgin soil as a profession is another matter, as Timothy Burke explains next.

Is the "Digital Turn" Truly New? (by Timothy Burke)

Some of the contributors to *Writing History in the Digital Age* surrender, to varying degrees, to the temptation to characterize the digitization of historical inquiry as a novel insurgency against a recumbent scholarly establishment. Many contributors emphasize the capacity of digital media to create novel forms of dialogic interaction between publics and scholars, to reroute the circulation of historical expertise, and to erode some of the privileged authority that the scholarly guild confers on itself. But many of these concerns are not new or entirely novel to digital media or information technology. I suggest, instead, that digitization offers a powerful new means to a long-articulated end and an investigative tool for the continued study of the wider circulations of historical representation.

By way of illustration, let me mention three specifically relevant bodies of scholarly writing that deserve to be in richer dialogue with advocacy for new modes of digital practice. The first is a well-established and wide-ranging body of work by historians, archaeologists, curators, archivists, and educators specifically concerned with controversies and practical problems in memorialization, museum design, and public history. Long-running discussions of public struggles such as those around the *Enola Gay* exhibit at the Smithsonian[7] or the problems intrinsic to "living history" and reenactment practices, for example, dovetail beautifully into the concerns of the contributors to *Writing History in the Digital Age.*

A second scholarly literature to consider in relation to advocacy of digital practice stands at the intersection between history and anthropology and is most visibly manifest in a series of international meetings and discussions in the late 1970s and 1980s between social historians and cultural anthropologists. The key takeaway in this older moment of historiographical ferment for "history in a digital age" is that it catalyzed, for many historians, a desire to make the relationship between historical sources and scholarly knowledge vastly more porous and unsettled. This turn went beyond conventional "history from below" to much more destabilizing projects. The first of these involved a dramatic expansion of what counted as valid historical evidence, often in pointed rebuke of existing scholarship. Raphael Samuel's polemical attack on his British colleagues for refusing to take on popular culture and textual ephemera as source material is an example, as is Luise White's appraisal of rumor and gossip as evidence for writing the history of colonial Africa.[8] The second move was the incorporation of testimony and other forms of evidence or bricolage within scholarly work in a manner designed to create epistemological parity between sources and scholars, as in Shula Marks's *Not Either an Experimental Doll* or Carlo Ginzberg's *The Cheese and the Worms.*[9]

Finally, a third literature, which grew out of this dialogue between history and anthropology, raised still more comprehensive questions about the relationship between scholarly historians and historically engaged publics and, in so doing, reimagined the historical guild as a mere subset of a much bigger "production of history." In works like Michel-Rolph Trouillot's *Silencing the Past,* David William Cohen's *The Combing of History,* or Amitav Ghosh's *In an Antique Land,* academic history is resituated as a limited, if valued, enterprise, one part of a vaster terrain comprised of public memory, lived experience of individuals and communities, amateur and specialist work outside of the academic world, diverse cultural imaginations and per-formances of the past, and much else.[10] Trouillot, Cohen, and others did not call on historians to master or incorporate this wider domain, nor did they ask historians to submit to it. They did, however, imagine that there might be far more generative or creative ways for scholarly historians to collaborate or converse with wider publics and circumstances. This last literature in particular very directly leads into the aspiration of some con-tributors to this volume that "history in the digital age" will underscore the limitations of scholarly practices and will permit radically new forms of relationship between academic historians and various sites of historical knowledge and production outside of the academy.

How Did You Encourage Public Discussion on a Book in Progress?

At present, the dominant work culture for historians is to produce single-author scholarship, often in isolation from others, and typically not revealed until final publication. We intentionally drew on web technology to interrupt this norm, by crafting a digital platform to make the stages of idea formation and peer review more public for our scholarly work. We proposed that constructing an edited volume of essays on the open web would make our writing more meaningful to others, more responsive to online commentary, and, as a whole, more intellectually coherent.

As we launched the site in spring 2011, our greatest fear was organizing a forum where no one showed up. So the coeditors timed our key events to coincide with the U.S. academic calendar, by holding our discussion of essay ideas immediately before the summer break and conducting our open peer review during the middle of the fall semester. Our low-budget com-munications strategy relied on varied forms of communication to reach different types of audiences. We sent over 100 personalized e-mail invita-tions to prospective contributors whom we already knew or identified to be working in the field of digital history. We connected with others through digital announcements (such as the H-Net networks) and blogs (such as a *ProfHacker* guest essay). We presented the work in progress at digital humanities gatherings, such as THATCamp (The Humanities and Tech-nology Camp) Prime 2011 and HASTAC (Humanities, Arts, Science, and Technology Advanced Collaboratory) 2011. But the most important lesson we learned was the power of a critical mass of contributors with their own social media connections. When we tweeted or blogged about new essay ideas on our edited volume, this information cascaded as several authors and commenters recirculated it on their Twitter, Facebook, and WordPress accounts. A typical solo-authored monograph would not have generated the same response.

With each phase of the project, we expanded the website for *Writing History in the Digital Age* to guide visitors into lively channels of discussion and also to document the evolution of our writing. During the initial "call for ideas" phase in May–June 2011, we invited readers to generate and respond to potential themes for the volume, and 73 participants posted 261 comments, which collectively generated over 60 paragraph-length topics. By late August 2011, we received 28 fully drafted essays from individual authors and coauthors, which we converted into WordPress posts. We then instructed our contributors on how to enhance them with digital media and web links. When combined with our introductory essay, the fall 2011 volume totaled over 120,000 words, far above the 90,000 permitted in our advance book contract with the University of Michigan Press. We publicly announced the open peer review, which ran from October through November 2011 and drew 71 participants who wrote 942 comments, the majority of them on substantive issues. The coeditors met in December 2011 to select 20 out of 28 essays (about 70 percent) to be revised and resubmitted to the press as the full manuscript. Newer versions of essays were posted online in spring 2012, with links to prior drafts and copyediting for the print version to be submitted.

The coeditors' editorial and intellectual property policy deliberately required essay contributors and commenters to use their full names and agree to our Creative Commons licensing. The combined objectives were to reward quality ideas by attribution, circulate them freely and widely, and maintain civil discourse online. Although we initially "primed the pump" to guarantee some comments at the spring 2011 launch, the flow ran nearly continuously during the fall of 2011, with minimal guidance from us.

Unlike a print-only text, our web-book format allows editors to track some general characteristics of the audience, how they arrived at the site, and which portions of the text generated the greatest interest. Based on anonymous Google Analytics data, over 8,500 unique visitors came to *Writing History in the Digital Age* during its developmental period from May 2011 through mid-January 2012. The number continues to rise as of this writing. Most of these web visits were brief. Only 1,000 unique visitors spent at least five minutes viewing our site, and of those, only 122 spent more than one hour on the site, which is comparable to the total number of individuals who have posted comments during all stages of the web-book.

Put into perspective, our user statistics are relatively small when compared to digital history websites, but they are larger than we anticipated for a volume of academic essays that have not yet been officially "published."

To what extent does this readership represent "the public" at large? We suspect that most readers who spent significant time on our 120,000-word site were other academics, but we can only infer this indirectly. The most popular sources of web traffic for engaged readers (who spent at least five minutes on the site) were direct links, most likely from an e-mailed announcement (32 percent), search engine keywords (28 percent), Twitter links (8 percent), and H-Net announcements (4 percent), followed by a range of institutional and individual blogs on history, writing, and digital publishing (totaling 24 percent). Some blog-driven web traffic came from sources familiar to us, while there were other sources we did not expect, such as two U.S. Civil War public history blogs that pointed directly to an essay of particular interest to their readers. Our English-language site engaged readers from the Western Hemisphere: most came from North America (72 percent), Western Europe (12 percent), and Northern Europe (7 percent), the home bases of the coeditors and most contributors. But we were pleasantly surprised to read that a Spanish historian translated several paragraphs from the introduction to share on a blog, as permitted under our Creative Commons license.[11]

What Types of Comments Were Posted, and by Whom, during the Open Review?

Readers of the volume had almost as much to say as the authors who wrote it. Taken together, the 942 open-review comments yielded 83,510 words of text (the equivalent of 148 single-spaced pages), or about three-fourths of the 120,000 words in the fall 2011 essays combined. Tracing the source of these comments reveals that the open-review process did not rely solely on the four expert reviewers designated by the University of Michigan Press. Of the 71 individuals who posted open-review comments, the majority were general readers (43 percent) and other contributors to the volume (41 percent), followed by the appointed reviewers (14 percent) and the book's coeditors (2 percent). We identified 10 individuals who posted 20 or more comments each: 6 were authors, 2 were expert reviewers, and 2 were general readers (including one who posted 244 comments, one-quarter of the grand total). One of the expert reviewers also required students in his graduate class on digital humanities to post a comment on the site, which boosted input from general readers. The median essay generated 31 com-

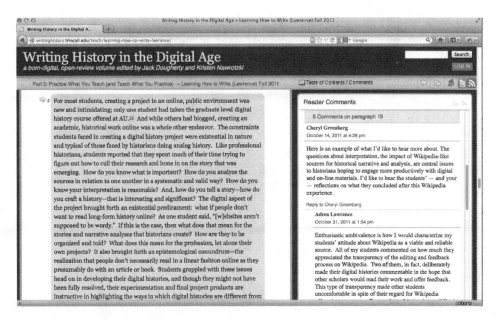

Fig. 10. Screenshot of text and commentary from the fall 2011 web-book version of *Writing History in the Digital Age*

ments, though the range varied widely from a low of 6 to a high of 66. When authors responded to their readers' comments, as they did in 23 out of 28 essays, it tended to generate more feedback from others. The CommentPress plug-in on our WordPress site gave readers the option of posting their remarks at three different levels of the text: general comments on the book (5 percent of the total), comments on a whole essay page (17 percent), and paragraph-level comments (78 percent). At least five essays contained paragraphs that generated eight to nine comments, signaling specific passages of the text that sparked vibrant discussion. The site allowed readers to browse comments along the margin of each essay or to view all comments by the individuals who wrote them (see fig. 10).[12]

What did these comments look like? When sorting all open-review comments by category, we found that 79 percent were substantive remarks on essays, in contrast to copyediting suggestions or brief acknowledgments to thank others for their feedback. Among the substantive comments, many were constructive or reflective, several probed more deeply with insightful questions, and a few were very critical or downright defensive. A typical constructive exchange between authors and readers focused on certain portions of the writing that should be further developed. For example, in response to Adrea Lawrence's essay "Learning How to Write Traditional and Digital History," Cheryl Greenberg posted this comment on paragraph 19:

> Here is an example of what I'd like to hear more about. The questions about interpretation, the impact of Wikipedia-like sources for historical narrative and analysis, are central issues to historians hoping to engage more productively with digital and on-line materials. I'd like to hear the students'—and your—reflections on what they concluded after this Wikipedia experience.

Two weeks later, Adrea Lawrence replied,

> Enthusiastic ambivalence is how I would characterize my students' attitude about Wikipedia as a viable and reliable source. All of my students commented on how much they appreciated the transparency of the editing and feedback process on Wikipedia. Two of them, in fact, deliberately made their digital histories commentable in the hope that other scholars would read their work and offer feedback. This type of transparency made other students uncomfortable in spite of their regard for Wikipedia editors' transparency. Too, students felt that it was difficult to identify and write for a particular audience on Wikipedia and in their digital history projects. What does a "general audience" look like, and what do they already know? This seemed to be one of the biggest initial issues for students, but it was one that they were able to work through after they began writing on Wikipedia and receiving feedback from other editors.

The next day, Cheryl Greenberg replied by affirming what she found interesting in the author's response and encouraging her to incorporate these insights into a revised version of the article.[13]

Other substantive exchanges occurred when readers disagreed about the significance of an author's main point or underlying assumptions. In response to the fall 2011 version of John Theibault's essay "Visualizations and Historical Arguments," commenters expressed a range of opinions. One contributor, Amanda Seligman, began by stating, "This article is at its strongest—and invaluable—in its discussion of mapping." But another contributor, Fred Gibbs, disagreed.

> Actually, I would say the opposite. Historians are probably as [if not more] comfortable with maps than other complex (and especially mul-

tivariate) visualization. It's the scatter plots and tree diagrams and representations of that nature that can be downright frightening to those who aren't familiar with them.

A third point of view came from Kathryn Tomasek.

> Quite a dense essay. I've clearly been reading too many student papers because I kept looking for a thesis, as some of my comments show. I do see the thread of argument: historians have supplemented their work with illustrations; digital visualizations are different, both from illustrations and from the displays of data of the cliometricians. As a reader, I need some help, though.[14]

Even some copyediting comments provoked strong differences of opinion. In Amanda Sikarskie's essay "Citizen Scholars: Facebook and the Co-creation of Knowledge," reader Jeremy McGinniss suggested two wording corrections to paragraph 12, which prompted Jonathan Jarrett to reply, "I don't agree with either of those corrections! . . . I submit that the sentence is correct as it stands."[15] We also found that some commenters (including one of the coeditors) struggled with writing feedback that was critical in content yet civil in tone. This problem is not specific to scholarly discourse on the web, as a review of heated exchanges in the "Letters to the Editor" sections of leading historical journals in past decades will attest. But our collective sense of "Internet etiquette" is still evolving and will continue to do so with the transparency of open peer review, where all can learn from reading the substantive commenting styles of others.

What motivated these commenters to voluntarily contribute their time and energy to the volume? Some may have wished to share a personal experience or a scholarly insight or to start up a connection to the field of digital history. Others may have sought public recognition for generating thoughtful feedback, as our policy that comments must be accompanied by full name encouraged. Some authors may have acted in self-interest, on the grounds that constructively raising the quality of the whole volume could also boost the status of their individual essays. Regardless of their particular motivation, all commenters engaged in historical writing as a collaborative creative process, rather than an isolated one. Yet this online sense of community did not appear instantaneously. During the two-month period, some readers gradually shifted from distant observers to highly engaged contributors. Charlotte Rochez recounts next how the process transformed her into one of the most prolific commenters on the volume, submitting over 11,000 words in feedback (or the equivalent of two entire essays).

How Did Open Review Transform Some Readers into Commenters? (by Charlotte Rochez)

When I first learned of *Writing History in the Digital Age*, I explored the website and read a few of the early articles; I recognized it as an exciting endeavor, and it sparked my thoughts, as well as a blog post, regarding how modern technology influenced my own writing processes. In summer 2011, a call was opened for article submission, and I suggested a paper focusing on the Internet and oral history. However, while grappling with the finishing touches, I realized that I did not wish to post it online in this way; I questioned possibilities of plagiarism and the notion of making criticism public and was uncertain about the use of digital, online citations. Moreover, I wondered whether, in the event that a piece was not accepted for final publication in this volume, it would be eligible for publication elsewhere, having already been posted online for public review. Through reading and reviewing the essays, I learned that this reluctance and wariness toward online publishing is shared by many students and by some more-experienced academics too.

Engagement in the open-review process helped me to address some of these concerns and altered my attitudes toward public online review. At first, I had preferred to make coded notes in a private Word document, but about halfway through the book, I felt inclined to post online. My misgivings were alleviated when authors responded positively to my comments, entering into a dialogue where further ideas, information, and links were shared. As I read Robert Wolff's claim that *Wikipedia* offered an opportunity "to peer behind the curtain and, if interested, take a place at the controls," it resonated with my experience in the open-review process, which presented me an unusual prospect as a student, something of a public apprenticeship in reviewing and editing.[16]

Through this apprenticeship, I advanced my understanding of how the processes of academic writing, editing, and publishing could better draw on conversation, community, and collaboration. The commenting during the open review served as a platform for public academic conversation, demonstrating how dialogic, discursive aspects of history could be electronically written in the digital age. In this way, the volume blurred the boundaries between a conference and a book. This increased the authors' ability to access and engage with some of the wider dialogues following from or contextualizing their initial essays and offered them the chance to incorporate aspects from these dialogues into their work before the more official publication. In this sense, the volume's open-review process showed how the digital age may foster a trend away from competition and toward collaboration in book publishing. Despite this, certain aspects of the volume's wider publication process suggested that we have yet to fully explore the collaborative potentials afforded by the web; for example, at least initially, few contributors took advantage of the coauthoring opportunities presented by the online volume. Perhaps this indicates that we are still coming to recognize and take practical advantage of such new opportunities and to explore their potential intellectual and professional benefits and risks.[17]

Did the Benefits of Publishing on the Web, with Open Peer Review, Outweigh Its Risks?

Without a doubt, publishing a book in its developmental stages on the web and opening it up to public criticism places its contributors in a precarious position. Some commenters on the volume wisely raised concerns about its potential downsides. Might unfiltered comments on an Internet forum, where poorly chosen words have consequences beyond their intended meaning, risk public humiliation for authors? Conversely, would an open-review process on the web—with full names of evaluators disclosed—pressure evaluators to be too nice, therefore discouraging opportunities for truly candid criticism?[18] As exemplified by the reflections of Kathleen Fitzpatrick and Katherine Rowe on their experience with *Shakespeare Quarterly*, even some advocates of open peer review have questioned whether the process inhibits untenured scholars from publicly critiquing ideas advanced by senior names in the field.[19]

Indeed, no review process is perfect, but we agree with the need for alternatives to the traditional blind system of peer review.[20] One problem is that in the age of Google, peer review has effectively reverted from double- to single-blind, because today's reviewers can usually decipher the author's identity, if desired, by searching online conference programs and departmental web pages. But the larger problem is that traditional peer review is invisible labor with very few institutional rewards. Because one's name does not appear on traditionally reviewed material, there is no public recognition for the quality of the work done. By contrast, our open-review experiment means that readers can identify the source of every comment, whether constructive or not. With this, we seek to create richer incentives for developmental editing, a commodity highly prized among authors (particularly in the time-starved academic economy), because it requires others to attend to one's writing with careful reading and thoughtful feedback. Historians and other humanists crave this type of feedback because so much of our scholarly value is based on our ability to clearly express our ideas in writing. Some historians contend that book and journal editors still play this role, but others argue that drastic changes in the academic publishing industry have sharply curtailed it.[21]

As Timothy has suggested elsewhere, if we lack sufficient cash to pay for developmental editing, we should consider an alternate form of currency widely recognized in the scholarly world: our reputation capital.[22] In our name-disclosed peer review, the value of our reputations rises or falls based on readers' and authors' perceptions of the quality of our feedback. Did the commenter make a fair-minded criticism of an essay, pose a deep question that calls attention to an unstated assumption, suggest an alternate way to frame the argument, recommend an overlooked source, or push aside the fluff? Instead of masking commenters' identities, open peer review flips the traditional model by creating a powerful incentive for scholars to invest time and energy in evaluating other people's writing, as the comments themselves become part of the scholarship.

Given the experimental nature of open peer review, the coeditors of this collaboration installed reasonable safeguards to protect our scholarly values of civil discourse and intellectual criticism. Our policy on editorial and intellectual property granted contributors the right to remove their essay from discussion at any point in the process (none did so) and clarified our right as coeditors to remove inappropriate language from the comments (which was neither requested nor necessary for this volume). Comments appeared as they were posted on our site, filtered only by our spam guard, with an occasional reminder to individuals to use their full name, as well as some typographical corrections by request from a writer or with a writer's permission. As coeditors, our most serious intervention was to redirect one heated exchange to the appropriate section of the volume and to invite a contributor to elaborate on the substance (rather than the style) of a specific comment. Our invitations to revise and resubmit essays were posted as public comments, but we informed authors by private e-mail when we decided not to advance an essay to the final manuscript.

We also made sure that the expert reviewers could freely speak their minds. Prior to the open-review period, we nominated 10 expert reviewers to the University of Michigan Press, which selected 4 of them and offered each its standard compensation of $200. Each expert received instructions that explained the mechanics of open peer review and its objective of encouraging all readers to participate in the evaluation process. But the letter also gave them the option, if desired, to send additional comments in a confidential e-mail directly to the editor in chief at the press, who would share them with the coeditors as anonymous comments. (To our knowledge, none of the expert reviewers chose this option.) Furthermore, when launching the open peer review, we intentionally did not announce the names of the expert reviewers, and none overtly revealed his or her identity during the two-month process, though one did at the end. In practice, this meant that most authors could not easily distinguish between comments from "official" reviewers and comments from general readers. After the review period, we informally polled several essay contributors about the process. Some correctly guessed the experts' identities based on their background, tone, or quantity of comments. Some correctly guessed only one or two and mistakenly assumed that other active commenters were the designated experts. Some reportedly neither attempted to guess nor cared who was who. While we have no definitive way of knowing if we succeeded, we strove for a meritocratic review process where the quality of the comment drove the status of the commenter, not vice versa.

Without a doubt, publishing this volume in stages on the public web enriched its intellectual coherence and scope beyond what the same set of authors would have produced using traditional practices. During the initial phase, when prospective contributors posted and discussed over 60 essay topics, the online forum led many to clarify, refocus, or abandon their ideas as better ones emerged. Moreover, the open peer review of full drafts demonstrated how crowdsourcing can improve our writing, as general readers and other authors posted valuable comments that never would have arisen if we had relied solely on traditional blind review with appointed experts. In their revised essays, several authors credited insights from noncommissioned commenters who they had never met in person.

Whereas a traditional press would rely primarily on comments written by its appointed experts to evaluate this volume, the "wisdom of the crowd" played an equal—or greater—role in shaping our thinking as coeditors. Several comments persuaded us that a particular paragraph or entire essay deserved more (or less) merit than we originally believed. Furthermore, general readers' comments demonstrated the degree of engagement with the writing by our intended audience, at least more clearly than any other means currently available to us. Yet, although we tracked the numbers and types of comments posted on each essay, our editorial decisions were not driven by popularity contests or computerized algorithms. Instead, our judgment was more traditional. We evaluated essays on how insightfully they responded to the guiding questions of our volume and on the extent to which authors demonstrated capability and willingness to incorporate rich ideas from the online developmental editing stage into their final revisions. Interestingly, some essays with relatively high numbers of comments were not invited to advance to the final round, while one essay with the lowest number was selected. Furthermore, some contributors anecdotally reported feeling more motivated to share their best work because their writing—at the stages of both preliminary idea and full draft—was publicly visible to all. We fully understand that this experimental format may not fit everyone and that individual perceptions of the process are linked to publication outcomes. But when framing it as an alternative to scholarship as usual, we agree with the assessment of contributor Shawn Graham: "The risk is worth the reward: . . . digital history takes place in a community, and this open peer review process represents a way of writing & crafting history in one step."[23]

What Is Next for Scholarly Publishing?

The Internet has changed the relationship between writers and readers, presses and libraries. With the click of a few buttons, scholars are sharing our writing online and commenting substantively on the words of others, which calls into question what we mean by the terms *publishing* and *peer review*. In response, all of the parties in academic book publishing need to rethink our relationships and financial arrangements with one another.

- *Authors:* We urge historians and other humanists to write more collaborative works or at least to coordinate individual works on related topics, treating writing similar to our customary task of creating coherent conference panels where contributors engage with one another. Furthermore, authors in the digital age should take on a larger role in preparing and formatting our writing for the web, as we required contributors to do for the online version of this volume. Both steps not only will reduce costs and speed up time to publication but will also serve our broader interest of creating more intellectually coherent works with richer communities of readers.
- *Readers and reviewers:* Peer review will always be the defining stage in the scholarly communication process. As illustrated by this volume, we recommend open-review processes that solicit feedback from designated experts and general readers on the public web, to raise the visibility of our highly valued labor of developmental editing and to fully credit it in stages of the work in progress. This pooling

together of established experts and rising newcomers, insiders and outsiders to the field, both legitimizes and strengthens our scholarly work.

- *Publishers and publishing services:* Academic book authors still require publishing services, but perhaps not as we have traditionally organized them. We have three primary needs: digital platforms to host and archive our writing, copyediting and technical assistance to meet production standards, and, most important, an impartial arbitrator of the open-review process to communicate with an editorial board on whether a work deserves its institutional stamp of approval. All three could be provided by a conventional publisher, a scholarly society, or an academic library that is funded to offer publishing services, as demonstrated by the University of Michigan. Whether or not these services can be financially sustainable under an open-access publishing model remains to be seen, and we will continue to closely watch other experiments.
- *Libraries and repositories:* If historians and scholars in other disciplines commit to open-access publishing in alignment with our scholarly values, the accumulated cost savings from library purchasing budgets potentially could be shifted to support their expanded role in publishing services. To be clear, this shift would not be instantaneous, and higher labor costs may still outweigh the projected budget savings. But a genuine cost-benefit analysis also needs to include the fiscal consequences of the status quo, where scholars are producing knowledge that fewer institutions can afford to provide to its intended audiences.

Writing History in the Digital Age has aspired to be a different type of book in at least three ways: it is born digital, open peer reviewed, and distributed by an open-access publisher. We believe that this model has enabled us to produce a more intellectually coherent and well-crafted volume than would have been possible with traditional means. Whether we have presented a thoughtful set of essays on how technology has transformed historical writing is to be decided by the readers. If this experiment has succeeded, we give credit to the community of contributors and commenters who decided against simply doing scholarship as usual. Given the growing fiscal crisis in academic publishing, we need more experiments to better understand which models might work, which ones will fail, and why. Accepting the status quo is not a fiscally sustainable option. If we truly believe in creating knowledge to be shared and engaged by others, it is our responsibility to realign our publishing practices to be more consistent with our scholarly values.

Notes

1. Granting the honor of writing the "last words" this way, rather than automatically turning to "famous names" in the field, stems from a suggestion by open-review advocates Kathleen Fitzpatrick and Katherine Rowe in "Keywords for Open Peer Review," *Logos: The Journal of the World Book Community* 21, nos. 3–4 (2010): 133–41, http://www.ingentaconnect.com/content/brill/logo/2010/00000021/F0020003/art00015.

2. Edward L. Ayers, "The Pasts and Futures of Digital History," 1999, http://www.vcdh.virginia.edu/PastsFutures.html.

3. Carl Becker, "Everyman His Own Historian" (annual address of the president of the American Historical Association, Minneapolis, December 29, 1931), http://www.historians.org/info/AHA_history/clbecker.htm; Roy Rosenzweig, "Afterthoughts: Everyone a Historian," web supplement to the book *The Presence of the Past*, 1998, http://chnm.gmu.edu/survey/.

4. Matthew Gold, ed., *Debates in the Digital Humanities* (Minneapolis: University of Minnesota Press, 2012), http://dhdebates.org.

5. Kathleen Fitzpatrick, *Planned Obsolescence: Publishing, Technology, and the Future of the Academy* (New York: NYU Press, 2011), 18.

6. Dan Cohen, "The Ivory Tower and the Open Web: Introduction: Burritos, Browsers, and Books (Draft)," *Dan Cohen's Digital Humanities Blog*, July 26, 2011, http://www.dancohen.org/2011/07/26/the-ivory-tower-and-the-open-web-introduction-burritos-browsers-and-books-draft/.

7. David Thelen, "History After the *Enola Gay* Controversy: An Introduction," *Journal of American History* 82, no. 3 (1995): 1029–35, http://www.jstor.org/stable/2945110.

8. Raphael Samuel, *Theatres of Memory* (London: Verso, 1994); Luise White, *Speaking with Vampires: Rumor and History in Colonial Africa* (Berkeley: University of California Press, 2000).

9. Lily Patience Moya, Sibusisiwe Makhanya, Shula Marks, and Mabel Palmer, *Not Either an Experimental Doll: The Separate Worlds of Three South African Women* (Bloomington: Indiana University Press, 1987); Carlo Ginzburg, *The Cheese and the Worms: The Cosmos of a Sixteenth-Century Miller* (Baltimore: Johns Hopkins University Press, 1980).

10. Michel-Rolph Trouillot, *Silencing the Past: Power and the Production of History* (Boston: Beacon, 1995); David William Cohen, *The Combing of History* (Chicago: University of Chicago Press, 1994); Amitav Ghosh, *In an Antique Land* (New York: A. A. Knopf, 1993).

11. Anaclet Pons, "La Escritura Histórica Digital: Teoría y Práctica," *Clionauta: Blog De Historia*, December 19, 2011, http://clionauta.wordpress.com/2011/12/19/la-escritura-historica-digital-teoria-y-practica/.

12. Read more about prior open-review experiments and about Comment-

Press, a WordPress plug-in originally developed by Eddie Tejeda and the Institute for the Future of the Book (http://www.futureofthebook.org/commentpress/), in Fitzpatrick, *Planned Obsolescence*, 116–27.

13. Cheryl Greenberg, comment on Adrea Lawrence, "Learning How to Write Traditional and Digital History," *Writing History in the Digital Age*, web-book ed., Fall 2011 version.

14. Amanda Seligman, Fred Gibbs, and Kathryn Tomasek, comments on John Theibault, "Visualizations and Historical Arguments," *Writing History in the Digital Age*, web-book ed., Fall 2011 version.

15. Jeremy McGinniss and Jonathan Jarrett, comments on Amanda Sikarskie, "Citizen Scholars: Facebook and the Co-creation of Knowledge," *Writing History in the Digital Age*, web-book ed., Fall 2011 version.

16. Robert Wolff, "Beyond the Historical Profession," *Writing History in the Digital Age*, web-book ed., Fall 2011 version.

17. Charlotte Rochez, "Online Conference: How Historians Research, Write, and Publish in the Digital Age," *Researching the Histories of Home Education and Learning at Home*, April 2011, http://historyofhomebasededucation.blogspot.com/2011/04/online-conference-how-historians.html; Charlotte Rochez, "Writing History in the Digital Age," *Researching the Histories of Home Education and Learning at Home*, November 2011, http://historyofhomebasededucation.blogspot.com/2011/11/writing-history-in-digital-age.html.

18. Cheryl Greenberg, comment on "Introduction," *Writing History in the Digital Age*, web-book ed., Fall 2011 version.

19. Fitzpatrick and Rowe, "Keywords for Open Peer Review."

20. Fitzpatrick, *Planned Obsolescence*, chap. 1.

21. See online debate about the publishing industry and developmental editing between Zachary Schrag ("Guest Post: More Babies in That Bathwater," *The Aporetic*, October 31, 2011, http://theaporetic.com/?p=2776) and Dan Cohen ("What Will Happen to Developmental Editing?," *Dan Cohen's Digital Humanities Blog*, November 17, 2011, http://www.dancohen.org/2011/11/17/what-will-happen-to-developmental-editing/).

22. Tim Burke, commentator at the 2012 symposium of the National Institute for Technology in Liberal Education, "Collaborations through Open-Access Scholarly Publications on WordPress," Arlington, VA, April 2012. See also Fitzpatrick, *Planned Obsolescence*, 40.

23. Shawn Graham, comment on "Introduction," *Writing History in the Digital Age*, web-book ed., Fall 2011 version.

Contributors

About the Editors

Kristen Dombkowski Nawrotzki teaches at the University of Education (Pädagogische Hochschule) in Heidelberg, Germany, and is a senior research fellow at the Early Childhood Research Centre at the University of Roehampton in London. She has published extensively on the history of early childhood education and related social policy in the United States and England.

Jack Dougherty is an associate professor of educational studies at Trinity College in Hartford, Connecticut. He is collaborating with students and colleagues on a public history web-book titled *On The Line: How Schooling, Housing, and Civil Rights Shaped Hartford and Its Suburbs*, which received funding from the National Endowment for the Humanities.

About the Authors

Timothy Burke, a professor in the Department of History at Swarthmore College, specializes in modern African history and also works on US popular culture and on computer games. He blogs at *Easily Distracted: Culture, Politics, Academia and Other Shiny Objects*.

Alex Sayf Cummings is an assistant professor of history at Georgia State University. His book *Democracy of Sound: Music Piracy and the Remaking of American Copyright in the Twentieth Century* was published by Oxford University Press in 2013. He is a coeditor of the blog *Tropics of Meta*.

Sherman Dorn is a professor of education at the University of South Florida in Tampa. In addition to his scholarship on education history, he has consistently blogged about scholarship since 2001 and is the former editor of the open-access, online Education Policy Analysis Archives.

Thomas Dublin is a distinguished professor of history at the State University of New York at Binghamton. He is the coauthor (with Walter Licht) of *The Face of Decline: The Pennsylvania Anthracite Region in the Twentieth Century.*

Ansley T. Erickson is an assistant professor of history and education at Teachers College, Columbia University, and an affiliated faculty member in the Columbia University Department of History. She is completing a book on the history of metropolitan educational inequality.

Nadine Feuerherm is a student in communications studies at Carleton University.

Fred Gibbs is an assistant professor of history at George Mason University and the director of digital scholarship at the Roy Rosenzweig Center for History and New Media.

Shawn Graham is an assistant professor of digital humanities in the Department of History at Carleton University in Ottawa, Canada.

Thomas Harbison is the interim assistant director for educational technology at the Bernard L. Schwartz Communication Institute, Baruch College. He earned his PhD in history from the CUNY Graduate Center.

Jonathan Jarrett is a departmental lecturer in medieval history at the University of Oxford and a career development fellow of the Queen's College, Oxford. His interests lie in frontiers, documents, and power, all of which he pursues especially in the tenth-century incarnation of what is now Catalonia. He is author of *Rulers and Ruled in Frontier Catalonia, 880–1010: Pathways of Power* and of various papers and articles, and he blogs at *A Corner of Tenth-Century Europe.*

Adrea Lawrence is an associate professor in Curriculum and Instruction in the Phyllis J. Washington College of Education and Human Sciences at the University of Montana in Missoula. Her research extends from the policy histories of American Indian education to research methodologies that include historical, ethnographic, and spatial history methods.

Leslie Madsen-Brooks is an assistant professor of history at Boise State University.

Sarah Manekin is currently a National Academy of Education/Spencer Foundation postdoctoral fellow and is on leave from Johns Hopkins University. She received her PhD in history from the University of Pennsylvania in 2009.

Guy Massie is an MA student in the History Department at Carleton University.

Trevor Owens is a digital archivist at the Library of Congress. He also teaches digital history at American University.

Natalia Mehlman Petrzela is an assistant professor of education studies and history at the New School university in New York City. She is currently working on a book entitled *Origins of the Culture Wars: Sex, Language, and the Creation of Contemporary Conservatism*. She received her PhD in history from Stanford University in 2009.

Stephen Robertson is the Director of the Roy Rosenzweig Center for History and New Media at George Mason University. From 2000 to 2013 he was a member of the Department of History at the University of Sydney. He is currently collaborating with his former Sydney colleagues Shane White and Stephen Garton on "Year of the Riot: Harlem, 1935," a project that will extend *Digital Harlem* into the 1930s.

Charlotte D. Rochez is a doctoral student and a supervisor at the Faculty of Education, University of Cambridge, Cambridge, UK. Her PhD research concerns the histories of home education and schooling at home. She is also a senior researcher on a project, Economically Disadvantaged Youth Living at the Fringe of Global Cities, funded by the Commonwealth Centre for Education, Cambridge. She blogs at www.historyofhomebasededucation.blogspot.co.uk.

Oscar Rosales Castañeda is an independent scholar/activist based in Seattle, Washington. He has contributed writing for the Seattle Civil Rights and Labor History Project at the University of Washington and was previously a contributor for HistoryLink.org. Presently he serves as communications director for El Comite Pro-Reforma Migratoria y Justicia Social, a social justice organization based in Seattle.

Lisa Rosner is a professor of history and the director of the Honors Program at Stockton College, New Jersey. She is the author of books and articles on the history of medicine and science, and she has received awards from the National Endowment for the Humanities, the American Philosophical Society, and the Chemical Heritage Foundation.

Martha Saxton teaches in the Department of History and the Department of Women's and Gender Studies at Amherst College. She is working on a biography of Mary Ball Washington, the mother of founding father George Washington.

Amanda Seligman teaches history at the University of Wisconsin–Milwaukee. Her books include *Block by Block: Neighborhoods and Public Policy on Chicago's West Side* (Chicago: University of Chicago Press, 2005) and *Is Graduate School Really for You? The Whos, Whats, Hows, and Whys of Pursuing a Master's or PhD* (Baltimore: Johns Hopkins University Press, 2012).

Amanda Grace Sikarskie is an assistant professor of public history at Western Michigan University. Prior to coming to Western, Amanda served as project developer and social media manager for the Quilt Index (www.quiltindex.org). She received her PhD in American studies from Michigan State University, where her dissertation research focused on the practice of quilt history in the digital age.

Kathryn Kish Sklar is the Bartle Distinguished Professor of History at the State University of New York at Binghamton. She is currently completing her book *Florence Kelley and Progressive Reform, 1899–1932*.

Stefan Tanaka is director of the Center for the Humanities, member of the Laboratory for Comparative Human Cognition, and professor of communication at the University of California, San Diego.

John Theibault is director of the South Jersey Center for Digital Humanities at Stockton College. His training is in the history of early modern Europe, about which he has written two books.

Hannah Ueno holds an MFA in graphic design from Washington State University and a BFA in visual communications from the Nihon University College of Art, Tokyo, Japan. She teaches courses in interactive media design, 3D computer graphics, image and typography, and package design at Stockton College.

Luke Waltzer is the director of the Center for Teaching and Learning at Baruch College. He earned his PhD in history from the CUNY Graduate Center.

Ethan Watrall is an assistant professor in the Department of Anthropology and an associate director of Matrix: The Center for Humane Arts, Letters & Social Sciences Online (www.matrix.msu.edu) at Michigan State University. In addition, Ethan is director of the Cultural Heritage Informatics Initiative and the Cultural Heritage Informatics Fieldschool at Michigan State University (www.chi.matrix.msu.edu).

Robert S. Wolff is a professor of history at Central Connecticut State University. His research explores slavery, abolition, and historical memory.

Laura Zucconi is an associate professor of history at Stockton College, New Jersey. She has authored a book on medicine and religion in the ancient Near East, in addition to articles on medicine and archaeology, and she has received an award from the National Endowment for the Humanities.